THE STATE OF THE ART
IN
FAMILY THERAPY RESEARCH

THE STATE OF THE ART
IN
FAMILY THERAPY RESEARCH
Controversies and
Recommendations

Edited by
LYMAN C. WYNNE

Department of Psychiatry
University of Rochester
Rochester, New York

FAMILY PROCESS PRESS
New York
1988

Book orders should be sent to the distributor, W. W. Norton & Company, Inc., 500 Fifth Avenue, New York NY 10110. Other correspondence and inquiries should be directed to Family Process Press, a Division of Family Process, Inc., 841 Broadway, Suite 504, New York NY 10003.

The text of this book was typeset in Century Schoolbook. Composition and printing were done by Science Press. Binding was done by Short Run Bindery.

Cover design by Rose Jacobowitz.

Printed in the United States of America.

Library of Congress Cataloging-in-Publication Data

The Start of the art in family therapy research.

(The Family Process Press monograph series)
Includes bibliographies and index.
1. Family psychotherapy—Research—Methodology.
I. Wynne, Lyman C., 1923–   . II. Series. [DNLM:
1. Family Therapy. 2. Research. WM 430.5.F2 S797]
RC488.5.S735 1988.   616.89′156′072 87-0951
ISBN 0-9615519-3-3

ACKNOWLEDGMENTS

I N THE Introduction to this volume, I describe some aspects of the process through which this volume came into being. Here I wish to give special recognition and express personal appreciation to several persons whose prepublication contributions are inadequately conveyed in the remainder of this volume.

First and foremost, Alice Lowery, who is currently Chief of the Psychosocial Treatment and Rehabilitation Program, Schizophrenia Research Branch, in the Division of Clinical Research of the National Institute of Mental Health, has provided crucial support throughout. Initially, she and John Docherty, then also at NIMH, helped plan the 1984 workshop on family therapy research from which this volume derived. Jointly sponsored by NIMH and the Board of *Family Process*, this workshop was opened by Alice with a positive, upbeat commentary on the status and prospects for family and marital therapy research in the NIMH portfolio of grant applications. Later, she summarized for her colleagues at NIMH the recommendations from the workshop and recommended that the workshop be a step in a series of program development activities sponsored by NIMH in the family therapy field. Finally, she has commented thoughtfully on the drafts of the manuscript and helped set a tone of constructive collaboration between NIMH and family therapists in the field.

Although Donald Bloch did not contribute a manuscript for the published volume, he participated actively in preparatory meetings and provided considerable impetus for the involvement of *Family Process* in this venture.

The burdens of actual preparation of the volume itself fell primarily upon the word-processing fingers of Margaret L. Toohey. She edited the manuscript for linguistic and conceptual clarity (within the constraints of the original material!) with great benefit for the contributing authors and particularly for me as Editor.

Finally, the advice and support of Judith Lieb at Family Process, Inc. and Susan Barrows at W. W. Norton & Company were invaluable in bringing to completion a complex editing task.

Lyman C. Wynne
Editor

CONTRIBUTORS

James F. Alexander, Ph.D.
Department of Psychology
University of Utah
Salt Lake City, Utah

Carol M. Anderson, Ph.D.
Western Pennsylvania Psychiatric
Institute
Pittsburgh, Pennsylvania

E. H. Auerswald, M.D.
Center for Applied Epistemology
San Francisco, California

Patricia Chamberlain, Ph.D.
Oregon Social Learning Center
Eugene, Oregon

Nathan B. Epstein, M.D.
Department of Psychiatry and
Human Behavior
Brown University
Providence, Rhode Island

Michael J. Goldstein, Ph.D.
Department of Psychology
University of California
Los Angeles, California

Alan S. Gurman, Ph.D.
Department of Psychiatry
University of Wisconsin
Madison, Wisconsin

Kurt Hahlweg, Ph.D.
Max Planck Institute of Psychiatry
Munich, West Germany

Neil S. Jacobson, Ph.D.
Department of Psychology
University of Washington
Seattle, Washington

David H. Olson, Ph.D.
Family Social Sciences
University of Minnesota
St. Paul, Minnesota

Gerald R. Patterson, Ph.D.
Oregon Social Learning Center
Eugene, Oregon

William M. Pinsof, Ph.D.
Family Institute of Chicago
Center for Family Studies
Chicago, Illinois

David Reiss, M.D.
Department of Psychiatry
George Washington University
Washington, D.C.

Robert G. Ryder, Ph.D.
Department of Child Development
and Family Relations
University of Connecticut
Storrs, Connecticut

M. Duncan Stanton, Ph.D.
Department of Psychiatry
University of Rochester
Rochester, New York

Frederick Steier, Ph.D.
Department of Engineering
Management
Old Dominion University
Norfolk, Virginia

Lyman C. Wynne, M.D., Ph.D.
Department of Psychiatry
University of Rochester
Rochester, New York

CONTENTS

PART V. DATA ANALYSIS

PART VI. RECOMMENDATIONS

INTRODUCTION

SEARCH AND RESEARCH:
Inquiry in the Field of Family Therapy

LYMAN C. WYNNE
Editor

INQUIRY, the process of searching by raising questions, includes both search and research (literally, "to seek out again"). An adventurous, exploratory approach to inquiry can energize increasingly meaningful and productive dialogue in the field of family therapy. This volume was motivated by a vision of family therapy in which networking and dialogue generate conceptual inquiry and empirical research that have diverse goals: to identify congruencies, contradictions, and gaps in our paradigms and theories; to examine the processes and checkpoints (usually called "outcomes") associated with our interventions; and to approach innovatively, as clinicians and researchers, problems that concern us but for which current interventions remain inadequate.

Thoughtful clinical observation, clinically relevant conceptualization, and systematic data collection and analysis can be viewed on a continuum as different varieties of inquiry about therapeutic processes and change. Neglect of any of these components will guarantee deficiencies in meaningfulness of inquiry and, reciprocally, will undermine the quality and credibility of clinical endeavors. Most therapists never personally participate in formal hypothesis testing. Nevertheless, most therapists will find their work more rewarding if they examine the premises, circumstances, and ingredients of their clinical activities. In so doing, they may be animated by this process to identify and formulate clinically significant hypotheses. At the same time, those researchers who are more oriented to systematic data collection need to be attentive and responsive to the inquiry of the more informal conceptual and clinical explorers.

A tension does exist in the family therapy field between those with differing stylistic and philosophic orientations toward inquiry. This tension is heightened by differences between family therapists about what has been called their epistemologic perspectives. There is also tension about differing approaches to gaining wider acceptance and credibility with the public, other health care professionals, and health care policy makers. This volume is predicated upon the belief that thoughtful research should derive from and contribute to sound theory,

1

and that credibility about health care approaches depend more than ever upon convincing, scientifically valid research.

THE NIMH-FAMILY PROCESS CONFERENCE

In 1979, at an Editorial Board meeting of *Family Process*, Don Bloch and I were musing about the issue of credibility for family therapy and the need for more convincing research. We commented on the enormous proliferation of clinical writings in family therapy and the highly attended, countless workshops and conferences demonstrating family therapy interviewing and proclaiming its merits to the newly converted. In contrast, we glumly conceded that research had not kept up in quantity or quality, that it was piecemeal and not cumulative, and that research progress was not keeping pace with clinical practice and theorizing in the field of family therapy. At the same time, research on other treatment approaches seemed to us to be comparatively active. For example, a new surge of research on individual psychotherapy was dealing with some of the issues that family therapy research also should confront, including new attention to process studies of the psychotherapeutic alliance. Furthermore, psychiatric research in pharmacotherapy was clearly influencing clinical psychiatric practice.

These reflections led us to conclude that family therapists interested in research had best bestir themselves and actively consider why, in 1979, relatively few first-rate applications were being submitted to NIMH and other research funding sources. We were aware that, rightly or wrongly, some family therapists with good research track records believed that peer review groups had developed unrealistic or inappropriate expectations for family therapy research. If so, this could become an escalating, self-fulfilling prophecy in which poorer quality applications would generate negative reviews that, in turn, would give family therapy researchers a sense of futility. (In Chapter 1 of this volume, Stanton gives examples of such discouraging scenarios.)

Given these kinds of concerns, Bloch and I concluded that it would be valuable to obtain a consensus of established family therapy researchers about what expectations are appropriate, that is, what is the current state of the art in family therapy research. Recommendations on this issue could be helpful to both prospective researchers and reviewers of family therapy research applications. Additionally, practicing clinicians and trainees/students might be interested in seeing what quality of study they should expect to find in research reports on family therapy.

In 1978, valuable literature reviews had been published by Gurman and Kniskern (1) and Jacobson (3). They observed that up to that time a depressingly high proportion of research in the family therapy field had been of poor quality. In 1979, the American Family Therapy Association (AFTA) had only begun to meet, and the American Association for

Marriage and Family Therapy (AAMFT) was giving only token attention to research. Rather than wait for someone else to begin a dialogue about how family therapy research might be strengthened, we proposed that the *Family Process* Board organize an informal consortium for the purpose of making research recommendations to the family therapy field itself as well as to such funding organizations as the NIMH.

The *Family Process* Board began with a series of small planning meetings to which we invited NIMH participants such as Morris Parloff and family researchers such as Alan Gurman and David Reiss. During the meetings of this loose "consortium," we gradually became aware that there were substantial differences of opinions about fundamental issues. For example, to what extent should family therapy and family therapy research identify disorders of individual family members as the targeted problem? Or should family therapy be directly, or primarily, concerned with treatment of impaired family systems? The dialogue in these planning meetings helped sharpen our focus on these controversial issues, issues that continue to resonate and, hopefully, are somewhat clarified in the present volume.

Thus, it appeared to the consortium participants that identification of appropriate concepts, goals, and methods in family therapy was precisely the kind of issue that deserved intensive discussion. What, indeed, do family therapists and family therapy researchers regard as primary criteria for change, that is, as the goals of family treatment? We concluded that the state of the art in family therapy research on this point and many other aspects of research design needed to be examined and illuminated, both for ourselves as family therapists and researchers and for others who are interested, concerned, and actively support improvement in the quality and efficacy of mental health care.

Later, as a result of our dialogue with NIMH staff, especially Alice Lowery and John Docherty, a plan evolved that NIMH and *Family Process* jointly would sponsor a small workshop on "the state of the art" of research on family therapy, that is, what is currently feasible and optimal and can serve as guidelines for recommendations to the family therapy field. The result was a two-day workshop held in January, 1984, in Bethesda, Maryland, jointly sponsored by NIMH and *Family Process*. The family therapist participants were James Alexander, Carol Anderson, E.H. Auerswald, Donald Bloch, Nathan Epstein, Michael Goldstein, Alan Gurman, Kurt Hahlweg, Neil Jacobson, David Olson, Gerald Patterson, William Pinsof, David Reiss, Robert Ryder, Margaret Singer, Carlos Sluzki, Duncan Stanton, Frederick Steier, and Lyman Wynne. In addition, there were ten NIMH staff persons, headed by Alice Lowery and John Docherty.

Each of the family therapist participants were asked to submit a position paper on a specified topic. These papers served as starting points for the conference discussion and, with many modifications, constitute most of the present volume. The original plan was to interweave the position papers and the lively and productive conference discussion into a volume that could capture the flavor of the meetings themselves. Unfortunately, as usually occurs with such efforts, the give-and-take of the face-to-face meetings appeared (on the written page) to be disjointed, repetitious, and, for this editor at least, uneditable. After abandoning this overly ambitious effort, I asked the authors of the position papers to review and update their contributions. Two conference participants, Alexander and Patterson, wrote entirely new, major chapters that have strengthened the volume substantially.

The problem of conveying the connectedness of the authors' contributions has been sporadically met by introducing Editor's Notes, an idea adapted from Gurman and Kniskern's *Handbook of Family Therapy* (2). At the end of the volume, more extended Editor's Comments are appended, including some points made by participants during the conference but not discussed elsewhere in the volume, together with some post-conference correspondence with authors. The intent in these notes has been to draw attention to points of consensus and continuing controversy. The overview and summary of recommendations in the concluding section (Chapter 17) similarly draw upon comments of the various authors but should not be regarded as fully representative of the views of these diverse contributors whose thinking actively continues to evolve.

My own ideas about many of the issues discussed in this volume have changed substantially since the original conference. To a considerable extent, this has been stimulated by my study of the material of the position papers and the transcript, as well as by reading fragments of the burgeoning recent literature. In taking a broad overview of a complex field, it is never possible to identify and give appropriate credit to those who have helped shape one's thinking. In any event, this is not a review of sources in the literature—even the literature on *recommendations* for kinds of family therapy research. Rather, more modestly, the intent of this volume is to convey selectively, but hopefully with acceptable representation, something useful about the state of the art in family therapy research.

REFERENCES

1. Gurman, A.S., & Kniskern, D.P. Research on marital and family therapy: Progress, perspective, and prospect. In S. Garfield & A. Bergin (eds.), *Handbook of psychotherapy and behavior change: An empirical analysis* (2nd ed.). New York: John Wiley & Sons, 1978.
2. _____, & Kniskern, D.P. (eds.). *Handbook of family therapy.* New York: Brunner/Mazel, 1981.
3. Jacobson, N.S. A review of the research on the effectiveness of marital therapy. In T.J. Paolino, Jr. & B.S. McCrady (eds.), *Marriage and marital therapy: Psychoanalytic, behavioral and systems theory perspectives.* New York: Brunner/Mazel, 1978.

PART I

CONCEPTUAL FRAMEWORK

1

THE LOBSTER QUADRILLE:
Issues and Dilemmas for Family Therapy Research

M. DUNCAN STANTON

University of Rochester
Rochester, New York

T HE FAMILY therapy field has been changing with an astounding fluidity—simultaneously growing, reevaluating, regressing, and advancing in various quarters. It is therefore not surprising that one of its generally more responsible wings, research, has had difficulty in keeping abreast of this ongoing metamorphosis. The changes have been difficult to integrate, much less to analyze.

As one committed to research, I will attempt in these pages to set forth some of the conceptual and practical challenges and considerations engendered by recent developments in this field. While we have thus far produced much credible research, there are a number of issues with which researchers in both family therapy and psychotherapy in general, as well as funding institutions, must eventually come to grips if family therapy research is to continue to develop a systematic, cohesive, sophisticated body of knowledge. Daunting as some of these challenges may seem, they are part of the charge and the excitement that keep researchers going. Discovery, consolidation, and validation are the essence of the endeavor.

The issues and points to be made will, ironically, be presented in a linear sequence—hardly in keeping with a systemic, nonlinear paradigm. However, many of them are interactive and overlapping, and the format is no more than a concession to the constraints inherent in a written presentation. Further, one may detect in the following pages a nonlinear, joining/disengagement dialectic between various viewpoints that is perhaps reminiscent of Lewis Carroll's (12) "Lobster Quadrille" ("Will you, won't you . . . join the dance?"). But more about that later. Let us first move out onto the floor.

DEFINING THE FIELD: A ROSE IS NOT A ROSE

One of the problems that occurs at the interface between those inside and those outside the family therapy field is that of definition. Nonfamily therapists often view family therapy as (a) a modality, that (b) usually involves the nuclear family. These assumptions are incorrect, particularly with regard to family approaches that derive, at least in part, from a systemic basis. Family therapy is not simply a "modality." Nor is it necessarily a set of modalities. More fundamentally, it is a way of construing human problems that dictates certain actions for their alleviation. Its conceptual and data bases differ from most other (especially individually oriented) therapies in that the interpersonal context of a problem and the interplay between this context and symptoms are of primary interest (2).

An index patient[1] is seen as responding to his or her social situation; those around the patient are noted to react to this response; the patient then reacts "back," and so on, in an ongoing, give-and-take process. Interventions designed to alter this process derive from such interactional formulations. As Beels and Ferber (6), Bell (7), Haley (21), and others have long asserted, this (a) concern with and (b) intervention in the system of interpersonal relationships surrounding a patient's symptom constitute a discontinuous change from more conventional, intrapsychic, and individually oriented approaches to mental health and behavioral problems. Further, Beels and Ferber have noted that the "goal of changing the family system of interaction is family therapy's most distinctive feature, its greatest advantage and, especially to those who come to it from other disciplines, its greatest stumbling block" (p. 283; original emphasis omitted).

Because most experienced family therapists emphasize a problem-oriented rather than a method-oriented approach (20), a good deal of flexibility is allowed in clinical operations and in decision about the people with whom they are applied. Consequently, and depending upon the problem, a family- or systems-oriented therapist may:

- treat (directly) only the person presenting with a problem (the index family member);
- see the family "sweater," that is, the one most bothered by the problem—the one who "sweats" the most about it, whether or not he or she is the index patient (8, 16);
- deal with one family member as change agent to the extended family (11, 28, 29);
- treat only a marital couple;
- deal with parents regarding their child;
- involve those family members living in the home;
- treat the nuclear family;

---

1. *Editor's Note*: See Editor's Comments, 1, at the end of this volume for a discussion of the use of this and similar terms, instead of the more traditional term "identified patient."

- deal with the extended family, including grandparents and other relatives;
- work with the whole family network, including friends, neighbors, other therapists, social agents, or any combination thereof (37); or
- shift to dealing primarily or solely with a system external to the family, such as a school or hospital (3, 9, 44).

Thus, attention has increasingly shifted to what I have termed the "systems of import" (38), that is, those people or interpersonal/social systems that directly or indirectly impinge upon the problem. Depending upon the approach taken, the system of import may not become clear until one has intervened and seen where, with, and from whom there is a reaction; identification of a system of import in any given case cannot always be ascertained beforehand. It should be noted, however, that these notions of orienting therapy toward the systems or context within which a problem is embedded can raise havoc with research aimed at specifically pinning down the essence of the family therapy "modality." The shoe doesn't fit because the issue is one of wardrobe, style, and the coordination of the components.

A Definition

In light of the above, let me take a stab at defining this field. Borrowing from Beels and Ferber (6), Gurman (Chapter 10), Gurman and Kniskern (19), Haley (20), and others, family therapy—perhaps more appropriately, *systems therapy—is an approach in which a therapist (or a team of therapists), working with varying combinations and configurations of people, devises and introduces interventions designed to alter the interaction (process, workings) of the interpersonal system and context within which one or more psychiatric/behavioral/human problems are embedded, and thereby also alters the functioning of the individuals within that system, with the goal of alleviating or eliminating the problems.*

This definition, while including ideas about symptoms, individuals, and families, allows for flexibility as to who is actually contacted in the treatment while preserving the distinctive features of interpersonal systems intervention that distinguish it from other approaches. From an operational standpoint, it also permits a researcher access to the process whereby a clinician specifies what a particular intervention is purported to do, whom it should affect, who might respond to it and in what way, and whether or not the intervention was effective.

THE CAUSE-AND-EFFECT ISSUE

Another reason for confusion between most family therapists and others pertains to the different views they may hold as to causality—

what or who "causes" what. Traditional thinking subscribes to the idea that certain causes lead, in linear fashion, to certain effects: "A leads to (or causes) B" or "A and B lead to (or cause) C." In contrast, present-day thinking in the family field follows a rationale more like: "A leads to B, B leads to C, and C leads back to A' (A prime)." This is the "circular" or recursive paradigm (4, 5).[2] In it, cause and effect are interchangeable. They are events within a chain or sequence, and selecting one or more of these events as the cause or the effect is spurious and misses the point; what is "cause" one moment is "effect" the next.

This dilemma regarding the definition of causality is paralleled by a difference between Western and Eastern thought. In Western (Aristotelian, pre-Einsteinian) thinking, a thing or process or entity either is or is not something. It is, for example, fast or slow, high or low, hot or cold. In Eastern thinking, it can be both simultaneously. It can be both fast and slow, low and high, hot and cold. Its definition may rest on its relation to other processes or entities. An example is clinical "ambivalence," which demonstrates the two sides of a bind, dilemma, or choice point. The ambivalent person is both happy and unhappy, attracted and repulsed, and so on. Although chains of events involve sequences and are, thus, linear at a microlevel, at a macrolevel the chain loops back recursively. From the latter viewpoint, the distinction between cause and effect, again, begins to lose its meaning.

Recently, Gurman (18) has asserted that, contrary to the position taken by some systems thinkers, nonlinear causality is not necessarily a problem for many present-day research methods and statistical tools. For instance, he notes that certain correlational techniques, such as multivariate analysis, can be used with a nonlinear paradigm because these techniques do not assume directionality of causation. From one standpoint, he is correct; one can partial out the relative degree of relationships. But this is not the same as identifying and predicting the contribution of an intervention in the actual flow of therapy where feedback and recursive processes lurk. Even present-day multivariate methods can have limitations when applied to the kind of complex interchange that occurs in a therapy situation, in which multiple variables are involved in sometimes symphonic, sometimes contrapuntal, and often cacaphonous ways. Without the parsimony that theory can bring, most such statistical methods (a) can lead investigators to include more variables than can be adequately handled, at least within a sample that is any smaller than the population of the state of Rhode Island, and (b) cannot adequately handle therapeutic processes such as timing, use of space, and a therapist's responsiveness to client feedback. Only through

---

2. *Editor's Note*: For a discussion of the concepts of circular causality and recursiveness, see Editor's Comments, 2.

well-developed theories that allow us to isolate the crucial factors and predict the response to interventions can we hope to reduce the myriad of potential variables to a manageable concentrate.

If one elects to investigate family therapy using mainstream statistical methods, however, one may encounter difficulties of a more insidious sort. The idea of linear causality is well entrenched within North American academia. The number of researchers and grant reviewers who insist on "clear-cut," one-way causality is legion, and their influence pervasive. Even a superbly designed bidirectional or nonlinear design is not always safe from the reviewer's or editor's blackball. The issue in question is not necessarily one of rigor, carefulness, or investigative integrity as much as it is one of a difference in values, conventions, and/or personal preferences. Such critics are ever on the search for the "cause that refreshes," even if that cause is inseparable from its effects, and vice versa. As a result, a disproportionate percentage of nonlinear research articles and proposals have all too often been rejected out-of-hand by nonfamily therapy journals and reviewers. As will be noted later, this may have made some family therapy investigators gun-shy about submitting grant proposals.

OBJECTIVITY

The ideal of absolute objectivity in research still lingers. Only gradually has mental health research swung over to the idea that objectivity is a relative thing. Schwartz and Breunlin (34) succinctly capture the issue:

> Underlying traditional research methods is a belief in an *absolute* reality that can be measured objectively, as opposed to the relativistic belief that the version of reality measured will be a function of one's point of reference and of the degree to which the act of measuring affects the phenomenon being measured. The methods of hard science are guided by a faith that breaking a phenomenon down to its most basic elements yields the most thorough understanding, and that it is both possible and useful to distinguish simple causes and effects. [p. 27]

In the interests of accuracy, however, it should be added that many investigators within the "hard" sciences shifted their viewpoint many years ago. Since early in this century, those in the "new physics" (43) have appreciated the role of values, philosophy, and experimenter effects in the investigatory process. As the physicist Werner Heisenberg (24), who formulated the uncertainty principle in 1927, put it:

> Science no longer is in the position of observer of nature, but rather recognizes itself as part of the interplay between man and nature. The scientific method of separating, explaining, and arranging becomes con-

scious of its limits, set by the fact that the employment of this procedure
changes and transforms its object: The procedure can no longer keep its
distance from the object. [p. 134]

Thus, in a research endeavor, the cause-and-effect process occurring in
therapy becomes complicated by the activities of the researcher. A
typical sequence might then be: The therapist intervenes with the family
(or client); the family reacts; the researcher assesses their response; the
family reacts to the researcher's input; the therapist revises his or her
intervention based upon the family's response to both the researcher's
and his or her own contributions; the researcher makes an assessment;
and so on. Here we have a complex interplay among three primary
components, each being affected by the other's preceding behavior and
affecting ("causing"?) the response that follows. The fact that the
therapist is part of the therapeutic system, that the researcher-observer
is part of a still larger system, and that all of them may interact together,
has definite implications for research design and highlights the relevance
of objectivity issues for family therapy research, perhaps even more than
for individual therapy research. Again, however, the nature of this
process does not preclude it from investigation and analysis. It merely
requires that we recognize what is occurring, bring it out into the open,
and adjust our methods accordingly. The march of science is not halted;
only the cadence, the formation, and the tune of the band are changed.

FEEDBACK PROCESSES AND EFFICACY

To make sense of the complexity that is therapy, one requires a
research design based upon a well-thought-out theory and a set of
hypotheses that allow examination of a manageable set of variables.
Therapy is a constantly flowing process. In a typical situation, the family
therapist intervenes, observes the family members' responses, possibly
modifies the approach, and intervenes again. The therapist must make
multiple, moment-to-moment decisions based upon the family's reactions and his or her own wits, propensities, and skills. Such feedback
processes are a subset of the nonlinear paradigm. As an example, if a
therapist asserts to a mother and father that their delinquent son needs
to have hard-and-fast rules set for him, the son is liable to protest. Or, if
the therapist attempts to get these same two parents to talk together, the
son may escalate with extremely distracting behavior. At such points, the
therapist must decide how to respond (or "not" respond). One option
would be to shift attention to the son in an attempt to "calm him down,"
a choice that would, of course, at least temporarily derail the original,
parent-directed intervention. Another option would be for the therapist
essentially to ignore the son and attempt to fortify the parents' resolve or
help them to continue talking despite their son's interruptions. Yet

another option would be to attempt both goals simultaneously or in rapid, alternating succession.

From the above example, one might ask upon what basis the therapist makes a judgment. Obviously, factors such as values (empowering parents versus greater "concern" for the adolescent), countertransference, and so on, come into play. However, the feedback process is crucial when the therapist attempts to assess whether the parents have been pushed too hard, whether they will join in the attempt to quiet the son, and whether the son can be pacified. Such determinations rest upon subtle cues that the therapist picks up in the flow of the process, cues that may be obscure to a third person who is not in the room or who cannot see the parents' faces and body postures, or whose observation is limited by what a videotape can provide. These determinations also depend upon the kind of conceptual spectacles worn. As Einstein admonished us years ago, what we see is contingent upon the theory to which we subscribe. Not only the variables and patterns to which we attend, but also the form or structure by which we construe or organize them, depend upon a set of a priori assumptions (13).

The point here is that the extremely complex feedback process that occurs in therapy involves multitudinous, split-second decisions based upon a variety of family, therapist, and external factors, all interwoven. While Kniskern (26) may have overstated a good case in asserting that research on recursive processes tends to be "overly subjective" (Kniskern fails to mention that that there may be many, perhaps untried, methods of assessment), the realization of such research in any quasi-objective sense could require a prohibitively lengthy list of therapist options and moderator variables. This might perhaps lead to analytic summaries like: "Given family reaction Q24 to intervention 124C, the therapist can respond with any of intervention Numbers 25–42, 89, 98, or 106, depending upon whether theory Number 4, 8, or 21 is to be applied, and given that the therapist has a heavy accent and is suffering from a hangover subsequent to drinking because his wife left him yesterday morning for the dry-cleaning delivery man." Although such a scoring schema might be, as the British put it, "a bit over the top," it illustrates the magnitude of the task that lies ahead for those who brave this domain without clear theoretical guidelines. Ironically, this is the kind of task that a family therapy supervisor faces on a daily basis, especially while conducting live supervision.

MODEL AND MANUAL PURITY VERSUS AMALGAMATION, SYNTHESIS, AND INNOVATION

In recent years, therapy outcome researchers have shown a strong preference for treatment models that have well-developed and established procedures that can be specified in manuals. Such models are valued because they allow the research to be both replicated by other investigators and applied by practitioners. Although well-intentioned, this requirement may, however, prove unduly restrictive in light of the emerging trend in the family therapy field of combining one or more approaches. In contrast to theoretical purists, most family therapists are pragmatic. They will not be restrained for long by proponents of a purist position. Younger clinicians in particular tend to incorporate from various models whatever seems to be demonstrating validity and efficacy. Sometimes a complete treatment model develops from such an amalgamation. This happened, for example, with structural therapy (32) in which behavioral tasks and psychodrama were incorporated within an overall family structural framework. What's more, these combinations may not be summative but may combine synergistically. (In fact, I would contend that this is exactly what occurred with the behavioral-structural-psychodramatic combination.) Therefore, efforts to break such synergies down into their essential components might reveal much about the components but little about the whole (31). Whereas we may be able to examine wholes, we cannot reduce synergistic phenomena to their basic elements as, in the language of his times, John Stuart Mill told us many years ago.

In short, ongoing changes in the field have begun to make the model purists appear as grumbling anachronists. In contrast, common stock in Amalgamated Therapies is on the rise and looks like a good bet for both short- and long-term gains. Let us then, as family therapy researchers, theorists, and clinicians, move to the next stage of developing methodologies for investigating syntheses and wholes.

Manual Control

All this has important implications for therapy manual construction. Synthesized approaches would seem to complicate the manual maker's job considerably—at least in terms of how the "ideal" manual has often been construed. Each time a family or systems therapist shifts to a different model or mini-model in treatment, a whole new set of rules and constructs would be required, each with its own manual. The whole could possibly rival the *Encyclopedia Britannica* in length. While this may not be an impossible task, given considerable manual dexterity, it would appear to be somewhat daunting.

Manuals also introduce the inherent risk that accompanies oversimplification. As Lebow (31) notes, they can become so specific that they do not make allowance for situations that deviate from their prescriptions. Accompanying this is the tendency, especially by less experienced therapists, to adhere slavishly to a manual, so that "examples" are taken literally and applied universally, perhaps at the sacrifice of good clinical judgment and appropriate professional flexibility.

A final note on the manual issue concerns the restriction that such aids can impose on innovation. As change occurs in the field in general, it can also take place within a given psychotherapy outcome study. Suppose an investigator uncovers something potentially important, but the therapy manual precludes following the lead. If the investigator decides nonetheless to pursue the lead, the case might need to be (nonrandomly) dropped from the study. If the case is retained, it may be so divergent that its inclusion violates the parameters established by the manual, thereby compromising the "purity" of the approach and limiting the generalizations that can be drawn from the study. In fact, such problems actually did arise in our own clinical research with drug abusers (41, 42). We found that we had both to refine and revise operations, rules, and procedures as the project unfolded. This is part of the discovery process and, I would hope, a part that is not blithely forsaken.

In sum, manuals, and those charged with seeing that they are adhered to, can put constraints on both the therapy and the investigative process, squelching exploration, innovation, and creativity.[3] Unfortunately, or fortunately, the psychotherapy field, whether involving family therapy or other approaches, has not reached the level of technical perfection toward which it seems to strive. There is still room for the unique, the creative, the uncalled-for. Attempts to tether the "intuitive leap" have not been wholly successful. In reaction, I can only exclaim, "Praise the Lord and pass the innovation."

SOME METHODOLOGICAL CHALLENGES

Some of the family therapy models that have emerged over the years may not be compatible with conventional research methods. Two prime examples are the Bowen (11) approach and the work of the Milan group (35).[4] These therapists have emphasized the importance of change that occurs outside the therapy session, even if it is initiated by in-session activity. For instance, in a Milan-type session, a possibly potent intervention is introduced by the therapists and the session is terminated. The therapists then wait to see what will shake down in the system during the

---

3. *Editor's Note*: A contrasting positive view of the use of manuals in family therapy research is discussed by Epstein (Chapter 9). This topic remains an unsettled controversy.

4. *Editor's Note*: Epstein (Chapter 9) and Gurman (Chapter 10) recommend that low research priority be given at present to these approaches. The *care* with which research can be carried out with different models of family therapy certainly varies, but ingenious and innovating research on those models that pose research design difficulties should be welcomed, as Stanton recommends.

ensuing month. Their position is that family and interpersonal systems—
which may include important members and coalitions that are unknown
to the therapists—are too complex to allow accurate prediction of what
the family will come up with. At the following session the therapists
assess what has happened and design their next intervention based upon
this new information. Such a treatment model presents formidable
obstacles to a researcher trying to assess systemic process because any
attempt to ascertain extra-session events could put him or her in the role
of intervener (31). Further, if the researcher is known to the family as an
agent or associate of the therapist, family members may put considerable
pressure on him or her to join them in neutralizing the therapeutic
intervention.[5]

Another model that elucidates the researcher's and the therapist's
dilemma is Landau's (28, 29) Link Therapy. This is a brief, problem-
oriented therapy in which a selected family member (usually *not* the
index patient) is trained and coached to be an agent or therapist to the
family system. It was developed in part to deal with families that will not
allow entry to the therapist, perhaps due to cultural differences between
family and therapist. The general idea is to empower the link therapist so
that he or she can operate effectively within the system. The information
that the therapist receives comes primarily from the link therapist; that
is, there may be little or no observed family interaction data. Therefore,
researchers who aim to investigate treatment process and family interaction could find themselves in the position of undercutting the therapy. If
the link therapist is to be elevated and treated as an authority, that is, his
or her word is to be considered valid, the question could be raised as to
why researchers are poking around in the system, even in the unlikely
event that they were welcomed by the family. Usually the link therapist is
trying to maneuver the family system subtly, and the well-intentioned
but undermining activities of researchers could easily disturb this activity. Such potentially reactive aspects of the research enterprise dictate
that different criteria and new investigatory methods be devised for
assessing therapy models of this sort.

OTHER VOICES, OTHER LOOMS

An issue that has, to date, received scant attention in the literature
concerns the inadvertent competition that can arise when two or more
treatment models, provided by different therapists, are applied with the
same case or family. An example is when an individual therapist sees the

---

5. *Editor's Note*: In Chapter 12, Pinsof discusses research in which extra-session
change is studied as part of a broadened concept of therapeutic process in an
effort to deal with the kind of difficulty Stanton describes.

index patient, another sees one parent, and a third treats the family—all at the same time. Contrary to the popular belief that "more therapy is better" and, therefore, the more therapists involved the better, I have found that such instances, on the whole, can detract drastically from the effort to bring about beneficial change. Too often the various models have different procedures and asynchronous pacing that work to neutralize each other. For instance, an individual therapist may work toward emancipating the index patient by trying to get him or her to leave the "destructive" influence of the home immediately. In line with this, the individual therapist may oppose the index patient's attendance at family sessions because this would tend to draw him or her back into the family. In contrast, many family therapists (for example, 10, 17, 23) tend to bring the index patient and family at least temporarily closer together as a means for effectively traversing the leaving-home stage by going through it again, but this time doing it "right." If these differing approaches are applied with the same case, we would have two concomitant therapies, with similar goals, subscribing to procedures that dictate that they do exactly the opposite of each other. It is as if two weavers, fashioning the complex cloth of therapeutic process, would jointly attempt to weave a tapestry while using different materials and working from different patterns. While their final product, if they could fit it on the same loom, might be admired by the most rabid Jackson Pollock fan, the rest of us would probably view it as confusing, disorganized, or even revolting.

How might a family respond to being caught in the pull between opposing therapies? At best, the two approaches might cancel each other out, resulting in no net change. More frequently the upshot is escalation of a dysfunctional pattern within the therapeutic system (that is, the aggregate of treaters and family members), leading to increased symptomatology and acting out on the part of the index patient or even other family members. And, of course, the therapists, when queried about the resulting mess, would likely retort that (a) it was "the other guy's fault," (b) "the family wasn't motivated," or (c) it was "another case of resistance."

These phenomena point to the importance of considering the whole therapeutic system when undertaking outcome research. The Milan associates (36) have highlighted one facet of this problem in their discussion of the person referring a case for family therapy—how this person often has to be considered a member of the dysfunctional family system and dealt with accordingly. Yet a broader conceptualization is indicated here, one that takes into account and provides management of *all* the various "helpers" (for example, teachers, counselors, clergy, self-help groups) involved with a case. (One recourse would be for outcome researchers to exclude cases with even one outside helper or therapist, but this would beg the question because such a sample would be abnormally skewed and preclude complex, multiproblem families and anyone with a history of chronicity.) In the final analysis, it must be recognized that parallel therapies that are not coordinated have little hope of success, no matter how well-intentioned the therapies and collegial the therapists. Even therapy that would otherwise be optimal can be negated by an uncoordinated, unwittingly competitive system of helpers.

This problem is reflective of the larger trend toward super-specialization taking place in society today (compare medicine, engineering, science). For the psychotherapy field it means that each therapist is striving to perfect his or her particular technology and apply it to one component of the system. In the process, the whole can be overlooked (except, hopefully, by the systems therapist), and the family and interpersonal system can be pulled in several directions at once. In my opinion, this ranks as one of the most important and potentially destructive developments presently facing the field of psychotherapy.[6]

DEGREES AND FREEDOM

In recent years, grant reviewers and funding agencies have shown an increasing preference to support only outcome research that uses therapists with advanced degrees, that is, beyond the bachelor's level. Indeed, some requests for proposals have specified that only advanced-degree therapists will be acceptable in the research design. While the rationale for this position is apparent, it does seem that the situation may have gone a bit far, given the nature and evolution of family therapy and those who practice it. This requirement may be unnecessarily restrictive. While most family therapists have advanced degrees, there are a number of competent ones who do not. Some of our own outcome research (41) employed therapists without conventional academic credentials, and their effectiveness was no worse, and often greater, than that of therapists who held masters or doctoral degrees. Further, there is a fairly long tradition in the mental health field of employing, and giving credentials to paraprofessionals and lay therapists—as has occurred with alcoholism counselors.

On the other hand, possession of an advanced degree is no guarantee that one is an effective therapist. In my experience, some of our multidegreed colleagues can be quite incompetent at this kind of work. This may be especially so if they are green at doing therapy, or

---

6. *Editor's Note*: On the other hand, there is also an opposite, constructive development in current treatment approaches to major, chronic psychopathology. There has been a heartening, recent willingness of clinicians and researchers to work together in coordinating their efforts. For example, current research of this kind, combining family therapy and pharmacotherapy for schizophrenia, has been sponsored by NIMH in a multicenter, collaborative research program.

inexperienced in performing the particular kind of therapy being investigated in a research project. (Some of the least credible research on individual psychotherapy outcomes that I have encountered used parvenu psychiatric residents as therapists, leading, not surprisingly, to equivocal results.) The relationship between holding an advanced degree and being a successful therapist is unclear, and may even be nonexistent.

In short, the call here is not for elimination of degree-bearing therapists from outcome research; rather, it is to allow some flexibility in this dimension in research projects. Instead of requiring advanced degrees, perhaps the prerequisite for such therapists should be that they have a certain amount of credible, appropriate, even "certified" experience in the therapy model they are to provide. Further, there is a need for more research that assesses the ways in which therapists actually function, regardless of degrees, credentials, or perhaps even experience (33).[7] As Haley (20) put it, "Since no particular profession has shown superior skill or better training in family treatment, why should one of them have more status or salary than another? A therapist is now often judged on his merit—the success of his therapy—not upon his professional background" (p. 284).

FUTURE RESEARCH: SOME RECOMMENDATIONS

In this section some suggestions will be presented about topics and areas within the family therapy field that are in need of conceptual and/or operational elucidation. They are included either because they have heretofore received little or no attention from a research standpoint or because I believe that the emphasis they have received has been inadequate.

The Decision-Making Process

One area that seems ripe for investigation is the process whereby therapeutic decisions are made, including the features of that process that are most likely to lead to a successful outcome. The reference here is

---

7. *Editor's Note*: Several other contributors to this volume have discussed the issue of using experienced versus inexperienced therapists in research, but no one else has brought up the point that academic degrees probably relate poorly to the ways in which therapists actually function. The literature on effectiveness of individual psychotherapy with paraprofessionals versus those with academic professional training, does not show distinctive differences; unfortunately, none of the studies on this matter has been definitive (Lambert, Shapiro, & Bergin, 1986). Additional variables, such as years of life experience, years working in the community, or being a parent or marital partner, probably are inversely correlated with academic training, and could usefully be studied as covariates relevant to therapist effectiveness.

not necessarily to the moment-to-moment, in-session decisions described earlier, but rather to the more molar decisions that set the overall direction for family treatment—the broad strokes rather than the brush strokes. Such decisions usually follow from a theory or conceptual schema, and there is a need for clarifying the kinds of information that such a schema would require in order to arrive at the most effective strategy for change. Several subsets of the decision-making process that deserve consideration are the following:

Treatment Inclusiveness

A prime question that the family therapist must answer early in treatment is who should be included in the therapy. Usually this can be ascertained by determining as precisely as possible what people, family subsystems, and extrafamily systems are actually involved in the problem—again, the *systems of import*. Does the interaction surrounding the problem involve, for example, parents, grandparents, siblings, relatives, schools, or courts? What "helpers" are included in the therapeutic system? If a therapist intervenes without obtaining such information, he or she may be misled into establishing a treatment plan that is directly subverted by the overlooked family members or helpers, if for no other reason than that the therapist failed to include them. One aid in making this determination is to assess the extent to which the index patient and accompanying family members are in contact with other family members. Do they all live in the same house, or around the corner from each other? Is there regular phone contact? Who lives with, calls, or sees whom regularly? Who can be depended upon for a response when the presenting problem flares up? Under what conditions should a couple's parents be included regarding a "marital" problem? Often such information can be quite revealing. For example, grandparents are likely to be "lurking" nearby, or actually in the fray, in families with a schizophrenic member, whereas this is less common with a school problem. Haley (22) notes that the greater the severity of the problem, the more likely there are to be three or more generations involved. In such instances, the grandparents should be either directly included in the therapy or carefully accounted for in the intervention. Further, if therapy becomes "stuck" at some point, it is often wise to enlarge the system being engaged—to become more inclusive. (I call this the *Principle of Inclusiveness*, as contrasted with a *Principle of Exclusiveness* in which the effort is directed toward a more and more molecular level of integration, for example, to a physiological or biochemical explanation.) Waxing inclusive is usually one of the quickest antidotes to a therapeutic paralysis.[8]

---

8. *Editor's Note*: In agreement with Stanton's concerns, Goldstein discusses in Chapter 8 the difficulties of data analysis in family therapy research that arise from the important variations in the composition of the "family."

Family Life-Cycle Stages and Transitions

Identifying the kind of life-cycle struggle a family is going through can be invaluable both in understanding why the family presents as it does and also in determining treatment direction. It is always legitimate to ask why a family is appearing for treatment now rather than, for example, six months ago or two years hence. What changes or transitional events prompted this reaction and, as a consequence, symptomatology in one or more members? Is a member leaving home, seriously ill, moving farther away, growing up, getting married, dying, or what? Unless one has obtained a good sense of the family's developmental stage, therapy runs the risk of operating in the dark and possibly floundering due to misdirection.

In addition, conceptual hypotheses and formulations concerning the life-cycle stage have implications for deciding who should be involved in treatments. For example, it is usually prudent to conclude that when no life-cycle event or change in the nuclear family can be identified as corresponding to the onset of the problem, it is time to examine the grandparental system. When one broadens one's scope and includes grandparents, one often uncovers events like a retirement, a severe medical problem, or a death, which had started an escalation in family stress. This puts pressure on one of the parents to attend to the oldster(s) and withdraw from his or her spouse. The "symptom," however, may crop up not in a parent but in a grandchild.

Points of Intervention

Research is needed to decide at what point or points in the family system an intervention should be aimed. Toward whom and at what juncture should an intervention be directed? For instance, should emphasis be given to dealing with the family matriarch, the parent-teacher interface, or the "powerful" uncle? Given that randomly scattered interventions will succeed only at the level of chance, what rules does one use for homing in on a key family member or subsystem? Where should the pressure be applied? Which family members need to be quelled? What rules can be identified for determining the points that are most likely to reap success?

Type of Intervention

Once a therapist has identified the system of import, the life-cycle transition, and an appropriate point for intervening, the next decision revolves around what to do about it. What intervention should be used? Or, is there a choice of several? Should one use a "compression" strategy—pushing certain members closer together—or a "diversion" approach—drawing firm boundaries (39)? Should several techniques be used concomitantly, such as organizing an extended family to undertake a suicide watch over their self-destructive daughter while helping the

parents undergo grieving over the recent death of a maternal grandfather
(30)? Although some existing family therapy models are fairly explicit
about such questions, others may be evolving out of experimentation and
exploration of precisely these kinds of questions.

Agnostic Diagnostic

The interplay between diagnosis and intervention often colors decision
making. This interplay is amplified by the difference between individual
and systemic diagnoses. Commonly, an outcome study lumps cases
according to a particular diagnosis and then assigns them to a treatment
condition. However, the diagnostic information obtained initially may be
inadequate both for proper compartmentalization and for real assistance
in the decision making about appropriate treatment. Auerswald (Chapter
4) provides an example of this in his description of six Filipino boys, all
from the same school and all simultaneously "diagnosed" as school-
behavior problems that, because of different antecedents and complexities, required three different kinds of interventions. To have assigned
these boys randomly to different treatment conditions (had they been
part of a research study) would have been naive and possibly ineffective
if only the primary diagnostic information had been relied upon for
assignment.

As another example, I examined the six most recent marital cases
treated at the University of Rochester Family and Marriage Clinic prior
to this writing. In four of them, treatment was proceeding in a more or
less conventional, marital-therapy way with the couple. With the other
two cases, however, the steps taken were quite different. In one case,
therapy immediately began with a network session involving several
dozen members. The wife had contacted us with the question of whether
to stay in the marriage with her alcoholic husband or to leave him.
Because a number of treatments had already been tried, we decided to
expand the system to include all the relevant figures. In contrast, the
second aberrant case was taken in the opposite direction, essentially
toward parallel individual therapy for the young couple. The wife was
clear that the marriage was over. She was working full-time and attending college while her husband, who had been unemployed for a long time,
was sitting at home most of the time and watching television. He had left
Puerto Rico 18 years before and had not been back except once when his
father had died. He had essentially no support system and was quite
depressed, with possibly suicidal and homicidal tendencies. We referred
him to a Spanish-speaking, individual therapist.

If the above collection of cases had been part of a marital therapy
outcome study, the latter two cases might, eventually, have been
excluded. And that is the point. The complexity of the decision as to how
they are to be handled is, to me, one of the most important aspects of the

whole clinical process. Certainly, four of these cases could have been dealt with adequately in a conventional design, but all six presented as marital problems. How should we have handled the two for which it was clear that standard marital therapy was not indicated? Or what might we have done with a multiproblem case, even with the marriage as a presenting problem, in which five or ten other therapists were already actively involved? Would standard marital therapy suffice when so much else is swirling around outside the couple's sessions? Commonly, important information like this is not revealed until therapy is well underway, but it may dictate that the mode of therapy initially selected be dropped and a new tack taken.[9] In fact, in my experience, any one—or possibly all—of the aforementioned six cases might evolve toward, or shift to, a different treatment approach at a later stage in therapy. How would we cope with that in a project requiring us to maintain therapeutic purity? These are the kinds of questions and decisions that crop up regularly in clinical settings. Whereas they often tend to be overlooked by researchers, their implications for outcome studies are immense. As my colleague Thomas Todd and I have commented elsewhere (42), life—and research—are inherently messy. We can ignore such realities only so long before we eventually have to come to grips with them.

Diagnosis, Immutability, and Intrasystem Fit

It is the usual practice for family therapy researchers to categorize cases according to some diagnostic schema, while also taking into account the degree of chronicity presented. If a case becomes a dropout, it is attributed to any of a number of reasons (chronicity, improper diagnosis, and so on) and may be disregarded in the outcome analysis. However, conventional diagnosis can be severely limiting because it addresses only one aspect or one person within the family part of the therapeutic system. The therapist and agency role in what occurs at intake is frequently overlooked. Often the problem lies less within the family itself than in the interface between the family and the "helping" system. Thus, therapists and other helpers need to calibrate their attempts at entry and their responses to the family *as it presents itself*. As noted earlier, seemingly similar problems may follow from very different antecedents and require different approaches and interventions.

Why is the family-therapist "fit" such a key issue? To begin with, we should not forget that psychotherapy is commonly perceived pejoratively—there is stigma attached. This is particularly so for families that feel isolated from society or that come from cultures different from the

---

9. *Editor's Note*: See Chapter 7 for a further discussion of the difficulties for family therapy research generated because the "presenting problem" changes, especially before treatment begins and during the early stages of treatment.

treatment system or the social surround. For such families, psychotherapy may be viewed as both shameful and as a policing activity by the larger society. Their definition of the problem and their perception as to who is responsible and who is to "blame" may differ greatly from the views of the helping system. Consequently, they become "resistant," and are then viewed as "unchangeable" by the agency (14, 15, 39). However, the categorization of some families as immutable and others as malleable may be no more than a function of the way the helping system views and presents itself to these various families. If there is improper fit at the nexus of the two systems, the family may be deemed immutable or unchangeable. Those who conform to the expectations and interventional preferences of the agency will be seen as malleable. But, like raw data, families must be regarded as "themselves," and responsibility for designing a workable fit and for practicing the flexibility that this implies must lie with the helping system. This issue has important implications for researchers who intend to study or treat families with ostensibly similar problems or diagnoses. It is difficult to separate definitions of diagnosis, problem type, and chronicity from (a) the style, biases, and preferred modus operandi of the helping system, and (b) the interaction between that system and the family system.

Self-Correction

If an intervention is made, how does one decide about its correctness? What criteria should we use to determine if it is working or not? If it appears to be failing, what provisions are there for self-correction? Is additional information needed, does the scope of the therapy need to be broadened, or would another intervention pitched at the same level or point suffice? Questions such as these have received little systematic attention in family therapy. Isn't it time that they be addressed more fully?

Cybernetics Versus Hierarchy

For some time, a controversy has been brewing among several family therapy schools over the issue of hierarchy. Proponents of a more cybernetically oriented theory contend that the notion of a family hierarchy has limited value because all members collude in putting a particular member "on top" or giving him or her more "power" (25). On the other hand, more structurally oriented therapists such as Minuchin (32) and Haley (22) posit that symptoms arise from a dysfunctional family structure in which, for example, one or more children are elevated and placed on a par with their parents. It seems that this theoretical issue may be amenable to experimental test. For example, from a pure family-cybernetics viewpoint, a task could be given and carried out by almost any family member with equal success because each shares a kind of equipotentiality. From this perspective, tasks and family members are essentially interchangeable. If one person changes through completing the task, all family members will change—presumably in a beneficial way.

In contrast, the hierarchically oriented therapist would assert that effective assignment and completion of a task must be predicated on a structural framework. A given task might, for instance, be best assigned to one or both parents rather than to a child. Otherwise, therapists might find themselves dictating that an eight-year-old manage the family budget and dole out allowances to the parents. An experiment could be conducted in which "cybernetic" cases had a task assigned randomly to any member, or members, *except* those to whom a "hierarchical" therapist would assign that task. The two groups could then be compared on the process, degree, rapidity, and cost-effectiveness of the subsequently observed changes. To my knowledge, such a test of this burning theoretical and operational issue has never been attempted. Why not?

Outcome Nets

Whereas there is general agreement that family therapy outcome research should give high priority to change in the presenting problem and even, to some degree, to change in the nuclear family, much less attention has been given to changes in the extended family system. This is somewhat surprising given the fact that one of the tenets of a number of family approaches has been that if the symptom changed, the system must have changed (1, 40); and in some views (for example, 10, 11, 17, 29), the term "system" also pertains to the extended family.

If we do not examine the family, we cannot tell if positive change in the index patient was offset by deterioration in another member; for example, a mother gets depressed when her son improves. Likewise, a more sensitive measure of change would be able to detect if multiple positive outcomes occurred in a family above and beyond a good outcome with an index patient. I know of a recent case in which the family with a suicidal, diabetic, incestuous teenage daughter began to make dramatic, positive changes across nearly all of its members. In addition to marked improvement of the index patient, each of a number of alcoholics in the family stopped drinking, several nonworking members got jobs, and two adult female members stopped taking tranquilizers. Information such as this would not have been obtained had a net of assessment measures not been spread. Further, if we are interested in measuring outcome, would not a case like this deserve more weighting than one in which improvement occurred only in the index patient, laudable as that might be? By overlooking the extended family, perhaps we in the field have neglected a source of powerful data that is not particularly difficult to obtain, and which could substantially improve the sensitivity of our outcome measures.

POLITICAL UNREALITIES

To many researchers or potential researchers in the family therapy field, obtaining support to conduct their investigations has led only to Sisyphean frustration. This has been especially so for those involved in cutting-edge thinking and exploration. As noted earlier, the prevailing research models, methods, and paradigms often do not fit. Among the most respected innovators and conceptualizers in family therapy is a group at the Brief Therapy Center of the Mental Research Institute in Palo Alto. John Weakland, one of the group's more candid members, is quoted by Schwartz and Breunlin (34) as saying:

> It's damn hard to make a living doing research in this field . . . After we were turned down on a couple of proposals . . . we finally came to the conclusion that it is less work to volunteer time than it is to keep beating your head trying to write a proposal that would be accepted. [p. 57]

The problem, however, does not always lie in design issues. Several years ago a proposal for a family therapy outcome study was described by an acknowledged expert in these studies as "a better design than any family therapy research presently in existence." It involved a large pool of subjects and random assignment in the comparison of four different therapy approaches, each to be provided by expert and committed therapists in their own given modality. This project was initially rejected "with communication." The revisions recommended by the first review group were then made and the proposal resubmitted. It was rejected a second time. The reasons given for this rejection were based upon nonfactual assumptions and an appalling misunderstanding of the (more or less standard) design. This experience illustrates a point: If supposedly superior family therapy research, using conventional methods and asking questions of general importance (for example, about the relative effectiveness of group, individual, and family therapy), encounters funding problems, we will need to redouble our efforts to secure support for family therapy research that employs new, less traditional, or less popular designs.

Naturally, the problem does not stop with the research funding blight. Publication patterns, especially in nonfamily therapy journals, also deserve scrutiny. (How many of us have had family therapy manuscripts rejected by mainstream psychiatry or psychology journals, not on issues of design, merit, or writing style, but because they were "not germane to the interests of the readership"?) Schwartz and Breunlin (34) note that many family therapy investigators

> face great constraints on their ability to stray from the "hard methodology." As Michael Berger says, "The kinds of research you can easily get published usually address questions of a different level than those clinicians need to answer." We are reminded of the Sufi story of the man who lost his key at one street corner but was looking for it at the other corner because the light there was better. [p. 57]

Of course, these are all classic manifestations of the resistance a field, or a subset of a field, must endure upon encountering a "paradigm shift." Kuhn's (27) insights continue to deserve our awe, even if they have not brought much comfort. It is therefore up to the researchers in the field both to encourage continuing shifts and to provide the solid underpinning and validation of those shifts that advance the field.

Exploration Versus Confirmation

As with psychotherapy in general, family systems approaches are still involved in the development of new techniques, methods, and theories. While the field continues to explore and unfold, however, a certain bias has begun to creep into agencies that provide support for research. The bias is to fund studies that confirm a treatment's efficacy, either by comparing it with a baseline or with other treatments. This is confirmatory research, and it is perhaps in line with the American propensity for the refinement of technology, as compared with the more European tradition of developing new and different concepts and paradigms. While confirmatory research is important and essential, in recent years it appears to have hogged the stage, crowding more exploratory efforts out of the limelight and into the wings.

If we are interested in breaking new ground, we are taking a risk by accentuating the confirmatory approach. It may be more amenable to existent research designs and methods for analysis, but maybe that is part of the problem. Many times, what is needed is not, or not only, further application of known methods of investigation, but also the development of new methods. As implied earlier, the rules for an innovative paradigm may not be identical to those for established paradigms. Different methods, following different rules, may be required, just as a positron scanner requires different methods and assumptions than does an X-ray machine. Further, if one is truly exploring, one cannot always state a priori just what one expects to find and precisely how one expects to measure it. In the process of discovery, one must sometimes discard one's map or plan or rulebook and enter the doors one finds ajar. That, supposedly, is what research is all about.

By embracing exploratory research, we would, of course, be playing the percentages. In the short run, a lower proportion of our studies might "pay off." From a longer-term perspective, however, the payoffs we do get have the potential to realize extensive gains. Certainly, if we are in need of innovative breakthroughs in therapy and quantum leaps that take the field to new heights, we are more liable to get them through the exploratory approach. Conversely, if we neglect exploratory research, attending primarily to the immediate gains yielded by confirmatory research, we knowingly or unwittingly sacrifice the future. That, my friends, is a high price. Is it really worth it?[10]

SUMMARY

At the risk of being cryptic, here is a list of some of the major points and recommendations propounded in these pages:

1. While family therapy may be an "approach," it is not simply a "modality." It is a way of gathering and organizing information in order to determine and apply interventions that alter interpersonal systems, contexts, and, as a result, individuals and the psychiatric/behavioral/human problems they face.

2. Cause and effect are essentially interchangeable. What is "cause" one moment is "effect" the next.

3. Conventional methods of data gathering and analysis will be severely taxed when used in the examination of family therapy phenomena. In some cases they may be either inadequate or overly obtrusive, thus dictating that new methods be developed.

4. Synthesized approaches to family therapy are on the rise. By nature, they present formidable problems for the development of detailed guides or manuals for specifying clinical operations.

5. It is absurd to limit oneself to breaking synergistic wholes into their parts. There can be much "truth" and value in the whole. Nonetheless, this issue will probably remain a bone of contention among therapy researchers for some time.

6. Competing therapies applied to the same case and asynchronous helping systems are often overlooked as factors in psychotherapy and family therapy failure. This phenomenon sorely needs attention.

7. Advanced degrees do not (necessarily) good therapists make. Effectiveness, not accreditation, is what counts. There is also a need for improved concepts and methods for assessing how therapists function, effectively or not, regardless of their degrees and credentials.

8. The conceptual and operational bases for making clinical decisions are greatly in need of investigation. They are the road signs to effective

---

10. *Editor's Note*: A strong consensus of the contributors to this volume supports Stanton's emphasis on exploratory versus confirmatory research in family therapy, given the present state of the art. In Chapter 12, Pinsof advocates this position most explicitly.

treatment; they also inform us as to where the field in general is heading.

9. Outcome studies should attempt to assess both the nuclear and extended family. Treatment methods that beneficially change not only the presenting problem, but also the broader system, are to be encouraged.

10. We must beware that our efforts to concretize, regiment, categorize, and analyze family therapy do not squelch its still untapped creativity or curtail its drive for exploration. Indeed, we must encourage and support its innovative potential.

11. The balance of research in this field must shift from its primary emphasis upon confirmatory research to at least an equal emphasis upon exploratory research. Otherwise, we sacrifice the future for the present.

12. Family therapy research has too frequently been given short shrift in the halls of both academic and funding institutions. It is time that we changed this.

Finally, an implicit question in much of the above discourse is that posed by the "Lobster" refrain: "Will you, won't you, will you, won't you, will you join the dance?" To what extent should family therapy research join the dance of the larger field of psychotherapy research and, beyond this, the even broader field of mental health research? To what extent should it, and can it, teach psychotherapy research a new dance? In either case, should the dance itself be rechoreographed and, if so, in what ways? However, while we ponder these questions, we must beware of tarrying, for even as we speak, the Mock Turtle beckons the throng. With or without us, the dance goes on!

REFERENCES

1. Alexander, J.F., & Parson, B.V. Short-term behavioral intervention with delinquent families: Impact on family process and recidivism. *Journal of Abnormal Psychology 81:* 219–225, 1973.
2. Auerswald, E.H. Interdisciplinary versus ecological approach. *Family Process 7:* 202–215, 1968.
3. _____. The Gouverneur Health Services Program: An experiment in ecosystemic community health care delivery. *Family Systems Medicine 1:* 5–24, 1983.
4. Bateson, G. *Steps to an ecology of mind.* New York: Ballantine Books, 1972.
5. _____. *Mind and nature: A necessary unity.* New York: E. P. Dutton, 1979.
6. Beels, C.C., & Ferber, A. Family therapy: A view. *Family Process 8:* 280–318, 1969.
7. Bell, J. Promoting action through new insights: Some theoretical revisions from family group therapy. Paper presented as part of a symposium on "More Imaginative Approaches in Consulting Psychology," American Psychological Association meeting, Philadelphia PA, August 29, 1963.
8. Berenson, D. The therapist's relationship with couples with an alcoholic

member. In E. Kaufman & P. Kaufmann (eds.), *The family therapy of drug and alcohol abuse.* New York: Gardner Press, 1979.

9. Berger, M., Jurkovic, G.J., & Associates. *Practicing family therapy in diverse settings.* San Francisco: Jossey-Bass, 1984.

10. Boszormenyi-Nagy, I., & Spark, G.M. *Invisible loyalties: Reciprocity in intergenerational family therapy.* New York: Harper & Row, 1973.

11. Bowen, M. *Family therapy in clinical practice.* New York: Jason Aronson, 1978.

12. Carroll, L. *Alice's adventures in wonderland.* New York: The Heritage Press, 1941.

13. Colapinto, J. The relative value of empirical evidence. *Family Process 18:* 427–441, 1979.

14. Dell, P.F. Family theory and the epistemology of Humberto Maturana. In F.W. Kaslow (ed.), *The international book of family therapy.* New York: Brunner/Mazel, 1982.

15. de Shazer, S. *Patterns of brief family therapy: An ecosystemic approach.* New York: Guilford Press, 1982.

16. Fisch, R., Weakland, J.H., & Segal, L. *The tactics of change.* San Francisco: Jossey-Bass, 1982.

17. Framo, J.L. Family of origin as a therapeutic resource for adults in marital and family therapy: You can and should go home again. *Family Process 15:* 193–210, 1976.

18. Gurman, A.S. Family therapy research and the "new epistemology." *Journal of Marital and Family Therapy 9:* 227–243, 1983.

19. _____, & Kniskern, D.P. Research on marital and family therapy: Progress, perspective, and prospect. In S.L. Garfield & A.E. Bergin (eds.), *Handbook of psychotherapy and behavioral change: An empirical analysis* (2nd ed.). New York: John Wiley & Sons, 1978.

20. Haley, J. Family therapy: A radical change. In J. Haley (ed.), *Changing families: A family therapy reader.* New York: Grune & Stratton, 1971.

21. _____. A review of the family therapy field. In J. Haley (ed.), *Changing families: A family therapy reader.* New York: Grune & Stratton, 1971.

22. _____. *Problem-solving therapy: New strategies for effective family therapy.* San Francisco: Jossey-Bass, 1976.

23. _____. *Leaving home: The therapy of disturbed young people.* New York: McGraw-Hill, 1980.

24. Heisenberg, W. The representation of nature in contemporary physics. In S. Sears & G.W. Lord (eds.), *The discontinuous universe.* New York: Basic Books, 1972.

25. Keeney, B.P. Pragmatics of family therapy. *Journal of Strategic and Systemic Therapies 1* (2): 44–53, 1981.

26. Kniskern, D.P. The new wave is all wet. *The Family Therapy Networker 7* (4): 38, 60–62, 1983.

27. Kuhn, T.S. *The structure of scientific revolution.* Chicago: University of Chicago Press, 1962.

28. Landau, J. Link Therapy: A family therapy technique for transitional extended families. *Psychotherapeia 7:* 29–36, 1981.

29. _____. Therapy with families in cultural transition. In M. McGoldrick, J.K. Pearce, & J. Giordano (eds.), *Ethnicity and family therapy.* New York: Guilford Press, 1982.

30. Landau-Stanton, J., & Stanton, M.D. Treating suicidal adolescents and their families. In M.P. Mirkin & S.L. Koman (eds.), *Handbook of adolescents and family therapy.* New York: Gardner Press, 1985.

31. Lebow, J. Issues in the assessment of outcome in family therapy. *Family Process 20:* 167–188, 1981.
32. Minuchin, S. *Families & family therapy.* Cambridge: Harvard University Press, 1974.
33. Pinsof, W.M. Family therapy process research. In A.S. Gurman & D.P. Kniskern (eds.), *Handbook of family therapy.* New York: Brunner/Mazel, 1981.
34. Schwartz, R.C., & Breunlin, D. Research: Why clinicians should bother with it. *The Family Therapy Networker 7* (4): 23–27, 57–59, 1983.
35. Selvini-Palazzoli, M., Boscolo, L., Cecchin, G., & Prata, G. *Paradox and counterparadox: A new model in the therapy of the family in schizophrenic transaction* (translator, E.V. Burt). New York: Jason Aronson, 1978.
36. _____, Boscolo, L., Cecchin, G., & Prata, G. The problem of the referring person. *Journal of Marital and Family Therapy 6:* 3–9, 1980.
37. Speck, R.V., & Attneave, C.L. *Family networks.* New York: Pantheon, 1973.
38. Stanton, M.D. Marital therapy from a structural/strategic viewpoint. In G.P. Sholevar (ed.), *The handbook of marriage and marital therapy.* Jamaica NY: SP Medical and Scientific Books, 1981.
39. _____. Fusion, compression, diversion, and the workings of paradox: A theory of therapeutic/systemic change. *Family Process 23:* 135–167, 1984.
40. _____, Steier, F., Todd, T.C., & Marder, L. Symptom versus system change: An investigation of the relationship between treatment outcome and changes in family interaction patterns. *Journal of Consulting and Clinical Psychology,* in press.
41. _____, Todd, T.C., & Associates. *The family therapy of drug abuse and addiction.* New York: Guilford Press, 1982.
42. Todd, T.C., & Stanton, M.D. Research on marital and family therapy: Answers, issues and recommendations for the future. In B.B. Wolman & G. Stricker (eds.), *Handbook of family and marital therapy.* New York: Plenum Press, 1983.
43. Tomm, K. The old hat doesn't fit. *The Family Therapy Networker 7* (4): 39–41, 1983.
44. Wynne, L.C., McDaniel, S.H., & Weber, T.T. (eds.). *Systems consultation: A new perspective for family therapy.* New York: Guilford Press, 1986.

EDITOR'S REFERENCES

Lambert, M.J., Shapiro, D.A., & Bergin, A.E. The effectiveness of psychotherapy. In S.L. Garfield & A.E. Bergin (eds.), *Handbook of psychotherapy and behavior change.* New York: John Wiley & Sons, 1986.

2

THEORETICAL VERSUS TACTICAL INFERENCES:
Or, How to Do Family Therapy Research without Dying of Boredom

DAVID REISS

George Washington University
Washington, D.C.

I N 1980, Smith, Glass, and Miller (22) published a monumental review of a generation of research on the outcome of individual, group, and—in small measure—family psychotherapy. They reviewed 475 published and unpublished, controlled studies and, among these studies, 1,766 comparisons between treatment and control groups. To sharpen their analysis, they converted each of the comparisons to a standardized metric called the "effect size." This is calculated by subtracting the average score on an outcome variable for the control group from the average score for the experimental group and dividing the difference by the standard deviation of the control group (22, p. 41). Three of the four conclusions reached by their penetrating analysis are worth quoting (with original italics omitted); the fourth conclusion concerns comparisons of psychotherapy and pharmacotherapy that are interesting but not germane to the goals of this volume.

> Psychotherapy is beneficial, consistently so and in many different ways. Its benefits are on a par with other expensive and ambitious interventions, such as schooling and medicine. The benefits of psychotherapy are not permanent, but then little is. [p. 183]
> Different types of psychotherapy (verbal or behavioral, psychodynamic, client-centered, or systematic desensitization) do not produce different types or degrees of benefit. [p. 184]
> Differences in how psychotherapy is conducted (whether in groups or individually, by experienced or novice therapists, for long or short periods of time, and the like) make very little difference in how beneficial it is. [pp. 187–188]

Jointly sponsored by NIMH and *Family Process*, the conference on family therapy, from which this volume was derived, hopefully may have marked the beginning of a new generation of psychotherapy research. Given a growing interest in family systems techniques and perspectives, a new wave of outcome studies could, directly or indirectly, be launched.

But, if the findings from a new generation of research duplicates—in form or content—the conclusions I have just quoted, count me out. I do not gainsay the enormous, practical importance of these robust findings. Nor should they be, I remind myself, surprising. We have always known that although the psychotherapy enterprise is variegated in the extreme, the ingredients of a successful psychotherapeutic encounter may still largely rest on highly charged and particularistic connections among human beings.

The current generation of psychotherapy research is a major scientific endeavor; surely we must count nearly 500 separate studies, many of them conceived and executed by some of the finest minds in clinical research, as precisely that. Yet the scientific yield is sadly disappointing. What I miss in this enormous corpus of conscientious research (some parts of it more conscientious than others) is any gathering sense of *how psychotherapeutic change happens*. Smith and her colleagues (22) reached a similar conclusion. In my view, the great psychotherapeutic research endeavor was pushed back on its haunches and became reduced to evaluation of outcome without research that illuminates the process and theory of change. It became preoccupied with demonstrating the efficacy of established techniques rather than exploring how people, groups, or families may be changed. In short, the absorbing inquiry into one of the most fascinating processes of human behavior—how some people can change others—was replaced by the boredom of compiling a ledger of such changes as they occurred across four decades.

As several other contributions to this volume make clear, family therapy has arrived on the psychotherapeutic scene with a fresh vision. It is not, as Stanton points out (Chapter 1), simply another therapy. It is, according to its proponents, a fresh conception not only of psychiatric symptomatology and its linkage to a broader social system, but also a new concept of how such symptoms and the social links that perpetuate them may be changed. In other words, family therapy constitutes an emerging perspective on the process of psychotherapeutic change. As enthusiastic family therapists (not unlike zealots before us), we are pleased and even proud when our brand of therapeutics is shown to be effective. Our true passion, however, is reserved for demonstrating to others by what mechanisms we have achieved effectiveness. More specifically, what we cherish and what we believe permits us to be effective is our insight into family life and its relationship to psychiatric symptomatology. The modest amount of family research in the literature does indeed document the effectiveness of family therapy. Although another ledger is building, it has not yet clarified the mechanisms by which effective change was wrought. Like a multigenerational family, the history of psychotherapy research seems to be repeating itself.

To avoid such disappointing repetition, to center psychotherapy research more firmly on the exciting quest for insight about how change occurs, and to focus this conference on a specific procedural blueprint, I propose that we examine two fundamental stumbling blocks that impede our progress. If these can be circumvented, then we have a chance to learn from the disappointments of past psychotherapy research and to harness the fascinating proposals about change that have been engendered by our emerging field. The first of these stumbling blocks is the nature of the psychotherapy research system itself. As I will try to clarify, this system, if left to its own devices, will continue to force its component research teams back on their evaluative haunches. It will honor nothing more or nothing less than a careful replication or extension of outcome ledgers until we run out of stone tablets, papyrus, and vaults in which to place them. The second stumbling block lies in the family therapy movement itself. I refer particularly to its cavalier treatment of theory, particularly *theory about family change* or, more accurately, *competing theories about family change.*

THE PSYCHOTHERAPY RESEARCH SYSTEM

Two salient facts about the psychotherapy research system are no secret to anyone. The first fact is that there is increasing competition for the mental health research dollar. There has been a veritable explosion of research activity in the mental health area, particularly in the neurosciences. Many apply for grants but few are chosen. Second, as family psychotherapy research becomes more sophisticated—with larger samples, better attention to therapy process, better controls, more exhaustive measurement, better follow-ups—it becomes more expensive. Some of the earlier studies were done on a shoestring. With a few devoted therapists or their shanghaied students, an available clinical sample, and one or two overworked secretaries, a lucky investigator might still pull off a publishable study, but those days are numbered. Good studies today require successful grant applications. Most of these grant applications are likely to be directed at NIMH, although other federal agencies and even some state agencies have supported family therapy research with sizable grants.

These two nonsecrets—the necessarily expensive and competitive nature of modern-day research and the importance of federal research dollars as support for a major new thrust in family psychotherapy research—have some important system consequences. First, in initiating a request for applications, staff members at the funding agency are under heavy pressure to justify the practical outcome of the research for which support is requested, as against *radically different approaches to the very same clinical problem.* I am not only talking about competing psychotherapies, but also about a broad range of biologic treatments as well as systematic efforts at prevention.[1]

Second, when applications are reviewed, the pressure to demonstrate efficacy becomes translated into an intense *preoccupation with methodology* and efforts to verify that any demonstrated treatment effect is attributable to the treatment itself and not to dozens of possibly confounding influences. What is more, this effectiveness must be *demonstrated to the widest possible audience.* This last requirement is particularly crucial because it usually dictates not only an emphasis on efficacy but also on a particular set of methods by which efficacy can be judged. These methods, when in common use, will be widely appreciated even if they are not designed to focus on the changes most important to the therapeutic process under study. It is for this practical reason that Todd and Stanton (23) have advocated the inclusion of a standard set of assessment instruments in family therapy research.

The psychotherapy research system, primarily because of the financial pressures and the review processes it engenders, is little interested in theory, that is, in detailed and specific concepts of therapeutic change. These specific concepts require immersion in broader theoretical contexts in order to be comprehensible, let alone interesting. Yet the mental health therapeutic enterprise is *divided* by its adherence to widely differing theories, while researchers and research review committees are *united* more by methodological concerns. In research and research review processes, theory often is a barrier to communication.

INADEQUATE THEORY WITHIN FAMILY THERAPY

The psychotherapy research system is a bog that we have not yet fully entered. The volume of transactions between family therapists and federal funding agencies is still too small to have had a major influence on the course of theory development in our field. Indeed, there are at least three features of intellectual work in the family therapy field that have slowed the development of usable theories of family change.

First, as thinkers we seem to take a connoisseur's delight in grand abstractions. Among these, first and foremost, has been general systems theory. Imported early in the development of the field, it has lingered as an intellectual backdrop for almost all discourse. But there have been

---

1. *Editor's Note:* As a pragmatic response to this issue, Goldstein (Chapter 8) recommends that low priority in family therapy research be given to those clinical problems for which competing, adequate approaches already exist. He suggests that we should instead emphasize research on problems for which other approaches seem inadequate, for example, marital conflict and the chronic, negative symptoms of schizophrenia.

other, equally mighty abstractions that have fueled our thinking: cybernetics, group theory, the theory of logical types, and now a plethora of "new" epistemologies. Although I believe that highly abstract schemas can be useful for orientation and integration of more concrete theories, they are inadequate for generating specific, testable hypotheses, and when attempts are made to apply them directly to data gathering, the results can be disastrous (18). The central, sad fact is that none of these grand abstractions are adequate for generating specific hypotheses that could guide enlightened inquiry about family and other social processes and social change. Surprisingly, in my view, the family therapy movement has produced relatively little in the way of systematic, specific theories that can be explored with careful and fastidious research. Several of us have, somewhat belatedly, recognized this. Hoffman's influential *Foundations of Family Therapy* (12) is an effort to render clear and specific theories that lie close to observable clinical phenomena *and* accord with grander schemas. Even more recently, Sluzki (21) attempted to clarify these contrasting, specific theories about family functions and change.

Second, the family therapy literature has been, from the outset, action-oriented. There has been, as a matter of style, a focus on the action of the therapist and not on the detailed and subtle rendering of a family portrait. Contrast the intellectual development of psychoanalysis. The most careful reader cannot learn very much about the conduct of psychoanalysis from reading Freud's entire corpus. Much of Freud's writing on psychoanalytic techniques appeared in a few short papers published between 1911 and 1915, and then again in a somewhat mournful essay written shortly before his death. A great proportion of the remainder was theory and vivid description of the patient—not of the doctor's technical prowess. Would there be much argument with my view that the family therapy field does not have a "Little Hans" or a "Dora" or a "Rat Man"?[2]

Third, and following from my second point, there has been relatively little interest among family therapists in systematic observations of families in nontherapeutic settings. In particular, there has been surprisingly little interest in the circumstances and processes that lead to major or substantial change in family patterns in natural settings—changes that, in some instances, might truly be called self-healing. A related area is the study of family healing as it may go on in primitive cultures. Frank (9) performed such an analysis for individual therapy in the service of identifying the healing processes in formal psychotherapy. Almond (1) performed an identical analysis for "healing communities," as con-

---

2. *Editor's Note:* See Editor's Comments, 3, for further discussion of the use of case material in the development of family therapy.

structed on psychiatric inpatient communities and as conducted in primitive cultures. The absence of such comparative studies in the family therapy field forces us to think of family therapy as a human process *sui generis*. Thus, what we learn about family process cannot help elaborate more general principles about the transactions of families with "healing systems."[3]

Our field, nevertheless, is not without its proto-models: small, still evolving ideas about family change. These conceptual nuclei, in my view, ought to be carefully elaborated to serve as the fundamental, conceptual core of the next generation of family therapy research. In delineating the problem facing theory construction in our field, I have implied that three criteria be applied to these emerging models of change.

First, they should be at the appropriate level. Broad and abstract notions are useful as anchors or backdrops; they are of little value in hypothesis-testing research. What is needed are specific and concrete theories that focus on the sequential processes of change in families and that lend themselves to operationalization and verification.

Second, the theories ought to deemphasize the pyrotechnics or high-wire acts of therapists and focus more equitably on both the family itself and the family in the context of the therapy system. (I use the term "therapy system" in a way that I believe accords with current usage: the set of relationships, interactions, and values that describe the thera-peutic team, its engagement with the family, and the institutional/community setting in which the work is carried out.)

Third, the most powerful theories will be those that conceive of therapeutic change as part of a broader and more general social process—the transactions of families with healing systems. To illustrate my remarks, I will briefly sketch two concepts of family change.

Disassembly and Reconstruction

These terms, as everyone will recognize, pay homage to the model of family change that is inherent in the work of the "classical" structural therapists. The term "disassembly" is taken from the work of Aponte and VanDeusen (2), which focuses our attention on the stable, often dysfunctional structures of boundary, hierarchy, and alignment in family life. In the end, change requires nothing short of disassembly of the structures, often with a blunt instrument. Perhaps the most dramatic exemplar of this model is the "lunch session" in the therapy of families with anorexia (16). As most everyone knows, there are two fundamental techniques

---

3. *Editor's Note:* In strong agreement with Reiss, during the conference discussion Patterson vividly described how quasi-anthropologic studies of families in natural settings have been invaluable in helping him and his colleagues identify key variables and plan research relevant to "real-life" family problems.

employed. The first is the dramatic staging of a confrontation between parents and anorectic child; a long, midday session (often two hours long) is staged in the therapy room and the lunch is served. In this powerful "overfocusing," the parents are instructed to get their child to eat. The second major tactic is to pepper the family with intrusions that block their structured routines of dealing with such confrontations: their avoidance of conflict, their overprotectiveness, the parents' habitual undercutting of each other's authority, and so on. Indeed, the dramatic staging and the fusillade of interruptions by the therapists both serve as blocks to family routines and, if successful, induce an unmistakable, iatrogenic family crisis. The crisis is a direct consequence of the family's inability to adapt its highly structured routines. This clinical example clearly underscores this concept of change, namely, that a precursor of change may be the disruption of family routines and the consequent induction of crisis.

There are a number of analogues to the sequence of disruption of structured routines followed by crises and then by long-lasting change. Among the most dramatic are the changes induced in family routines by the presence of chronic illness or disability. A variety of observers are beginning to document how these interruptions in routines produce profound family crises (13). For our analysis, it is even more important that substantial changes in family structure (as in families with an anorectic child) ensue and endure. Darling's (7) work on families of severely disabled children documents that these changes in family patterns can often be characterized as positive growth by anyone's standard.

The model of disassembly and reconstruction is perhaps weakest in its failure to specify the reconstructive process itself. It needs to delineate the origin of the new structures and the specific mechanisms by which they "harden" to become enduring. One suspects, in examining the clinical evidence, that it is the *routines* of the therapeutic transactions themselves that form a nucleus, and that the hardening process is due to their reinforcement. If all goes well, the new patterns are experienced by the family members as deeply and poignantly rewarding.

Projection, Disowning, and Conversion

Whereas the disassembly model of change focuses on family patterns as the structures that are to be transformed, the model of projection and disowning focuses on another source of stability in families: the set of shared constructs or beliefs that shape the family's conception of reality while justifying and reinforcing its values, standards, and many of its patterns of transactions. Indeed, this process is truly circular because the family's actual transactions reinforce, in turn, its conception of the world. One component of this process was delineated some years ago by Ferreira

(8) as the "family myth," a concept that has been adopted with great élan by the Milan group (20). But family myths are only one of many components of shared family constructs. Included in these covert but intensely charged experiences are shameful family secrets, assumptions about morality, experiences of mastery or victimization in relation to the family's social context, and a shared conception of the future. I and my colleagues have referred to these congeries of shared though ineffable experiences as the family "paradigm" (17). Each family has its unique paradigm that serves as its guide to many of its transactions. Clues to the paradigm are particularly abundant in the family's patterns of transactions with outsiders, although they are also manifest in the family's conception of its own history and ritual life, for example, its dinnertime and holiday ceremonies (3, 24), and in its treasured possessions (6).

A family's paradigm cannot be "disassembled" by a therapeutic onslaught. Indeed, the paradigm has an almost infinite capacity to protect itself by the ways it "defines" any attempt to attack or disrupt the family; that is, therapists or any other components of the social world are construed in ways *consistent* with the family's paradigm. Yet clinical experience suggests that, under special circumstances in both the therapeutic and natural settings, the family may partially or completely disown part or all of its paradigm. The fundamental mechanism seems to be projection; that is, what the family once experienced as inside them, what they experienced as a critical component of their inner and most personal core, is subsequently experienced as if it were located outside the family.

Bowen (4) as well as Zinner and Shapiro (25) have called attention to projective processes within the family. They particularly focused on the projection by the parent onto the child of experiences and feelings that were intolerable for the parent. Indeed, most authors who have commented on projection of this sort regard it as a mechanism undergirding a very rigid and pathological family system. I think that they have failed to recognize that these same projections may be a mechanism of positive change. We have, for example, tracked several families over time and shown how the blaming and scapegoating, which are frequently part of the projective process, are the essential mechanism by which outsiders are drawn or sucked into the family.

For example, a couple comes to blows in the course of a bitter and mutual projection of feelings onto each other. At the zenith of this bitter process, the wife may call the police. I believe that there is now evidence that if the policeman can maintain an outsider role (that is, can remain firmly anchored in the community) by arresting the husband and putting him in jail for a night, that the couple can undergo a series of enduring changes when the husband returns. However, if the policeman becomes drawn into the family by becoming a "mediator," no change ensues.

I am suggesting that projection is a critical step in this process. Both spouses must disown, through projection, a binding sense of identity with, and commitment to each other (and perhaps a wider circle of kin and neighbors) in order to bring things to a boil—particularly to the point of calling for help from an outsider.

The Milan group has presented a particularly interesting example of the therapeutic use of these projective processes (20). Over three generations, the Casanti family had moved from a rural and isolated farm to the city where they started a family construction business. In the first generation, on the farm, the family was held together by a shared conviction of family power through stolid mastery: "The survival, safety and dignity of [our] members depend on the family. Whoever separates himself from the family is lost." Although fully functional in a rural setting, this paradigm persisted into the second and third generation even though family members had moved to the city. Its persistence produced devastating effects on the younger daughter of one of the Casanti brothers, and therapeutic intervention became necessary. The extended Casanti clan regarded the initial therapeutic contact as a violation of their self-concepts.

The specific therapeutic intervention was the now-famous prescription of a ritual for the family. The prescription had two parts. First, it required the family to set aside one hour a night for sharing feelings among themselves in a rigorously prescribed way. Second, it required the family to behave with even greater reverence toward the extended Casanti clan. This paradoxical instruction, I believe, helped the family to project what was once felt as theirs onto the therapy system during the course of their own change. By its instruction, the therapeutic team is not putting something into the family. Rather, something is being taken out. The therapists are saying, in effect, "It is *our* standard to honor the clan that must be honored." Such prescribed rituals, I suspect, allow the family to disown implicitly and temporarily this standard of loyalty to the extended family by projecting it onto the therapeutic team. At the same time, the ritual gives them a behavioral arena, the prescribed family discussion, in which to define their separateness as a nuclear family.

In nontherapeutic settings the same sequence of transformations of families can be observed. For example, the migration of a family from one cultural setting to another offers a rich opportunity for studying this process of disowning (14). In fact, the Casantis were going through precisely this form of migration but apparently could not, unlike most other familes, accomplish the necessary conversion on their own. I refer to the change process as a conversion, drawing upon the connotations of that term to emphasize two components of this change. First, it reflects an alteration of beliefs and convictions; second, and equally important, if successful, it represents a radical alteration in the social community in which the family is embedded. As in religious conversion, the beliefs change as one joins with a new, extended community. It is the membership of the family in a new group (the nuclear family left the rural setting of the Casanti clan to become more embedded in an urban community) that both initiates and sustains the change.

The family therapy setting can be viewed as a new community with its own rules and beliefs. The Milan group's ritual prescription suggests that these beliefs can be manufactured or tailored to accomplish specific therapeutic aims, but I remain skeptical. Did the paradoxically prescribed ritual given to the Casantis have its impact because it reflected some basic value of the Milan team? This now becomes a research question of paramount importance, along with the parallel question of whether the team approach—because the team may be, in effect, a natural "belief community"—is critical for the induction of conversion through projective processes. In other words, it is possible that the conversion mechanism depends upon the presence of a therapeutic team to provide a vivid sense of entering a new community (perhaps heightened by the mystery of why most of the team is invisible—hidden behind a one-way mirror).

RECOMMENDATIONS

Even when fully realized, these two sketches of change models will at best be only partial—in the sense that it is unlikely that either alone accounts for all or most of the change in the course of family therapy. Further, they are partial in the sense that they do not mention other processes that may be equally or even more important for change. For example, Hoffman (11) has begun to sketch a model of change that focuses not on disrupting stable features of the family but on trying to immobilize certain, constantly changing features of the family system.

Likewise, these models contain nothing about the social learning principles that have shaped a number of clear models of change in the more behaviorally oriented family therapy approaches. Finally, these models focus entirely on psychosocial mechanisms, although there is recent evidence that biologic mechanisms may also be involved in perpetuating family stability and may have to be addressed in more complete models (15, 19).

Nonetheless, I hope that I have made my point about the importance of models of family change, and that I have adequately grounded my pleas that they become central in the next generation of family therapy research. To concretize my position, however, I would like to make several specific recommendations; these are addressed simultaneously to investigators and their would-be patrons, the funding agencies.

1. Theory construction is not a back-room activity. It must be moved

front and center in the family therapy research enterprise. Investigators should be funded for time and effort spent in theory construction. Reviews and conferences should be sponsored that focus on theory construction. Note should be taken of the systematic attempts within the family and social field to improve methods for constructing testable theories (5, 10). Hopefully, the theories that emerge from these efforts will be free of conceptual language that ties them too closely to specific schools; perhaps even the systemic and learning approaches may be reconciled in part. It may be Panglossian to hope that such theories might also embrace nontherapeutic models of the change processes in families.

2. Family therapy research should be primarily process research.[4] Outcome and efficacy are crucial, of course, but *understanding change* is primary. Theories should specify those processes that we most want to measure during the course of therapy and, more importantly, what inferences about change can be legitimately drawn from such measurements.

3. All grant applications, whether for outcome or process research, or both, should be required to have a well-developed theory section. Applicants must offer concepts and evidence that support more than the feasibility of their study, the psychometric purity of their instruments, and the logic of their design. Further, they must go beyond optimistic estimates of the efficacy of their approach. All applicants should clearly state the mechanisms or processes they believe responsible for the effectiveness of the therapies they are studying. In order to anchor the work in broader inquiries concerning the transaction between families and nontherapeutic healing communities, preference should be given to research teams composed of family therapists and social scientists with interest and experience that includes but goes beyond the clinical setting.

4. Review committees should not be stacked with theory-hating methodologists. Research-trained clinicians from within and without the family field will always be necessary. But why not also include a few persons with a passionate interest in general or specific processes of human change?

REFERENCES

1. Almond, R. *The healing community.* New York: Jason Aronson, 1974.
2. Aponte, H.J., & VanDeusen, J.M. Structural family therapy. In A. S. Gurman & D.P. Kniskern (eds.), *Handbook of family therapy.* New York: Brunner/Mazel, 1981.

---

4. *Editor's Note:* The contributors to this volume share consensus on the importance of process studied in family therapy research. Pinsof (Chapter 12) and Alexander (Chapter 13) especially emphasize this view.

3. Bossard, J.H.S., & Boll, E.S. *Ritual in family living.* Philadelphia: University of Pennsylvania Press, 1950.
4. Bowen, M. *Family therapy in clinical practice.* New York: Jason Aronson, 1978.
5. Burr, W.R., Hue, R., Nye, I.F., & Rews, I.L. *Contemporary theories about the family* (Vol. 1). New York: Free Press, 1979.
6. Csikszentmihalyi, M., & Rochbert-Halton, E. *The meaning of things: Domestic symbols and the self.* Cambridge: Cambridge University Press, 1981.
7. Darling, R.B. *Families against society.* New York: Sage Publications, 1979.
8. Fereirra, A.J. Family myth and homeostasis. *Archives of General Psychiatry 9:* 457-463, 1963.
9. Frank, J.D. *Persuasion and healing: A comparative study of psychotherapy.* Baltimore: John Hopkins University Press, 1961.
10. Hage, J. *Techniques and problems of theory construction in sociology.* New York: Wiley-Interscience, 1972.
11. Hoffman, L. "Enmeshment" and the too richly cross-joined system. *Family Process 14:* 457–468, 1975.
12. _____. *Foundations of family therapy: A conceptual framework for systems change.* New York: Basic Books, 1981.
13. Korn, S.J., Chess, S., & Fernandez, P. The impact of children's physical handicaps on marital quality and family interaction. In R.M. Lerner & G.B. Spanier (eds.), *Child influences on marital and family interaction: A life-span perspective.* New York: Academic Press, 1978.
14. Landau, J. Therapy with families in cultural transition. In M. McGoldrick, J.K. Pearce, & J. Giordano (eds.), *Ethnicity and family therapy.* New York: Guilford Press, 1982.
15. Levenson, R.W., & Gottman, J.M. Marital interaction: Physiological linkage and affective exchange. *Journal of Personality and Social Psychology 45:* 587–597, 1983.
16. Minuchin, S., Rosman, B.L., & Baker, L. *Psychosomatic families: Anorexia nervosa in context.* Cambridge: Harvard University Press, 1978.
17. Reiss, D. *The family's construction of reality.* Cambridge: Harvard University Press, 1981.
18. _____. Critique: Sensory extenders versus meters and predictors: Clarifying strategies for the use of objective tests in family therapy. *Family Process 22:* 165–172, 1983.
19. _____, & Oliveri, M.E. Sensory experience and family process: Perceptual styles tend to run in but not necessarily run families. *Family Process 22:* 289–308, 1983.
20. Selvini-Palazzoli, M., Boscolo, L., Cecchin, G., & Prata, G. *Paradox and counterparadox: A new model in the therapy of the family in schizophrenic transaction* (translator, E. V. Burt). New York: Jason Aronson, 1978.
21. Sluzki, C. Process, structure and world views: Toward an integrated view of systemic models in family therapy. *Family Process 22:* 469–476, 1983.
22. Smith, M.L., Glass, G.V., & Miller, T.I. *The benefits of psychotherapy.* Baltimore: Johns Hopkins University Press, 1980.
23. Todd, T.C., & Stanton, M.D. Research on marital and family therapy: Answers, issues, and recommendations for the future. In B.B. Wolman & G. Stricker (eds.), *Handbook of marital and family therapy.* New York: Plenum Press, 1983.
24. Wolin, S.J., Bennett, L.A., & Noonan, D.L. Family rituals and the recurrence

of alcoholism over generations. *American Journal of Psychiatry 136:* 589–593, 1979.

25. Zinner, J., & Shapiro, R. Projective identification as a mode of perception and behaviour in families of adolescents. *International Journal of Psycho-Analysis 53:* 523–530, 1972.

3

THE HOLY GRAIL:
Proven Efficacy in Family Therapy

ROBERT G. RYDER

University of Connecticut
Storrs, Connecticut

THERE ARE a variety of agendas related to an interest in demonstrating that family therapy works and what there is about it that works. This chapter touches on several of these agendas, all oriented to this same goal of proven efficacy. Nevertheless, I believe that pursuit of this Holy Grail may be a distraction from other pursuits, some of which may be more valuable, for example, doing therapy, doing other kinds of research, thinking, or teaching. Obviously, it is also possible that some alternative pursuits are less valuable or downright awful, but that is not the emphasis to be taken here.

THE POLITICAL AGENDA

Suppose that it is a good thing for family therapy to be well regarded and respected. Should we then undertake to accomplish this goal by doing politically motivated research? One answer to this question is that such research is not science. According to Gergen (2), who believes that there are no empirical facts whatsoever in the social sciences, it is rhetoric. We may even say it is morally questionable. Nevertheless, if such an enterprise were attempted, what would be its feasibility? Not great, I would say. The reason for this judgment is that social science research does not have a great track record of convincing and converting heathens. It may offer a totally convincing record to the already converted without attracting many new converts (college sophomores excluded).

I believe that there is no such thing as a totally unassailable research project. Perhaps most of you will at least agree that such an animal is rare. The complications of doing causal research (I mean experimentation) are mostly well known; and causal studies, with people, with independent variables believed to be capable of producing help or injury, are going to be susceptible to major assaults. The "enemy" can be counted on to attribute apparently positive findings to poor statistics, inadequate randomization, evanescent enthusiasm (the old Hawthorne effect as applied to therapists), dropouts, trivial or fakable measures, and on and on into the night. When strongly held beliefs or values are at stake, or an argument is about something other than its substantive content (which is almost always true and false), one side is going to accept null findings and demolish affirmative ones, whereas the other side will tend to do the opposite. No one wins in political research efforts. Eventually, they just die of old age.

On the other hand, it is possible to lose politically in social science. The way to do this, I think, is to do a lot of shaky work that is eventually subjected to severe criticism or that fails to get anywhere in the long run. In the short run, we may have studies, or reviews, or meta-analyses, and so on, that we proudly wave about as banners. In the long run, we run the risk of destroying the credibility of ourselves, of social science (or some aspects of it), of the therapy we hoped to assist, and perhaps even of the funding process that let us do the work in the first place.

It is possible that most people already believe that family therapy is valuable (though perhaps only in its proper place). If so, is it reasonable to engage in one more social science exercise to try to turn general belief into legitimate, "proven" fact? Apparent attempts to prove what seems obvious (if only in retrospect) have not usually been a big political plus, if cocktail-party gossip is to be believed.

Perhaps, just perhaps, the long view of self-interest dictates the doing of work that is not obviously self-serving, that is more interesting than rhetorical, and that is slow, modest, and mostly nonintrusive. Rather than pull together 50,000 "subjects" (as has been done, in effect, with individual therapy research) and attempt to prove ourselves irrefutably (as has failed in the individual therapy meta-analyses—see 1, 3–5, all in one issue of *The American Psychologist*), we may do ourselves more of a favor by being subtle and interesting.

DOGS AND TAILS

As many have noted before, system effects are everywhere. For example, the doing of research can have unintended consequences that, in turn, further support similar research. For example, the tendency to urge the *study* of what can be studied may be followed by the urge to *do* what can be studied (which, in turn, makes the research more plausible). Thus, structured therapies, well defined in terms of observable behaviors, can be elevated to an exalted status not otherwise deserved. Such therapies are also said to be more teachable, which is used as another argument for them. To think linearly for the moment, the tail, in effect, wags the dog.

Easily measurable outcomes can be demonstrated more readily than outcomes that are very difficult to measure. Should we then specialize in trying for outcomes that are concrete and objective? The conceptualization of therapy itself can fall victim to reductionism. We can come to think of therapy as some kind of summing of various discrete, coded behaviors, or tasks accomplished, or phases completed. Certainly, this is not a necessary consequence of detailed studies, but it may not be such a far-fetched view either. With the current emphasis on behaviors (concrete, countable things that people can do), the more subtle texture of what occurs can be lost from sight, or noted only as a research agenda for mañana.

The idea of experimentally cutting up therapy into pieces to be separately manipulated, compared with a more gentle approach to studying what happens, seems reminiscent of the distinction made recently by Stierlin (7). I refer not to the distinction he draws between science and art, but to the distinction between an orientation to power and an orientation to curiosity. These orientations may shape both therapy and research, and help to mediate between them.

Even definitions can be the result, rather than just the basis, of research efforts that are overly concerned with self- justification. What is family therapy? If it is to be studied, it must be (re)defined as something procedural. Indeed, if it is to be taught "properly," it must be similarly defined (see the latest AAMFT accreditation policies). The idea that family therapy is a point of view can be deemed unacceptable for the simple reason that we have no idea how to "prove" a point of view with our empirical social science. Perhaps a better idea would be to use the family therapy point of view to do more interesting research on all therapy.[1]

SCIENCE AND VALUES

Values and values may be a better heading for this section. The issue is, how important is the question of family therapy efficacy. Before getting a stake at which to burn this heretic (or to use for shafting him or driving it through his heart), it may be productive to consider this question. No doubt, efficacy is of social importance. Questions of relative costs and benefits of various therapeutic procedures are or may be of great social importance. But, is efficacy—much less efficacy that is complicated by cost considerations—of any *scientific* importance?

Let me approach this question from another angle. It is utterly implausible that therapy, as that term is generally used, has no effect

---

1. *Editor's Note:* Ryder seems to say that if family therapy is defined as "something procedural," then it can't *also* be regarded as a "point of view." I would argue that family therapy, as a point of view, can be defined as having procedural *aspects* that can be studied (see Stanton's definition in Chapter 1). However, consideration of a family therapy point of view in *all* therapy certainly would be highly interesting—and probably would bring to light previously neglected issues.

whatsoever. The effects may be trivial or not, helpful or not, intended or not, but it is simply unreasonable to believe that there are absolutely no consequences. Is there, *can* there be any doubt of this? What then is our warrant for assuming that (some, most, all) effects are best described by some dimension that we, or society as a whole, consensually value? Carl Rogers (6) said, some 30 years ago, that the first task is to learn *what* therapy does, and then to worry about whether or not we like it. To say that therapy "improves" some people/marriages/families is to say almost nothing about its consequences.

Such a focus is worse than boring. It creates more rather than less difficulty if we try to find out what is going on in therapy. The urge to pass judgment on results can be so strong that the results themselves never even make it to an integrative review, or do not form a central part of the review, or are so variously studied that they are not cumulative at all.

Issues of social importance certainly need to be addressed. However, here (as in considering the political pragmatics of research) an *Umweg*, a more circuitous path, is well advised. Rather than accumulate drawers of unconvincing evidence about what is best and what is not, doing work that is of scientific interest—that is, enlightening about therapy process and/or about families—may have a greater ultimate effect on the enlightenment of therapists and their clients. Years of social science efforts relating to individual therapy have not led to much of central importance to the average, work-a-day clinician. Let us follow Reiss's (Chapter 2) suggestion and go another way.

CAUSALITY AND INDEPENDENT VARIABLES

Demonstrations of causality are among the things that are much desired but little achieved in social science research. Except under rather special circumstances, attempts to study causality tend to be fruitless. They are relatively easy only when the manipulations of independent variables are so trivial that no one worries about possible negative effects. Otherwise, having both the power and the hardness of heart to maintain adequate equivalence between treatment groups is difficult and, hence, rare (properly so, in my opinion). Dependent variables that are unambiguously meaningful yet gross enough to be well measured are also rare. Independent variables that are meaningful and well-enough defined to provide an unambiguous interpretation of results are virtually unknown. Achieving conceptual specifications of what is studied, without begging the question of what causes what, may be the most difficult problem of all.

Psychotherapy research results that have been consensually regarded as useful, important, and correct, that have been dependably replicated, that do involve more than crass variables, and that have maintained this status over many years—these have not been frequent. Yet the logical models and measurement techniques have not much changed over the years. It may be too early to determine whether family therapy research results will stand the test of time. However, there does not seem to be a unique research model for family therapy that is greatly different from models applied to other forms of therapy (assuming for the moment that family therapy is indeed a form of therapy).

As is well known, the problems involved in executing an effective, classical study of therapy outcome, with clearly defined independent and dependent variables, are serious and usually insurmountable. Also rare are adequate control over the actions of clients, service provision choices, and measurements of various kinds. Meaningful diagnostic distinctions among kinds of clients (prior to getting hard data about the results of different therapies) require a kind of logical bootstrapping or lucky guesses.

Suppose that one is interested in a classical outcome study and has somehow solved all pertinent measurement problems, and the problems of defining success, improvement, and the like. Independent variable manipulations must be limited to those that are totally independent (by definition) of client actions, or of therapist actions once the therapist has been confronted by the clients (and, hence, may be responding to them). Therapists in different experimental conditions may be trained differently, be given different instructions as to how to deal with clients, perhaps be thought to have different personalities (by prior measurement), and so on.

I want to call attention to two problems with such studies. First, they are intrinsically quite crude because they are limited to what can be specified *before* therapy begins. Once an interactive dance or information exchange between therapist and client has begun, what the therapist does can no longer be regarded as independent. Second, such a procedure may rest on the model that therapy is an identifiable, consistent, substantive, replicable thing that can be applied to a particular party, and with specifiable effects upon that party.[2]

There seem to be some in the family therapy camp who may leap to accuse this model of being linear, and who may condemn it out of hand. Others may simply shrug because we do, after all, accept a linear model at some level. But at what level? There is no doubt that therapists make a career out of providing something to people. Is that something a service

---

2. *Editor's Note:* The contributors to this volume seem to agree with Ryder that such "classical" outcome studies are misguided and inappropriate. The therapist must be *part* (not "independent") of the therapeutic system. This is essential to studies of therapy process (and process/outcome) and is recommended as the "state of the art."

in the usual sense, as might be provided by a piano tuner, an orthopedist, or a prostitute? Is that something a collection of techniques presumably drawn from some substrate of scientific or esthetic understanding that can be *applied* to clients, and with definable results? If so, then we are talking about a fundamentally linear process in the actual interaction between clients and therapist. This is, I think, a questionable view as applied to most talking therapies, including most family therapy.

Note that I am not asserting that this linear view is wrong in any absolute sense, only that it is questionable—that is, not clearly consensual. It is entirely possible to suggest that what therapists provide, what they have a reasonable claim to be paid for, is something else. For example, a therapist may claim to be providing his or her own human presence in a family or other grouping, restricted by various boundary conditions but enlightened by a wealth of previous personal and vicarious experiences with other persons. What happens then is merely what happens. It may be special because of who the therapist is (in terms of background, attitudes, and so on), and because of the special way that the therapist enters the group. Nevertheless, there may be no reasonable basis for thinking that any given concrete action by the therapist is a unidirectional service provided by the therapist to the clients. Depending on one's epistemology, everything that happens in the therapy, including actions by the therapist, can be regarded as information about everyone, about the clients, about the therapist, or about some other individual or grouping.

I imagine that most therapists regard their thinking as varying from time to time, and that they are somewhat in between the linear and nonlinear extremes. Strictly speaking, only the second of these two points of view, the nonlinear point of view, is susceptible to study with a classical outcome design. We can sometimes provide unambiguous experimental control over who sees what clients, but not over the details of therapist actions with clients. These details remain vulnerable to the traditional, methodological accusation that they may be influenced by clients. They are no longer clear, independent variables with linear effects.

The trouble with using a classical design with a nonlinear point of view is that there may not be much point to it.[3] To assert that therapy is "effective" from a nonlinear point of view may not be much more

_____

3. *Editor's Note:* Perhaps the trouble comes if one attempts to apply a "classical" design to *outcome* research and neglects to look at the *processes* of therapy, where a nonlinear point of view is more clearly relevant. Then the results may even become interesting, especially, I believe, if these processes are linked to selective measures of outcome. When outcome assessment is limited to giving improvement rates, without understanding the processes and context associated with these rates, outcome becomes uninterpretable.

meaningful than to assert that marriage, as some sort of generalized "service," is successful. Sometimes it is, and sometimes not, due—it must be surmised—to aspects of who is paired with whom and why, and to poorly understood emergents coming out of the dyadic or family process.

Suppose, however, that the research enterprise is undertaken from a more unidirectional point of view, namely, that therapy is the appropriate provision of certain techniques that will alleviate disorders. Then, part of the advance preparation of therapists, that is, part of the independent variable manipulation, may be to instruct them to use different techniques under different experimental conditions. Subsequent significance tests that compare experimental conditions may show that they differ according to the techniques used, and that the differences cannot be attributed to differences in clients (if clients are really randomly assigned to conditions, and the assignments are firm). If so, a therapist with a nonlinear point of view would be likely to regard all the therapies studied as inadequate. That is, if one regards therapy in part as the provision of one genuine human being to another, under various boundary conditions, any external impetus to specify in advance one technique versus another (almost regardless of the technique) is to reduce the quality of the therapy. "Real" therapy, from such a point of view, is thus omitted from the study.[4]

The kind of outcome study described begs the question of what therapy is all about, by assuming that it is the more-or-less mechanical (which is not to say stupid) application of definable interpersonal procedures. Anyone who disagrees with this view will find such studies wanting.

Obviously, not all therapy research is outcome research. However, the therapeutic process may be studied, even in exquisite detail, with causality in mind. One may want to learn, for example, which therapist interventions were most effective with a particular family. However, nothing done by the therapist can be regarded with certainty as an "intervention," if by intervention is meant something entering an interactional system from outside of it. There is no way of demonstrating that

---

4. *Editor's Note:* There is no agreement among the contributors to this volume about whether it is ever appropriate to assign therapists randomly to use differing treatment models. The hope is to include the therapist's "personality" as a constant across techniques. However, differences in a therapist's skill, experience with, and enthusiasm for one model versus another are likely to undermine such research designs. Additionally, the "personality" of the therapist, as manifest in the therapy, and which may or may not be efficacious, is likely to fit one approach differently than another. Obviously, I share Ryder's dim view of such efforts at randomization of therapists.

the therapist has not been led to her or his action by the interactional system of which the therapist has now become a part.

Although therapy may be difficult to study in a classical model, therapists are feasible objects of study. Without ever worrying about generalizing from people to procedures (a questionable step), a sufficiently determined agency could study who among its therapists was more or less successful, and turn its hardheartedness to appropriate personnel policies (keeping the good therapists and sacking the others). All(!) that would be needed would be a clear and well-measured idea of what the agency wanted its therapists to accomplish.

Personally, I think we would do well to step back a little from the therapy research enterprise and ask ourselves what it is we are about and why. Many subtleties are not going to yield to experimental research. Not now and not in the foreseeable future. Outcome research will not generate evidence about causality. Are there other goals of some importance? I would say that the answer is yes. Should causality as an objective of family therapy research (not to mention other research) be eschewed as a goal except in fairly restricted contexts? I would give that question the same affirmative answer. There is a great deal of "mere" description of therapy process to be done before we can achieve some sense of certainty regarding the nature of therapeutic encounters, or of any other important human encounter.

REFERENCES

1. Dawes, R.M., Landman, J., & Williams, M. Reply to Kurosawa. *American Psychologist 39:* 74–75.
2. Gergen, K.J. *Toward transformation in social knowledge.* New York: Springer-Verlag, 1982.
3. Kurosawa, K. Meta-analysis and selective publication bias. *American Psychologist 39:* 73–74, 1984.
4. Landman, J., & Dawes, R.M. Reply to Orwin and Cordray. *American Psychologist 39:* 72–73, 1984.
5. Orwin, R.G., & Cordray, D.S. Smith and Glass's psychotherapy conclusions need further probing: On Landman and Dawes' reanalysis. *American Psychologist 39:* 71–72.
6. Rogers, C., & Dymond, R.F. *Psychotherapy and personality: Change coordinated research studies in the client-centered approach.* Chicago: University of Chicago Press, 1954.
7. Stierlin, H. Family therapy—A science or an art? *Family Process 22:* 413–423, 1983.

4

EPISTEMOLOGICAL CONFUSION AND OUTCOME RESEARCH

E. H. AUERSWALD

Center for Applied Epistemology
San Francisco, California

THE PURPOSE of the conference leading to this volume was to meet a challenge that originated in the sociopolitical "surround" we inhabit. The challenge was to come up with data, derived from solid research, to show that family therapy is an effective means of alleviating human distress and that it should be taken seriously by the power-wielding funding organizations in and out of government. I believe this task is complicated by a situation that has developed in the field of family study and treatment, which I would describe as an epistemological split that currently is creating considerable confusion.

This split, I believe, is not confined to the field of family study and treatment. It expresses an epistemological split that has developed in Western society in this century. Although the predominant reality system of the Western world remains rooted in Cartesian/Newtonian mechanistic and reductionistic "common sense," the basis for a new nonmechanistic and nonreductionistic reality system has been forming in twentieth-century science and philosophy. I believe that the emergence and early growth of family therapy signaled the entry of the thinking immanent in the new reality system into the behavioral sciences.

As we all know, the rapidity of growth of family therapy as a field has been astounding. As the field has mushroomed and become for many a means of livelihood, the epistemological origins of the field—as a revised way of thinking, a revised reality system—have remained visible in theoretical conversation. To a large extent, however, both clinical work and research have given way pragmatically to the need to remain congruent with the generally predominant Cartesian/Newtonian mechanistic/reductionistic edition of reality. More and more, the field has been subsumed by that reality and defined as simply another—hopefully more effective—modality of treatment for individual and family disorder. Much of the thinking in both the clinical and research realms, and, for pragmatic reasons, nearly all of the actual research now being done, reflect this subsumption.

I believe there is a need for research that is based in the still emerging nonmechanistic and nonreductionistic system of thought that originally gave birth to the field. In fact, as you will see from my later comments, I believe that research based in this epistemologically altered reality will be, in the end, more generically useful than research that is now being done. Such research, however, cannot be designed or its significance understood as long as the current epistemological confusion is maintained.

This chapter, then, is an attempt to clear up some of that epistemological confusion, and to present some thoughts on a methodology of research carried out in the emerging nonmechanistic and nonreductionistic reality system. I will later refer to research in which the outcome, in order to have meaning, must be concerned with if, how, when, and under what conditions the therapy works to reach this therapeutic end.[1] The key question in the design of outcome research is, of course, "outcome as related to what." The answer to this question requires a clear definition of the distress that therapeutic intervention is attempting to alleviate.

Keeping this issue of problem definition in mind, if one looks through ecological glasses, first at the large variety of people, families, and communities that make up our nation, and then at the large variety of public and private professional health-care offices to which people come for help, one observation stands out above all others. The definitions of distress that emerge in homes and on the streets of communities, and the definitions that emerge in professional offices, more often than not differ dramatically.

The incidence of such definitional discrepancy is highest, as one would expect, in impoverished ghettos, where virtually no one has ever heard of Freud, and lowest in the middle- and upper-class Caucasian neighborhoods where therapy is part of a way of life, where people have more power to control their environment, where distress is less often rooted in conditions outside the family, and where diagnostic labels have become part of the common vocabulary.

If one has the freedom and inclination to move about from vantage point to vantage point in the field of a given community, one can watch this definitional hiatus develop. The split occurs during the reductionistic sequence of events we call diagnosis, and the degree of definitional

---

1. *Editor's Note:* What Auerswald describes as research that is concerned with if, how, and under what conditions a therapy works is what other contributors to this volume call "process" research. A consensus emerges in this volume that "outcome" research should not continue to be carried out in the traditional, narrowly reductionistic way in which *only* improvement rates are reported without attention to the contextual conditions to which Auerswald refers. Several authors, such as Reiss (Chapter 2), Pinsof (Chapter 12), and Alexander (Chapter 13) make this point. However, Auerswald's epistemologic critique goes farther than most others in his call for an ecosystemic reorientation.

discrepancy is sometimes related to the number of steps in this sequence. The following case illustrates these points.

Case Example

A nine-year-old boy is in trouble. His behavior is distressing to his family and to the school he attends. His family defines the distress as a situation in which the boy refuses to mind his mother and is failing in school.

The child's teacher in school agrees with the family's definition, but adds another dimension. The boy's behavior is less than exemplary in the classroom, and, as is the practice, she defines him as a "disruptive child." After talking to the boy's mother, she refers the child to the school's guidance counselor. The guidance counselor reads the child's school records, talks to the child and to his mother, and then adds another facet to the school's definition by including "possible dyslexia" in her write-up for referral to the local child guidance clinic.

The child is then seen by a child psychiatrist who continues the process of redefinition. His definition is that the boy is afflicted with a "behavior disorder." The family's definition is now reduced to the status of "chief complaint," and the school's definition is abandoned, except for "possible dyslexia," which the psychiatrist retains, and on the basis of which he refers the child to a clinic psychologist for testing.

The testing psychologist adds two more definitional labels based on IQ testing and some angry and bizarre fantasies he extracts from the child on a projective test. These are "borderline intelligence" and "possible incipient schizophrenia." The psychiatrist then attempts to meet with both parents, but only the mother arrives for the session, saying that the father couldn't get the time off from work. The psychiatrist reports all of the above to her, and introduces her to another clinic psychologist who is assigned as therapist.

This psychologist, who bills herself as a "family systems therapist," is a former teacher who had returned to school to acquire a Ph.D. in psychology, and then spent a year in a family therapy training program. She is interested in dyslexia, and she is putting together a research project for which she hopes to acquire a postdoctoral fellowship. She wants to measure the usefulness of family therapy in the treatment of dyslexia. As a "family systems therapist," she is unimpressed with the usefulness of the array of diagnostic definitions applied to the situation of this child, but she is intrigued by the "possible dyslexia" definition. She has been talking to a pediatric neurologist who is also interested in dyslexia, and from whom she hopes to receive referrals for her proposed study. She refers the child to him with the request that he nail down the equivocal diagnosis.

The pediatric neurologist reports that his work-up reveals that the boy *is* dyslexic, and suggests that this hitherto unrecognized dyslexia is the basis for all that has happened. Accordingly, this "family systems therapist" designs her therapeutic intervention toward the goal of providing a context that will reframe the problem in this way and assist the child to overcome his dyslexia.

The therapist then obtains her postdoctoral fellowship, and this family becomes part of a cohort of families that are treated and studied for the purpose of determining the efficacy of family therapy in the treatment of dyslexia. After 6 months of weekly family therapy sessions, supplemented by individual sessions with a remedial reading specialist, this child's reading skills evolve from a first-grade to a fourth-grade level. General impressionistic statements in the records of the therapy state that the child is now doing well in class, and that his war with his mother has ceased. The ongoing notes of the therapeutic process contain periodic references to dyslexia, but they are rare, and in one note the therapist remarks that, despite her early explanations, the family does not seem to have comprehended what dyslexia is all about.

In the dyslexia study, the data collected in work with this child and his family are included in the larger body of data that, when analyzed, suggest that family therapy is effective in the treatment of dyslexia. However, the results are never published because the advisor for the postdoctoral fellowship changes, and the new advisor raises questions about the validity of the diagnosis of dyslexia (because this child and others had progressed so rapidly) and notes that controls were lacking and that the study of family therapy was contaminated by the addition of remedial work for the child alone.

Research Implications

I think it is fair to say that if I asked most researchers in the family therapy field to respond to the above story, the response thus evoked would be a discussion of the inherent methodological problems of such research attempts, and of the ways that these problems could be at least partially solved by the use of tighter and more sophisticated research methods. Although a better project design might have given more acceptable results, it seems that there are *always* unanswered methodological questions in such studies. In fact, careers are made by contemplation of these problems.

What bothers me much more about this case story, which is not exceptional, is that this family, given a different sequence of diagnosis and with different personnel involved, could have become part of a cohort in a study of the outcome of family therapy in the treatment of "disruptive" children, or behavior disorders, or prevention of adolescent schizophrenia, and so on. This difficulty is more serious than how to design research on treatment of a specified kind of problem.

More fundamentally, one must look at the reductionistic processes immanent in the way this boy and his family were defined by the professionals they encountered on their trip through the linear sequences of diagnosis and treatment. The family's definition of the problem had been totally lost by the time the family got to therapy. Yet, the clinical work done with this family was primarily related to that definition and, in fact, achieved a successful outcome.

If some researcher had designed a project to study whether family therapy was useful in situations in which a child refused to mind his mother, or for children in trouble in school, the work done with this family would have contributed to an outcome result achieved with minimal methodological problems. The methodological difficulties were created during the reductionistic process of professional diagnosis! There is, however, virtually no chance today that a trained researcher would design a study this way. First of all, such a study would be considered naive, too global, and, probably, nonprofessional. Secondly, what organization that funds research would release money for "A Study of Children in Trouble in School and Who Won't Mind Their Mothers"?[2]

In the above context, a certain irony surfaces when one looks at the timing of the conference that produced this book. In this era of parsimony in spending for human concerns and extravagance in spending for weapons, what is being demanded is "proof" of the effectiveness of various methods of therapy. Professionals in the family therapy field, along with a spate of others with convictions about other methods of therapy, are rising to the challenge, getting together for the purpose of documenting the outcomes of their work, by collating what data exist, and by planning how to acquire more impressive data. The irony is that the kind of study that would most impress nonprofessionals would be one that convinced them of the effectiveness of family therapy in helping families whose children are in trouble in school and/or who don't mind their mothers.[3]

---

2. *Editor's Note:* The gist of Auerswald's story is familiar, I hope, to all psychotherapy researchers and psychotherapists, of whatever stripe. There can be little doubt that some researchers would respond much as Auerswald fears. On the other hand, I also agree with Auerswald, as he goes on to say, that appropriate research on such therapy can, nonreductionistically, keep the family's definition of the problem in sight. In Editor's Comment, 4, at the end of this volume, I include further discussion with Auerswald about this issue.

3. *Editor's Note:* The irony is compounded by the fact that prominent nonprofessional health-care lobbies, such as the National Alliance for the Mentally ill (NAMI) are not impressed with therapy oriented to "problems of living." Instead, the family self-help movement regards such problems as trivial and forcefully demands more biologic research on the "brain disease" of major psychopathology such as schizophrenia, without diverting funds to the "worried

We *can* do such research, and it can be very useful; but we cannot do it in academic settings under laboratory conditions, and we cannot do it without a major shift in how we think about research, or about therapy for that matter. The shift is epistemological. Because family therapy is about the only field in the behavioral sciences that has paid serious attention to epistemological issues, one would think that it would be precisely the site in which such a shift has been tested. Unfortunately, such is not the case; and I think the reason for this is that our forays into epistemological issues have only created splits and massive confusion.

As I have already stated, because I believe much can come from an epistemological shift, and from research and clinical practice freed from reductionistic requirements, I would like to attempt a definition of some of the sources of that confusion. I also will present some thoughts about outcome research carried out in an alternative, nonreductionistic framework. Let it be understood that I am basing this attempt on some controversial assumptions, which, for the sake of brevity, I will not defend here, but which I can defend if pressed to do so.

NOTES FOR AN ECOSYSTEMIC EPISTEMOLOGY

The first assumption is that the study and treatment of families are at least partially rooted in science, and that ideas born in the arena of science have relevance. The second assumption is that events characterizing the evolution of the field of family study and treatment cannot be separated from the events that have characterized the evolution of physical and biological science in this century. The third assumption is that each time we humans build a structure of any kind, be it concrete or abstract, we are engaging in the contruction of an "edit" of the universe, and that these structures (edits) can be local or universal.

Within the context of these assumptions, then, I must also define some of the terms I will use, terms that are in common usage in our field, but for which there is a lack of definitional consensus. I will use Bateson's modified definition of the term "epistemology" (7, 8) to denote a set of rules used by a specific group of people to define reality, but I will limit its use to the denotation of a set of rules used by the members of a group in their definition of *universal* reality. I will use the term "paradigm" to denote a set of rules, again used by a specific group, to define a subunit of

---

well." Nevertheless, Auerswald may be right about the ordinary, day-to-day preoccupations of the nonorganized, nonprofessional public that is not burdened by major illness in a family member. In any event, it should be clear that family therapy and family therapy research are not inherently limited to attention to *any* single form of presenting problem, whether viewed and experienced by the family members as parent-adolescent conflict, impending divorce, or schizophrenia in a family member.

a universal reality. I will use the term "theory" to denote an idea or a set of ideas that actually or potentially contribute to a paradigm. And I will use the term "model" to denote a concrete metaphorical representation of an epistemology, a paradigm, or a theory. I am not wedded to these definitions, but their use allows me to write with more clarity. Since about 1959, five paradigms have surfaced within the field, each of which is based on a different definition of a family. They are as follows: 1) a *psychodynamic* paradigm in which a family is defined as a group made up of the interlocking psychodynamics of its members who are at various developmental stages; 2) a *family system* paradigm, which defines a family as a system that operates independently, and from which individual psychodynamics, including those that create symptoms, emerge; 3) a *general systems* paradigm in which a family is defined as a system that shares isomorphic characteristics with all systems, and which arranges systems in a hierarchy according to classes—from quarks to universe—and with "higher" systems containing those "lower" in the hierarchy (for example, sociocultural systems "contain" families, which "contain" individuals who "contain" a psyche, and so on); 4) a *cybernetic systems* paradigm, which defines systems, including a family system, in terms of circular information flow and regulatory mechanisms; and 5) an *ecological systems* (or *ecosystemic*) paradigm, which defines a family as a coevolutionary ecosystem located in evolutionary timespace.

In the last decade, paradigm 1 has been largely abandoned by family therapists.[4] Paradigms 2 through 4 have been merging into what is being called "family systems therapy." Paradigm 5, which is rooted in "new science," is becoming recognized as more than just a paradigm for use in family therapy. It appears to be rooted in an emerging, alternative reality system that has major implications for how we humans organize a knowledge base as a species, including, of course, how our thinking about families and family therapy is organized.

Major additions to paradigm 5 have emerged in the work of scientists outside of family therapy such as Maturana and Varela (13, 16), Brooks and Wiley (10), Prigogine (14, 15), and a large group of physicists who, in their search for a unified theory, have been developing what they have named "the anthropic cosmological principle" (6, 9). There is also work that roots the paradigm epistemologically within identifiable currents in Western philosophy.[5]

---

4. *Editor's Note:* As viewed from California, this abandonment of the psychodynamic paradigm may be complete. However, in Boston, New York, Washington DC, and London, psychodynamically oriented family therapists still thrive.
5. Further discussion of these interesting developments are unnecessary in this chapter and would require too much space. I will be publishing such a discussion elsewhere in a book to be entitled "Beyond Peace and War."

Some of the confusion in our field has resulted from a failure to differentiate these paradigms. Most family therapists seem unaware of the profound difference between "family systems therapy" (combining paradigms 2 through 4) and the ecological systems framework of paradigm 5. This difference is the only difference which is truly epistemological.[6]

Another source of confusion began, so it seems from my vantage point, when some of us in the family therapy field became interested in the remarkable events that have characterized the evolution of science in this century, beginning when Planck and Einstein stepped through the cracks in the Cartesian/Newtonian view of physical reality and laid the groundwork for a new view of reality that superseded the old. To some of us, this transformation in physics became an important metaphor. We were looking for methods of intervening that could create transformations to improve the lives of people in the families that came to us. For ourselves, we wanted to validate ourselves as scientists, not as mystics. And here was an event-shape that satisfied both these criteria. It was rooted in science, and it contained a large-scale transform.

Furthermore, within our field we were already experimenting in a small-scale arena with similar interventive actions that we called "reframing." The isomorphic connection was that in both the large-scale arena of physics and the small-scale arena of the family the method of transformative intervention consisted of the introduction of ideas, in words or action, that changed the basis of reality definition in the target field.

Most of us were attracted to the work of that irrepressible nudge, Gregory Bateson, who had come into family therapy and the behavioral sciences through the side door; like Socrates, he kept questioning our tendency to settle for labels that precluded further thought, and he kept insisting that we pay attention to how we knew what we thought we knew.

What has created the ensuing confusion is that what is contained in this ostensive merging of ideas from physics, from Bateson's model of evolution, and from the work of family therapists, is what Hofstadter (11) calls a "strange loop." As a result, the current field of family study and treatment at times resembles the strange loop of an Escher drawing in which the stairs we climb lead us to the bottom landing.

The most obvious and well-documented events that created this strange loop began in 1900 when Planck studied the black body radiation phenomenon and proposed the "theory" of the quantum as a unit of energy. In 1905-1906, Einstein expanded the quantum idea and proposed

---

6. *Editor's Note*: See Editor's Comments, 2, for another view of the shortcomings of paradigms 2–4, which Auerswald groups together as "family systems therapy."

his Special "Theory" of Relativity (followed in 1915 by the General "Theory" of Relativity). Both Planck and Einstein considered their ideas to be theories. There was, however, no "paradigm" to which these "theories" could contribute. The paradigm in general use in physics until then was that proposed by Newton and Descartes. Neither Planck's quantum theory nor Einstein's Theory of Special Relativity fits into that paradigm. Thus, these ideas, which began as theories, became the basis for a new paradigm in physics. So far, no strange loop.

The evolutionary sequence, however, did not stop there. It soon became apparent that the paradigm of what was identified as "new physics" was useful in other branches of science. New physics became "new science." Further expansion occurred when it was recognized that new science formed a basis for a new set of rules that could be used to define a universal reality—that is to say, the basis for a new "epistemology." This event set the stage for the formation of the strange loop in the following way.

Newtonian physics had both emerged from and contributed to the rules governing the universal definition of reality used by Western civilization—the Western epistemology. This epistemology contained a rule of single truth and a rule of dualism, which demanded that a theory or a paradigm be either true or not true. There was, under these rules, no way that a theory or paradigm that was discontinuous and incongruous with the model of the Western/Newtonian universe could be subsumed. Such a theory or paradigm had to be labeled untrue.

When it became clear by experiment that the paradigm of new physics could not be discarded as untrue, and, subsequently, that it provided the basis for a new epistemology, the predominant Western epistemology demanded an either/or reckoning. When experimental evidence further confirmed the usefulness of the new epistemology, Newtonian physics and, by implication, Western thought, faced a crisis. From a vantage point within that reality edit, both epistemologies could not be true. There *could not* be two realities. It was the resolution of this crisis that created the strange loop.

Fortunately or unfortunately, depending upon one's vantage point, the new science epistemology contains a rule of monism and a rule that truth be defined as heuristic. These rules demanded a *both-and* rather than an either/or perspective, and they endowed both the Western/Newtonian and the new science epistemologies with the status of heuristic truth. When, in the world of science, *new* science became the predominant basis for the expansion of knowledge into micro- and macro-phenomena in the universe, Newtonian science lost its claim to predominance. It was not, however, abandoned—for two reasons. First, it remained highly useful and, second, with the redefinition of truth as heuristic and the abandonment of dualism, there was no reason to discard it. However, in science, the Newtonian reality rules could no longer be used as the basis for an epistemology. The Newtonian reality system therefore became a *paradigm* within the new science *epistemology*.

Thus, the reality system of new physics/new science, which was made possible by the Western/Newtonian reality system, became the predominant reality context that allowed the latter to survive. Put analogically, the Western epistemology, through Newtonian physics, gave birth to new science, which, in the world of science, became the parent to its former parent who became the child. Or, put yet another way, Western thought/ Newtonian physics came first, and was the ground within which the figure of new physics appeared. As new physics became new science and subsequently grew to the status of an epistemology, new science became the ground and Newtonian physics became the figure. Again, an Escher drawing comes to mind. This sequence of events in science thus represents more than simply a shift from one paradigm to another, as described by Kuhn (12). It contains the strange loop that creates a confusing sense of "sleight of hand."

I think the early stages of the same sequence can be seen in the general arena of nonscientific Western thought, as represented by the 1960's phenomenon of youth who glimpsed an alternative reality, in the rise of holism in the 1970s, in some of the less vacuous ruminations of "new age" people, and in the writings of a group of popular authors such as Ferguson, Capra, Zukov, and others. It can also be seen in the growing public awareness that the institutions of Western society, based as they are in the old epistemology of Western thought, are increasingly anachronistic and, in our nuclear age, downright dangerous.

Enter Bateson, in his quest for a nonmechanistic theory of evolution. I have argued elsewhere (3–5) that if one constructs a model of evolution as contained in Bateson's writings (which Bateson from his Socratic stance never described in detail and/or in one place), and then examines the rules of thought immanent in that model, these rules turn out to be those of the new science epistemology. Also, in contrast, the rules of thought immanent in mechanistic Darwinian evolution are those of Western/ Newtonian thought. I also argued (5) that any "chunk" of Bateson's model of evolution turns out to be an ecosystem, and those "chunks" that have a clearly established boundary are potentially viable. Thus, I believe that Bateson, by dipping into our field, provided a conceptual link between the thinking of family therapists and the epistemology of new science. What emerged in our thought has acquired the label of the "ecosystemic epistemology."

Another source of confusion, I think, arises when ecosystemic writers revert to the system of thought in which they were originally programmed, and violate the epistemological rules they espouse. For example, some, Bateson included, write about "epistemological error." In the new science (ecosystemic) thought system, there is no "epistemological error." The concept of epistemological error is based on the rule of single truth and the rule of dualism. There is, instead, incongruity, or lack of synchrony. In an ecosystem, whether it is a river bed, a family, or a complex of ideas, the both-and rule prevails. Ejection of a subsystem from an ecosystem may occur, as a reaction to a foreign body, when the entering species or idea does not "fit" and cannot adapt, but there are no confrontations at boundaries, no wars.

Still another source of massive confusion is the aforementioned lack of consensus in the definition of terms. My hope is that by beginning with definitions, I have made my views intelligible. My definitions in this chapter, however, are just that—my definitions, not consensus definitions. There is a need for a conference to begin the process leading to such consensus.

More confusion can be seen in the frequent, undifferentiated use of the term "systems approach." Most writers in our field, and others who use this meaningless term, seem blissfully unaware that there is a profound difference in the way a system is conceived depending upon what paradigm or what epistemology is in use in the field in which the term is used. The differences are far from trivial. For example, the "systems approach" that evolved in economics (now in nationwide use in the mental health field) is totally rooted in mechanistic Western thought. Its use by the Pentagon during the war in Southeast Asia gave us the "kill rate." It is not *eco*systemic at all!

SUGGESTIONS FOR ECOSYSTEMIC THERAPY RESEARCH

One of the reasons I have used all this space in an attempt to clarify epistemological confusion is that such clarity will allow us to answer a question that must be answered before we can begin to do meaningful research. That question is an old and familiar one. Is family therapy simply another modality of treatment among the many, or is it a radically different way of thinking? The answer is that any family therapy that uses the reality rules of the predominant Western/Cartesian/Newtonian epistemology can only be another new modality of treatment, and family therapy that uses the reality rules of the ecosystemic epistemology espouses a radically different way of thinking—different, that is, from the predominant thought system.

With this question answered, each of us can choose what definition he or she wishes to use as a base for research design. Those who choose to use the predominant Western/Cartesian/Newtonian thought system in their work, a choice that at present is certainly wise in pragmatic terms, will seek out basic information by means of traditional, reductionistic research methods. In therapeutic work, they will engage in reductionistic classification and treatment of individual or family system pathology; in outcome research, they will study the modality's usefulness in the treatment of various conditions as defined within the professional paradigms of the health and mental health fields. The major problems faced by this group will continue to be methodological.

On the other hand, those who choose to work ecosystemically will study the effectiveness of work—based in the ecosystemic thought style—with children in trouble in school and/or children who are at war with their parents, or, for that matter, any other situation of individual or family distress, without the need for reductionistic redefinition of the problems as first defined by those who seek help. Methodological problems in research design in this way of working are at a minimum (as I will attempt to show below).

There is, however, a different and very difficult problem. In order to do such research, a site must be developed that consists of a community-based health or mental health delivery system designed to operate ecosystemically and staffed by people who can think ecosystemically. What makes this problem so difficult is that such programs are ecologically out of synchrony with the general society in which they are formed. Even when they can be developed, in my experience, they cannot be sustained.

I make that statement somewhat ruefully because I have developed two such programs, into each of which a system for studying outcome was introduced. In neither program was I able to sustain its use long enough to collect a meaningful body of data, but both programs lasted long enough to show that the format was feasible and that it worked.

The first was part of a Neighborhood Health Center in New York City funded by the United States Office of Economic Opportunity (OEO) during its early days, when money was given without programmatic strings and with the charge to do something different in the delivery of health care to poor people. That program died when Richard Nixon entered the White House and OEO policy changed. The program was forced back into the standard, reductionistic mold of health care delivery (4).

The second was a state-run Mental Health Center serving an island in Hawaii. I took over the directorship of the Center on the basis of an initial contract that permitted me to develop an ecosystemically based program. In this instance, because I had to convert an already existing conventional program, the development of the delivery system took a long time. Nevertheless, I was able to get it in place, but only for a short time. I had been naive in my expectation that this contract would be honored. The leadership of the state's mental health system changed, my contract was forgotten, and the Center was forced to revert to the standard, reduction-istic, illness-oriented mode of operation.

In the course of this experience, however, I did learn a simple way to set up the kind of research I am promoting. (The method might even be called simple-minded, but the context in which it is used is not.) Two forms are built into the routine record-keeping of such a system, one of which is specifically designed to measure outcome.[7] This form has six columns. *Column 1* contains a detailed statement of the problem(s) for which help is requested, written in nontechnical language and agreed upon by client and interviewer. *Column 2* contains a listing of desired outcomes, again in plain language and agreed upon by client and helper(s). *Column 3* lists the cast of characters in the drama that contains the distressing problem(s). *Column 4* details the plan generated to reach the desired outcome(s). *Column 5* lists the tasks contained in the plan, who will carry them out, and who will coordinate if more than two helpers are involved. *Column 6* details what happened when the plan was carried out—the outcome. The actual outcome in Column 6 can then be matched with the desired outcome(s) in Column 2.[8]

In the pilot use of this form in the short-lived settings I described, in roughly 25% of the cases only one run-through was required for attain-ment of the desired outcome(s). In the remaining 75%, desired outcomes not attained, or newly generated during the first run-through, had to be identified and entered in Column 2 in order to set the stage for a second run-through. The first run-through almost always reveals information that explains what prevented the desired outcomes from coming to fruition, and this information goes into the formulation of the plan detailed in Columns 4 and 5 on the second run-through. Sometimes the process continues with a third run-through and, in the pilot effort, only rarely a fourth run-through.

In the course of the work done in accord with the requirements of the above form, an *ecological story* emerges. I have characterized these stories as "event-shapes in timespace," and have written about them and their use elsewhere (1–5). Thus, the second form built into routine record-keeping is simply a blank page on which the story in each case is

---

7. The first rudimentary version of the record-keeping system (described below) was suggested to me by Carole Haber and Larry Long, who had introduced it for use in their work in the West Side Crisis Center of the Jewish Family Service in New York in 1971.

8. *Editor's Note:* I believe that Auerswald's method of record-keeping is similar in certain respects to Goal Attainment Scaling (GAS). Although GAS has been enthusiastically recommended as a clinical and teaching tool, it has not yet been used extensively in therapy research. See Editor's Comment, 5, for a further discussion by me and Auerswald about these methods.

first written in narrative form. Then, an outline of key events that make up the event-shape, which includes the distress, is extracted from the narrative story and entered on the form. Over time, when collated, these stories are found to contain common elements that provide etiological and psychosocial, epidemiological data. Such data are highly useful to a basic understanding of the phenomena encountered and for planning and calibrating the program so as to meet the idiosyncratic needs of the people in the area served. Data collected in a program that delivers full health care are especially useful in this regard because data detailing distress ordinarily identified as biological can also be included.

As you can see, identification of outcome in this system is simple. The actual outcome achieves the desired outcome, or it does so partially, or it does not. What is also useful is that, when the outcome is only partially achieved, or is not achieved at all, that which prevented the achievement is usually identifiable. Such observations are available for ongoing program planning. Also, as data accumulate, clusters of similar types of problem definitions are formed, and a spontaneous classification system emerges that differentiates forms of distress germane to all families, to families from differing ethnocultural and socioeconomic environs, and, idiosyncratically, to families who reside in the community served by the delivery system.

One characteristic of work done in this ecosystemic framework is that interventions are not infrequently made at sites distant from that in which the distress (for which help has been requested) is located. Also, the interventions are additive, which is to say that the helper is thought of as entering and becoming a part of the ecological field and, by his or her presence and behavior, adding to the events occurring therein in such a way as to achieve the desired outcome(s). By thinking this way, it is often possible to design and carry out interventions that benefit not only individuals and single families, but also groups of individuals and/or families (1–5), thus providing another order of data for research purposes. I think the following story will illustrate this.

Case Example: An Ecological Story

Six children from six immigrant Filipino families are referred by an elementary school to the Children's Team of a community mental health center over a span of two weeks. It is noticed that the six children come from one of two classrooms, fifth grade or sixth grade. It is also known that the decision to refer these children occurred at a single staff meeting at the school. In each referral the child referred is described as unwilling or unable to conform to classroom rules. Members of the Children's Team, who work within the community they serve and seldom in an office, are aware that the school is run by a principal of Portuguese heritage, a former Marine who believes in strict discipline, and that the school is staffed by an unusual number of male teachers, also of Portuguese heritage.

The Children's Team worker, thinking ecologically, and beginning with the above information, suspects that an element in the children's ostensibly aberrant behavior might be some sort of cultural clash. He explores specific incidents in the classroom with each of the two teachers, both of whom turn out to be men of Portuguese heritage. He discovers that both teachers, with the support of the principal, use spanking as a means of discipline. The teachers are upset because the children do not respond to such disciplinary measures. They hit back or run out of the school. Afterward, the children do not seem to pay attention to what is going on in class. They are falling behind in their schoolwork, and when the teachers try to give them special, individual attention, they become even more inattentive.

The worker then visits the families of the children. He discovers that they all live in run-down houses in what had once been a sugar plantation village, now scheduled for demolition. Because the children speak fairly good English, he is surprised when he learns that all families had recently immigrated over a two-year span. He questions the families about how they discipline their children and discovers that once a child becomes old enough to understand rules clearly, no corporal punishment is used. Instead, children who disobey are taught to feel shame. The families report no disciplinary problems at home with the children in question.

The worker can now construct a story that contains the following event-shape that explains the children's behavior. The core events (the event-shape) in the story are:

- the disciplinary methods of the teachers in their local version of Portuguese culture
- the disciplinary experience of the children in their Filipino culture
- the immigration of the families from the Philippines to their new country
- the entry of the children into classes taught by Portuguese men
- the principal's support for and the teachers' use of corporal punishment
- the children's behavior

The Children's Team worker can now plan an intervention, an event or events that, when added to the event-shape, will achieve the desired outcome, which is the success of the children in school. He chooses to call a meeting of families, principal, and teachers at which participants can discuss how the children's behavior in school can be controlled. The meeting is held, and it results in an agreement that the teachers will use the disciplinary method of the parents. They will not spank the children (who revealed on questioning at the meeting that they did not consider the spankings as outcomes of their behavior but, rather, as meanness on the part of the teachers, of whom they had become afraid). They will, instead, shame them.

When this agreement was carried out, the behavior of five of the children became exemplary. Two of them, however, one in each class, continued to have serious problems in learning, and one of these two, the sixth-grader, continued to engage in somewhat lessened but nevertheless troubling conflict with both the teacher and the other students.

The worker then assumed that the event-shape he had uncovered was incomplete in these two cases and he continued his exploration. He discovered another event in the families of each child. He learned that in the family of the sixth-grader, the parents had been forced by their families to go through with an arranged marriage neither of them had wanted. Following the birth of their only child, they had turned away from each other and focused their lives on the child in a manner that created increasing pressure on the boy to be "perfect." In an effort to establish some sense of individual identity, the boy was rebelling in all situations outside his home. Thus, the additional event was the unwanted marriage. The worker visited this family for 10 weeks to work with the triadic bind. After the sixth week, the teacher reported that the boy's rebellious behavior had disappeared and that he was catching up in his classwork.

The family of the fifth-grader, on the other hand, seemed to be functioning very well. The boy's two siblings were bright and successful in school, and there was much affection and clear organization in their family life. However, the family reported that the child in question had seemed to develop slowly following an accident in his fifth year. He had fallen from a tree and landed on his head, and he had been unconscious for nearly an hour and dazed for several days. The family had taken him to the emergency room of a Manila hospital. They had been told only that he would be all right. Based on this information, the worker arranged for the boy to be examined neurologically, and for a battery of psychological tests to be administered. The boy was found to have an abnormal EEG and other signs of brain damage. In this instance, the additional event was the sequelae of the fall from the tree. A remedial educator was assigned to work with the boy. A year later he had been promoted to sixth grade but continued to learn slowly, and transfer to a special class was being contemplated.

CONCLUDING COMMENTS

The points I want to make by recounting this story are that (a) the events that comprise the story are themselves the data for outcome research (the outcome in five of these cases in relation to the problem on referral is clearly documented; the outcome of the sixth case will become clear only with long-term follow-up); (b) these data were collected in routine record-keeping; and (c) the information collected in this story will sensitize those who staff the delivery system to the possibility of similar, or analogically similar, situations they may encounter in future work, a process that is cumulative over time.

I think there is not only a place, but also a need for this kind of research. Given a couple of years of operation, a project that collects such data could provide the kind of information the funders and politicians are looking for—and a great deal more.

By this time, I suspect that the reasons I have written this article must be obvious. I am hoping to seduce some family therapy researchers into the group that chooses to do ecosystemically based research. I am also hoping to stimulate some thinking in funding agencies about how ecosystemic projects, such as those I have briefly described, might be supported.

Currently, there is no channel for such funding. Organizations that fund research usually set up review committees that look for methodologies that conform with the standard rules of more academic, reductionistic laboratory research, and the research I have described in broad strokes above does not conform at all to such criteria. Unfortunately, a similar statement can be made with regard to organizations that fund epidemiological research. This kind of research does not meet standard criteria in that arena either.

I know that it is possible to design and implement a HMO program into which such research can be built, because, as I noted above, I participated in such a project in the 1960s when relatively unfettered money was available for health services in the Johnson administration's War on Poverty. Now, however, part of the popularity of HMOs is that they are able to be self-supporting. As I mentioned above, the HMO design necessary for carrying out research of this kind must include an applied behavioral science component that can operate using an ecosystemic, not a biotechnical, medical model. Such a program cannot be self-supporting, and thus requires subsidy. Currently, there is no funding source for such subsidy.

The question can be raised: Why bring these notions to researchers in family therapy rather than, say, to a conference on HMOs? My answer is that I believe family therapy would not exist had there not been a major epistemological shift in the thinking of those who pioneered the field. That shift I think is what has made the movement important. It allowed for the development of new and effective ways to help people in distress. But, not only that. It is the site of connection of the behavioral sciences with the epistemological shift that has taken place in science in general.

Finally, one more time, and with passion! The ecological systems paradigm is more than a paradigm. It is an epistemology, a new system of thought rules used to define universal reality. It is sufficiently developed to make it usable in the design of community-based health and human services delivery systems. More than that, it is sufficiently developed to be used as a basis for solutions of even larger human problems.

We know, these days, that all species on earth are endangered, including humans. If the bombs go off, we are all finished. We know also that our predominant system of thought is not able to extricate us from such paradoxes as: In order to stop building nuclear weapons, we must build more nuclear weapons. We humans need a new system of thought, a new edit of the universe for our very survival. There is such a system of thinking aborning. Its use provides ways to solve little wars, in families and island-school classrooms. I have been thinking about how its use might prevent big wars. I think it can. So, I strongly believe that we should try it out wherever and whenever possible.

REFERENCES

1. Auerswald, E.H. Interdisciplinary vs. ecological approach. *Family Process 7:* 202–215, 1968.
2. _____. Families, change, and the ecological perspective. *Family Process 10:* 263–280, 1971.
3. _____. Thinking about thinking about health and mental health. In G. Caplan (ed.), *American handbook of psychiatry, Vol. 2: Child and adolescent psychiatry, sociocultural and community psychiatry.* New York: Basic Books, 1974.
4. _____. The Gouverneur Health Services Program: An experiment in ecosystemic community health care delivery. *Family Systems Medicine 1* (3): 5–24, 1983.
5. _____. Thinking about thinking in family therapy. *Family Process 24:* 1–12, 1985.
6. Barrow, J.D., & Tipler, F.J. *The anthropic cosmological principle.* New York: Oxford University Press, 1986.
7. Bateson G. *Steps to an ecology of mind.* New York: Ballantine Books, 1972.
8. _____. *Mind and nature: A necessary unity.* New York: E.P. Dutton, 1979.
9. Boslow, J. *Stephen Hawking's universe.* New York: Quill/William Morrow, 1985.
10. Brooks, D.R., & Wiley, E. O. *Evolution as entropy.* Chicago: University of Chicago Press, 1986.
11. Hofstadter, D.R. *Gödel, Escher, Bach: An eternal golden braid.* New York: Basic Books, 1979.
12. Kuhn, T.S. *The structure of scientific revolutions.* Chicago: University of Chicago Press, 1962.
13. Maturana, H.R., & Varela, F.J. *Autopoiesis and cognition: The realization of living.* Dordrecht: Reidel, 1980.
14. Prigogine, I., Nicholis, G., & Babloyantz, A. Thermodynamics of evolution. *Physics Today 25* (11): 23–28; 25 (12): 38–44, 1972.
15. _____, & Stengers, I. *Order out of chaos: Man's new dialogue with nature.* New York: Bantam Books, 1984.
16. Varela, F.J. *Principles of biological autonomy.* New York: Elsevier North Holland, 1979.

PART II

SELECTION
OF VARIABLES

5

CAPTURING FAMILY CHANGE:
Multi-System Level Assessment

DAVID H. OLSON

University of Minnesota
St. Paul, Minnesota

A LTHOUGH the field of family therapy research has generally demonstrated the overall efficacy of marital and family therapy, the research has failed to tap adequately the rich complexity of the specific approaches to marital and family intervention or their differential effectiveness with various marital and family systems or presenting symptoms of their members. We have not yet achieved a specificity of conceptual or therapeutic methods that would enable us to know what kind of family intervention works best with what kind of family systems having what kind of presenting symptoms. We are operating, therefore, much like a physician who would prescribe an aspirin for a wide variety of ailments.

In order for the family therapy field to make continued progress as a science, we need to look more seriously at baseline and outcome variables relevant to the complexity of the family systems and therapeutic change. I will propose (a) a framework that takes into account several of the variables crucial to any family therapy outcome study and (b) two major dimensions or spheres—the *system level* and the *therapeutic domain.*

The *system level* includes the individual, marital, and parent-child relationships, the family system, and the community level. The *therapeutic domain* includes three major categories: (a) symptoms and presenting problems, (b) mediating goals or first-order change, and (c) ultimate goals or second-order change. These two dimensions provide a framework that enables one to specify the particular assessments for a comprehensive picture of change in marital and family systems (see Table 1).

Table 1 illustrates the major baseline and outcome variables that could be considered in any family therapy study. This framework builds upon the ideas about mediating and ultimate goals initially proposed by Parloff (8), the multisystem level discussed by Cromwell, Olson, and Fournier (1), and the excellent review of family therapy by Gurman and Kniskern (2).

In terms of any outcome study, it is important to identify initially the

TABLE 1

Baseline and Outcome Variables for Family Therapy Studies

	Symptoms and Presenting Problems	Mediating Goals: First-Order Change	Ultimate Goals: Second-Order Change
Individual	DSM-III symptoms and categories	Specific treatment goals developed for each symptom level by therapist with some degree of consultation with family members.	Change in presenting problems/symptoms
Marriage	Marital issues		Change in type of marital system
Parent-Child	Parent-child issues		Change in type of parent-child system
Family	Family and extended family issues	Goal-attainment scaling (GAS) could be used to specify goals.	Change in type of family system
Community	Community and social supports		Change in social support system

symptoms and presenting problems. At the individual level, the DSM-III can be useful as a standardized approach. At the marital, parent-child, and family levels, there need to be checklists that indicate presenting problems and symptoms identified by both the family members and the therapist. These would represent the initial issues that brought the couple or family to treatment.

In the second important domain are the *mediating goals,* as described by Parloff (8). These goals represent first-order change and they can be linked to therapist-specific goals at each of the system levels—individual, marital, parent-child, family, and community. Goal Attainment Scaling (GAS; see 3) is a useful methodology for operationalizing these specific goals.[1]

In terms of assessment, it is assumed that the mediating goals would be uniquely related to the therapeutic approach, type of family, and presenting problem. Therefore, the goals representing first-order change would not be standardized but they would be unique and more relevant to the specific therapeutic situations.[2]

---

1. *Editor's Note:* See Editor's Comments, 5, at the end of the volume for further discussion of Goal Attainment Scaling.
2. *Editor's Note:* Olson's appropriately cautionary note here should not leave the reader with the impression that the "unique" content of mediating goals takes

Whereas the mediating goals represent first-order change and can be altered in the course of treatment, the *ultimate goal* would represent second-order change. These ultimate goals relate to the more underlying dynamics in the individual and family systems. The specific variables selected as ultimate goals might include ones identified and used explicitly and/or implicitly in family therapeutic and theoretical models, that is, family *cohesion* and family *adaptability* (5). They might also include *satisfaction* and *communication* in the marital and family systems.

Because the ultimate goals would be selected from more generally agreed-upon variables, a "common battery" of instruments should be sought across these studies. In spite of the difficulties in agreeing upon these concepts and methods, meaningful comparison across studies is very limited without a common conceptual and measurement approach.

Having assessment on both mediating and ultimate goals would enable a study to have the best of both worlds. The mediating goals would provide the specificity related to therapeutic approach, the type of family, and the initial presenting problems. The assessment of the ultimate goals would provide common methods and variables for cross-study comparisons. Also, assessing both mediating and ultimate goals could facilitate a comparison of change on these two important dimensions, a proposal strongly advocated by Gurman and Kniskern (2).

As Parloff (8) and Gurman and Kniskern (2) have indicated, it is important to measure both mediating and ultimate goals because this enables an outcome study to focus on both first-order and second-order change. In some studies, it might be possible to find first-order change but not second-order change, or vice versa. The ideal therapeutic intervention aims to achieve both kinds of change. Until studies incorporate both of these domains, it will not be possible to assess the total impact of any family therapy intervention.

In general, there is a *hierarchy* of increasing complexity as one moves from individual treatment to treating an entire family. As more family members are included in treatment, this necessitates incorporating assessment of these units and subunits. Therefore, if the focus of

---

them out of the realm of systematic, empirical research. As indicated in Olson's Table 1, it is here that the targeted measures, unique for each case, in Goal Attainment Scaling need to be brought into use. Additionally, as discussed elsewhere in this volume, process research is, indeed, primarily concerned with the step-by-step changes as mediating goals are sought and achieved. In the "therapeutic domain," these goals involve the therapist-family system, as an alliance and unity, and they cannot be adequately conceptualized in terms of the "family" as a system level disconnected from the therapist. As a means for implementing process research, Olson's schema can be explicitly expanded to emphasize the therapist's participation in therapeutic systems and goal attainment at each of the system levels that he has described.

treatment is the marriage relationship, assessment should be done at the marital level as well as at the individual level. For family therapy, it would be necessary to assess all five levels—community, family, parent-child, marital, and individual.

This hierarchical model enables one to capture the increasing complexity as treatment moves from the individual, to the marriage, and to the larger family unit. It also means that all relevant individuals within the family system should be involved in the assessments. This can provide a wealth of data that should reveal more of the complexity of a family system; but because of the low correlation between family members on self-report inventories (6), the inclusion of multiple family members necessitates sophisticated scoring procedures that can take into account the couple and family as a unit. Although very few studies to date have relied on *couple* and *family* scores, we have developed a variety of couple and family scores as alternatives to the traditional reliance on individual scores. (For more details, see 6.)

To increase the scientific rigor of these outcome assessments, it is important to obtain both self-report and behavioral assessment on the most important variables. Whereas self-report data provide an insider's perspective on family life, the behavioral data provide more of an outsider's perspective. Another issue that adds to the complexity of marital and family studies is the fact that the inside and outside perspectives have low correlations with each other (4). Rather than using these two approaches to validate or invalidate the other, it is becoming clear that they represent two different but important realities of marital and family life, both of which should be incorporated into a study.

Additional insight about the meaning of the traditional pre/post assessments of outcome research can be gained by doing multiple assessments during the treatment process. As Pinsof (9) so clearly demonstrated, studies of process clearly should be made a high priority in family therapy research.

Lastly, this proposed conceptual framework encourages investigators to identify presenting symptoms in relation to specific system levels (7, 10). Specificity of this kind will increase the clarity and usefulness of family therapy outcome studies. Only with such linkage can we move beyond the traditional statement that family therapy seems to be useful for a variety of emotional problems.

In summary, the proposed framework described in Table 1 was developed to illustrate the range of areas and issues that need to be evaluated in order to obtain a comprehensive assessment of the efficacy of family therapy. The two dimensions include the *system level* and the *theoretical and therapeutic domains*. Combining the two dimensions helps us to identify the critical areas to be assessed. Because each dimension has several levels or components, this framework suggests a hierarchy that can be used to assess *generalization of effects* across the levels. This comprehensive approach to assessment will, hopefully, provide useful information that can lead to greater specificity in treatment and to progress in generating a "theory of change" in the field of family therapy.

RECOMMENDATIONS

The form of outcome assessment of family therapy that I recommend should provide a comprehensive picture of the rich complexity of change in family systems. The framework proposed in Table 1 indicates two salient dimensions and the relevant areas for each. Table 1 also identifies the specific issues that should be assessed; such an assessment will facilitate the study of the generalization of effects across levels and across the dimensions. It also will provide specificity regarding the *kind of family therapy that works best with a given family system and given presenting symptoms*. This kind of specificity will help the field build a more adequate theory of change.

In summary, the following recommendations are proposed for future family therapy research:

- assess all of the appropriate system levels (individual, marital, parent-child, family, and community)
- assess presenting symptoms, mediating and ultimate goals
- use self-report *and* behavioral assessment for the most important outcome variables in order to capture both insider and outsider perspectives
- include as many family members as possible in assessment procedures
- use couple and family scores that better match the methodological assessment with the theoretical constructs
- use more sophisticated and powerful statistical models and methods.

REFERENCES

1. Cromwell, R.E., Olson, D.H., & Fournier, D. Tools and techniques for diagnosis and evaluation in marital and family therapy. *Family Process 15:* 1–49, 1976.
2. Gurman, A.S., & Kniskern, D.P. Family therapy outcome research: Knowns and unknowns. In A.S. Gurman & D.P. Kniskern (eds.), *Handbook of family therapy.* New York: Brunner/Mazel, 1981.
3. Kiresuk, T.J., Smith, A., & Cardello, J.E. (eds.). *Goal attainment Scaling: Application, theory and measurement.* Hillsdale NJ: Lawrence Erlbaum Associates, in press.
4. Olson, D.H. Insiders' and outsiders' view of relationships: Research studies. In G. Levinger & H.L. Raush (eds.), *Close relationships: Perspectives on*

the meaning of intimacy. Amherst: University of Massachusetts Press, 1977.

5. _____. Circumplex Model VII: Validation studies and FACES III. *Family Process 25:* 337–351, 1986.

6. _____, McCubbin, H.I., Barnes, H., Larsen, A., Muxen, M., & Wilson, M. *Families: What makes them work.* Beverly Hills: Sage Publications, 1983.

7. _____, Russell, C.S., & Sprenkle, D.H. Marital and family therapy: A decade review. *Journal of Marriage and the Family 42:* 973–993, 1980.

8. Parloff, M.B. The narcissism of small differences—and some big ones. *International Journal of Group Psychotherapy 26:* 311–319, 1976.

9. Pinsof, W.M. Family therapy process research. In A.S. Gurman & D.P. Kniskern (eds.), *Handbook of family therapy.* New York: Brunner/Mazel, 1981.

10. Russell, C.S., Olson, D.H., Sprenkle, D.H., & Atilano, R.B. From family symptom to family system: Review of family therapy research. *American Journal of Family Therapy 11:* 3–14, 1983.

6

THE SELECTION OF MEASURES IN FAMILY THERAPY RESEARCH

CAROL M. ANDERSON

Western Pennsylvania Psychiatric Institute
Pittsburgh, Pennsylvania

I N RECENT YEARS, most family and marital therapy clinicians and researchers have tended to concentrate on mildly distressed or "worried well" populations. Whereas these efforts have promoted the development of interesting theories, interventions, and research tools, in order for family therapy to remain credible, it must be proven efficacious in the context of definable disorders.[1] Baseline and outcome measures must be selected or developed that will answer three main questions: Does family therapy have any effects? Are they desirable? How are they achieved?

To demonstrate effects, family therapy must be compared to treatments of proven efficacy for the problem under consideration. If family treatment is no better than individual treatment, medication, or Aunt Mathilda's kind support, why bother? To determine the comparative impact of family intervention, the following five categories of information should be considered.

1. **Measures of patient functioning:** This category of information should include measures of diagnosis and symptoms as well as data about the presenting complaint, an essential part of any measure of the efficacy of family therapy. Whatever changes or improvements in functioning that therapy achieves are irrelevant if the issue that brought the family to treatment is not at least partially resolved. Measurements of a presenting complaint, however, are not necessarily simple. In families without severe disorders, complaints may be vague and even contradictory. How can the

---

1. *Editor's Note:* Here Anderson forthrightly is at odds with what appears to be the continuing mainstream of family (and marital) therapy—which is to be concerned primarily *not* with "definable disorders" but with relational difficulties that are usually not viewed as "disorders," especially in the DSM-III sense. Some family therapists believe that the solution lies in developing a typology of relational or family disorders. Meanwhile, however, because there is no consensus about such a typology, a credibility problem does exist for family therapy in the eyes of other professionals and at least some of the public. See the Introduction and chapters 7 and 8 for further discussion of this issue.

complaint "we don't communicate" be measured in a way sufficiently specific to allow us to determine that improvement has or has not occurred? How is the researcher or therapist to know if the goal has been reached? In addition, in many families, various members have different presenting complaints: a wife desiring more intimacy, a husband wanting more freedom, parents wanting greater control over an adolescent who wants more autonomy. Clearly, presenting complaints must be translated into specific and attainable goals that can be measured.

The inclusion of specific diagnostic criteria is also crucial in order to make the results of family treatment studies comparable with one another and with studies of other interventions. Diagnoses are more frequently used as criteria for inclusion in a study, rather than as baseline measures. Nevertheless, the presence or absence of the symptoms that make up a diagnosis, along with ratings of their severity, are legitimate and important variables.

The use of diagnostic labels and criteria, however, raises two problems for research in this field. One problem, common among family therapists, particularly those who practice some of the more recent, interesting and creative approaches, is the belief that psychiatric nosology is irrelevant for those who practice a family-systems orientation. Not only do these clinicians avoid using psychiatric labels themselves, but they also object to researchers who apply labels to families or patients in treatment.

Even if there could be general acceptance of the need to use diagnostic criteria for efficacy studies, the question of which diagnostic system to use would remain. If studies are to be truly comparable, it would be beneficial for researchers to use the same criteria. In schizophrenia research, for example, the diagnostic system used will result in great differences in the populations studied. In general, those patients who meet Research Diagnostic Criteria (RDC) for schizophrenia will also meet Present State Examination (PSE) criteria, whereas all of those meeting PSE criteria will *not* meet the more narrowly specified RDC criteria (5). Thus, researchers using PSE criteria are studying a much broader group of patients and families. Are the results from these two kinds of studies really comparable?

2. **Measures of individual functioning of other family members:** The study of treatment effects must not be limited to the measurement of improvement in the patient, as is common in most individually oriented research. Several other possible ramifications of family treatment must be included as part of the measurement of baseline and outcome if a genuine test of treatment power and effectiveness is to be made. If, as is commonly assumed, one of the advantages of family treatment is the development of a family system more supportive of the health and growth of each of its members, then measures of *all* family members, not just the patient, are relevant. Even if family

treatment only results in diminished stress experienced by other members with regard to the presenting patient, these ratings would be important indicators of the positive impact of family interventions. Without ways to rate separately the functioning of individual family members, it will not be possible to prove that system changes result in individual gain.[2] Because the notion of a relationship between family variables and individual pathology is central to most models of family therapy, it is crucial that this relationship be documented. Whether or not etiologic or pathophysiologic relationships can be demonstrated, family functioning at least must be shown to have an influence on the course of an individual disorder, the manner in which the disorder expresses itself, and the functioning of other family members.

3. **Measures of overall family functioning:** Because a primary goal of most family treatment includes some change in the family system, measures of overall family functioning must be a part of the baseline/outcome package. Measures of structure, process, and distress are all relevant and need to be developed and refined for use across studies, theories, and methods. Additionally, the measures should be selected on the basis of the family therapy researcher's a priori notions of the instruments' sensitivity to the particular therapy and to the clinician's goals and theory of change. Currently, many measures are chosen because they are widely used, have become standard instruments, and so on, not because they provide the best test of the impact of a particular family treatment.

In a study of any family treatment modality, it is important to establish specific, expectable, and acceptable outcomes before selecting instruments; only in this way can we insure the collection of data to document whether or not the outcomes occur. The baseline and outcome dimensions chosen also must depend to some extent on the nature of the problem. Clearly, there must be at least some different baseline measures for families of patients with serious disorders as compared to families that are simply suffering from disharmony. The need for specificity in measures is a problem because it also is desirable to support the development of standardized assessment tools that may yield comparable data about a wide variety of families being exposed to dramatically different interventions in a wide range of settings. Any measure about which a larger number of family clinicians or researchers could agree would probably be too general to provide much genuine information

---

2. *Editor's Note:* This point is well taken but will be difficult to implement in comparative research on family therapy versus other forms of intervention. It is more difficult logistically to obtain measures from all family members when family therapy is not provided, especially at follow-up. Simple measures, such as the Hopkins Symptom Check List, may have to suffice.

about the impact of any particular treatment. Even though there is a need to develop a fund of knowledge across studies that may help us to address common issues in the effectiveness of family treatment, attempts to achieve such a goal may generate measures that are so general that they do not adequately address the targets of specific interventions or the hypotheses on which particular models of family therapy are based.[3]

4. **Measures of patient and family satisfaction:** Although it probably should not be regarded as a primary factor, some rating of family satisfaction with treatment and treatment outcome is relevant. Minimally, satisfaction with treatment will relate to compliance and use of services. In studies that compare family treatment to other types of psychotherapy, measures of compliance, dropouts, and "no-takes" are of particular interest because it is expectable that family treatment will achieve better results in these area. Specifically, family treatment is not solely dependent on the motivation of the patient, a factor that should be particularly advantageous in treating such problems as schizophrenia, drug and alcohol addiction, or other disorders in which patients may not accept the fact that they are ill.

Measures of satisfaction with family life present a different set of problems. Whether increased satisfaction with family life is a sufficient gain in the absence of improvement in presenting syptoms or problems is questionable. From a specific family's point of view, it is probably valuable that family members feel better about their lives and problems, even if no change has occurred in the presenting complaint. From a political point of view, however, the field has a responsibility to address the issue of how many resources it is willing to commit to a given modality if the number and significance of its benefits are limited to a greater acceptance of the status quo. If a schizophrenic patient does not improve but family members feel less guilty and cope more easily with the illness, should this be regarded as a favorable outcome and/or an outcome that makes this treatment worthy of public support?[4]

---

3. *Editor's Note:* Other contributors to this volume were more optimistic, for example, Olson (Chapter 5), about the possibility of generating a core battery of family measures. I believe that Anderson's concerns are well founded. Core measures should not be used as scientific window-dressing; they must be documented as having differentiating properties relevant to treatment change. Most family measures suggested for a core battery originated in nonclinical family studies and have not yet been applied to a wide range of families in treatment.

4. *Editor's Note:* In the NIMH/*Family Process* conference discussion, Carlos Sluzki warned that taking patient-family satisfaction into consideration "by itself" could skew in favor of therapeutic approaches that establish a "nice," warm, kind relationship, as contrasted with approaches that may energize families into constructive change, which the family can regard as its own

5. **Measures of the researcher/clinician:** Although not generally a part of a package of baseline/outcome measures, qualities of the researcher and participating clinicians have an impact on treatment outcome and the manner in which results are presented and interpreted, and they probably should be measured.[5] In particular, the impact of the value system of the researcher in selecting targets and measures are of concern. In the study of marital therapy, for instance, is divorce always a negative outcome? It may, in fact, be a good outcome for some patients (the chronically abused, for instance) and poor for others. Likewise, the emancipation of young adults, a process that is highly valued in our culture in general and by clinicians in our field in particular, may or may not be desirable. If two parents have finally united to set limits on an acting-out, drug-abusing adolescent by throwing him or her out of the home, this may well be a positive step. On the other hand, if schizophrenic patients are ejected from the family into poorly organized transitional living arrangements, the result may be a weaker support system for the patient, and perhaps exacerbation of patient symptoms and parental guilt. If divorce rates and/or "appropriate" developmental moves are being used as measures of outcome, are clinicians encouraged to reinforce behaviors in order to obtain "good" results even though they may not be in the family's or patient's best interests?

SUMMARY AND RECOMMENDATIONS

All studies should involve multiple measures, particularly those insuring that data will be collected in the following areas:

- sets of measures of universal significance to family functioning (developed and refined for use across studies, theories, and methods)
- measures that relate to the specific problem being addressed, its relevant family ramifications, and the kind of interventions being used
- multiple methods of data gathering for all studies, particularly combinations of self-report and observational data

---

accomplishment, and for which they may feel little gratitude toward the therapist or satisfaction with the therapy. Such outcomes sometimes are explicitly sought in systemic and strategic models of family therapy. Anderson does not regard satisfaction as a *primary* measure, and commented that measuring family satisfaction does not mean it has to be positively valued by the researcher. If, indeed, one saw a strong correlation between negative feelings about treatment and positive change, then that finding would be quite interesting and should be explored in further detail.

5. *Editor's Note:* I strongly agree except that I would say these measures *certainly*, not just "probably," should be obtained. The researcher's qualities have been especially neglected in all forms of treatment research.

There is evidence that different methods of gathering data yield different and sometimes contradictory findings.[6] For instance, self-report measures of the marital interaction of depressed women suggest that they are dominated by their husbands (1, 4). On the other hand, one of the few studies using direct observation suggests that the spouses of these depressed women were not more controlling and that depressed women themselves actually engaged in more verbal and nonverbal attempts to control their spouses than did control subjects (2, 3). Thus, depressed women perceive themselves as being controlled even though they actually are not dominated during observed interaction. Because both of these factors have validity and relevance, it would be important to include both kinds of data-gathering processes in attempts to measure baselines and outcomes. We need strategies that include measures of perceptions *and* behaviors.

The timing of the administration of baseline and outcome measures should be carefully specified. The timing of baseline measures can have a major impact on what is observed. In schizophrenia, for instance, measures of family variables taken on the patient's admission to a hospital, at a time of crisis when the family has been coping with a seriously decompensated member, will differ dramatically from those taken two weeks after they have had a respite from the patient's behavior.

All studies should include a priori hypotheses about the specific, anticipated impact of therapy. Without great specificity in this area, it is too easy to present results in ways that make them look more significant than they are, or in ways that make the researcher look good. Retrospective reanalysis of data based on hints already found in initial analysis is a belated search for meaning that can yield misleading results that only further confuse and discredit the field of family therapy research.

REFERENCES

1. Collins, J., Kreitman, N., Nelson, B., & Troop, J. Neurosis and marital interaction: III. Family roles and functions. *British Journal of Psychiatry* 119: 233–242, 1971.
2. Hinchcliffe, M.K., Hooper, D., & Roberts, F.J. *The melancholy marriage: Depression in marriage and psychosocial approaches to therapy.* New York: John Wiley & Sons, 1978.

---

6. *Editor's Note:* In the conference discussion, Reiss took the position, somewhat contrary to the consensus of the participants, that "multiple level measures should not be used unless we have a clear concept of what we are going to do with discrepancies in the measures." (See Chapter 11, Editor's Note 4, for further commentary on this problem.) The example of a discrepancy that Anderson gives here appears to have been unanticipated but, nevertheless, was generative of a fresh idea.

3. _____, Hooper, D., Roberts, F.J., & Pamela, W.V. A study of the interaction between depressed patients and their spouses. *British Journal of Psychiatry 126:* 164–172, 1975.
4. Hoover, C.F., & Fitzgerald, R.G. Marital conflict of manic-depressive patients. *Archives of General Psychiatry 38:* 65–67, 1981.
5. Kendell, R.E., Brockington, I.F., & Leff, J.P. Prognostic implications of six alternative definitions of schizophrenia. *Archives of General Psychiatry 36:* 25–31, 1979.

7

THE "PRESENTING PROBLEM" AND THEORY-BASED FAMILY VARIABLES:
Keystones for Family Therapy Research

LYMAN C. WYNNE

University of Rochester
Rochester, New York

T HE CONCEPT of the "presenting problem" can be a meeting ground for family therapists, family researchers, and families themselves. Writing as a therapist, Haley (22) "assumes that the therapist has failed if he or she does not solve the presenting problem" (p. 2). Writing as a researcher, Jacobson (Chapter 11) agrees with Haley that "the primary criterion for successful therapy is whether or not the family 'got what they came for'," that is, "that the presenting (or emergent) problems have been eliminated." Families too, voicing their expectations through rapidly growing self-help consumer organizations such as the Alliance for the Mentally Ill (AMI), are highly critical of health care professionals, especially family therapists who divert attention from, or are not directly responsive to the family's presenting concerns (see 23, 26).

"Problem" will be my generic term for whatever it is that someone believes needs professional attention. Obviously, this means that there may be multiple presenting problems in any given case, and guidelines for identifying a useful research definition are essential. To be sure, the patient's or family's presenting problem, or chief complaint, is traditionally the starting point for clinical reports (after a notation of demographics—"white, single, 28-year-old female"). Nevertheless, medicine, psychotherapy, and family therapy have rarely, if ever, made research use of this routinely obtained information about presenting problems. Auerswald (Chapter 4) vividly describes the ways in which the family's definition of the presenting problem can become lost during clinical assessment and be neglected with detriment to both clinical care and research.

Despite such wide agreement about the importance of the presenting problem for therapy research, there are two major sources of dissent. The first comes from those family therapists and theorists who have been loosely called humanistic and experiential in orientation, and who strongly emphasize subjective experience (36), esthetic epistemology

(27), family growth (41), or family connectedness (1). These therapists prefer to set aside attention to presenting problems as soon as possible, either regarding them as transient or secondarily important, or expecting that they will recede when broader family patterns have shifted. By and large, these therapists are skeptical about the merits of empirical research on therapy.

A second source of dissent comes from therapists who support therapy research but believe that consistent attention to family system principles calls for primary emphasis on family system variables rather than on complaints of families, which may be about individual family members' symptoms or behavior, or about some extrafamilial event. Kniskern (29), for example, believes "that the primary criterion for the evaluation of success in family therapy should be change in family patterns of interaction," although he adds that if "the presenting problem is not alleviated, one must question whether the most relevant elements of family interaction have been altered" (p. 161).

In this chapter, I shall attempt a critique of the presenting problem as a criterion of change in family therapy assessment. I also shall recommend a second criterion for change, which involves theory-based family variables in addition to—not instead of—the presenting problem. (For further discussion of this issue, see Chapter 11, Editor's Note 12.)

PROBLEMS WITH THE "PRESENTING PROBLEM" IN FAMILY THERAPY RESEARCH

Although the idea of the family getting "what they came for" seems appealingly straightforward at first glance, a host of issues about this concept are not yet clarified or agreed upon by researchers. (Family therapists and families have not clarified these issues either, but researchers are under much more duress to be specific.) The major issues include:

1. *Multiple problem perspectives:* How does the researcher select from and integrate the multiple perspectives about the presenting problem?

2. *Problem change over time:* When should the baseline and process/outcome assessments be carried out in order to assess therapeutic change? How does problem reconsideration by the family and reframing by the therapist affect the meaning and usefulness of any initial definition of the presenting problem? The researcher must recognize that the problem that is labeled as "presenting" is a function of the time and circumstances of its presentation.

3. *Theory-based family variables:* How can family therapy research and theory deal with change in presenting problems that are framed as individual problems or extrafamilial problems, not as family problems? Can (or should) change in theoretically meaningful family variables be

integrated into family therapy research in a consistent way *regardless* of the form of the presenting problem?

4. *Political and pragmatic considerations:* Which political and pragmatic factors should be given weight in establishing priorities in family therapy research, favoring certain presenting problems rather than others? Examples of such factors include high public visibility of a problem, availability of research funds for some problems but not others, high prevalence of a disorder, high severity of distress or impairment, high cost/low efficacy of current standard treatment programs, and practical difficulties in generating samples of families of appropriate size for treatment research.

MULTIPLE PERSPECTIVES TOWARD PROBLEMS IN FAMILY THERAPY

Strupp and Hadley (38) have proposed that the perspectives of at least three interested parties need to be considered in mental health treatments: (a) the individual patient; (b) the mental health professional; and (c) society. Family therapists would subdivide society and identify a fourth perspective, that of the family (43). The family's perspective is often distinctively different from perspectives of "society" beyond the family, for example, of referring agencies, schools, and courts. In addition, the therapeutic alliance or therapeutic system of family and therapist together evolve still another perspective during their transactions with one another. Finally, the researcher's perspective necessarily has distinctive sources and qualities.

Family Perspectives

The perspective of the family *as a unit* usually is difficult to characterize initially. Reaching a family consensus about the nature and locus of problems, what should be done about them, and who should do it, is usually part of the process, or one of the end results of therapy, rather than the starting point. The baseline perspective of the family about the presenting problems usually involves a *constellation of individual viewpoints*. Because of the complexity of characterizing the family's view, most studies have rather casually assumed that a therapist's or researcher's perspective about the problem under treatment will suffice. I believe that this assumption is dubious and that therapists and therapy researchers have an ethical responsibility to give high priority to the assessment of change as desired and perceived by family members themselves.

As contrasted with individual psychotherapy, relational problems are more distinctively central for family therapy. Family therapists are more likely than other mental health professionals to view the primary problem as evident in repeated sequences of behavior between people

(22), but such sequences are not the *initial* presenting problem as perceived by the family. Because problems at other systems levels (biological, psychological, or extrafamilial) may have reverberations for the family, it is entirely consistent with clinical experience and with general systems theory[1] that consultation with the family and possibly family therapy be considered as an option regardless of how or what problems are initially presented. Despite the introduction of systems theory into medicine in terms of the biopsychosocial medical model (11, 12), an exclusive, individually oriented, biotechnical model still holds sway in medicine and psychiatry: that individual symptoms and individual disorders call for primary and often exclusive, individual consultations and treatment. Family therapists, nonfamily therapist professionals, and the public all need to recognize that, given the concept of multiple system levels, *it is entirely appropriate to proceed with family consultation or therapy when the targeted, presenting problem is the illness of an individual family member.*

This point is applicable even when there is little prospect of significantly modifying the course of the individual illness, for example, cancer, multiple sclerosis, Alzheimer's disease, congenital problems such as Down's syndrome and spina bifida, irreversible injuries such as paraplegia, and so on. These disorders, and those that may be more modifiable (such as schizophrenia), are often profoundly burdensome for families and are likely to have major developmental consequences for future family functioning. Family therapy and consultation are highly relevant to the care of ill family members and to the issue of preventive intervention with other family members (5, 44).

In assessing change in the family's perspective about their presenting complaint or problem, certain additional caveats for the unwary researcher are in order: (a) Presenting problems are described at levels of abstraction and concreteness that vary widely within and between families, for example, "Johnny smoked marijuana last night" versus "We have a communication problem." (b) Some families are inarticulate and portray the presenting problem in their behavior rather than in their speech. (c) Many families report the problem in a form that they believe the therapist would prefer to hear, or that will test the therapist, or that will show compliance or loyalty toward someone who referred them.

---

1. The concept of a hierarchy of systems levels is most explicit in *general* systems theory, which is not the only version of "systems theories" that are currently advocated. See Chapter 4 by Auerswald and Editor's Comment, 2, for further discussion of these variations. However, there is no controversy about the main issue that is relevant here, that biological, personal, familial, and extrafamilial factors interpenetrate and influence one another. Hence, treatment need not, and should not, be limited to a single level of functioning.

Perspective of the Therapeutic System

The presenting problem in which family therapists are likely to be most interested is the family or marital system's inability to cope as a relational system.[2] The usual initial lack of consensus among family members about a presenting problem may be compounded by a lack of consensus with the therapist. For example, a husband may come to marital therapy with the idea that the presenting problem is how to help his wife's depression; the wife may view the problem as her husband's excessive preoccupation with work; and the therapist may want to frame the presenting problem in terms of some aspect of the couple's relationship.

Usually, family therapists try to reach a consensus (for the therapeutic system) by identifying a shared ingredient in what the individual family members have stated to be their goals for change. Failing to reach such an agreement, therapists sometimes define the presenting problem as the conflict between family members over their goals. When the members remain in great conflict or are highly vague about their perspectives, the family clinician may suggest that the presenting problem is their difficulty in deciding what they want from therapy, or whether they want family therapy at all. However, such a "presenting problem" would be relevant only in studies of pretreatment or of treatment through the phase that Alexander calls Assessment/ Understanding (Chapter 13).

Later, when the family members and therapist have reached a consensus about the goals of therapy, this perspective about the presenting problems (or their solution) can be defined, for research purposes, as a baseline for family therapy. The contacts or work with the family up to that point can be defined as family consultation (45) or, more traditionally, as assessment or evaluation.

Some psychotherapists slide into therapy or they contend that "therapy" begins with the first telephone call or contact. It is possible to argue that any interpersonal contact may have therapeutic (or antitherapeutic) effects. However, I, with McDaniel and Weber (45), have pointed out that the concept of "therapy" implies that therapeutic effects are deliberately sought and that this goal is an agreed-upon, primary basis for the relationship. It is presumptuous and unwarranted to assume that everyone who contacts a mental health professional wants, or even has implicitly agreed, to participate in any form of therapy. Advice, informa-

---

2. The other side of this coin, to which de Shazer (8) has brought attention, is not presenting problems to be solved but, rather, solutions to be achieved. He recommends that therapists move quickly on from a statement of the presenting problem to a "solution statement" describing what the clients will be doing more of when the problem is solved. This is an attempt to expand the perceived area of satisfactory or competent functioning.

tion, consultation, education, and counseling about a specific problem, illness, person, or relationship are some of the alternative frameworks for contact with mental health professionals.

The quality and degree of consensus about treatment goals between family and therapist are obviously relevant information for understanding the processes and outcome of therapy. For example, "therapy" dropouts that take place before family members have agreed to be in family therapy are clearly not comparable to dropouts after agreement has been reached about a treatment plan. These differences in perspectives about the presenting problem should be made explicit in any therapy research design. Most studies have failed to do so and thereby confuse the meaning of the findings.

Thus, on both theoretical and clinical grounds, it is essential to regard the presenting problem from the therapist's (and supervisor's) perspective as a function of the therapeutic system. As a function of the process of therapy, the locus of the problem necessarily lies in the therapeutic system of family and therapist transacting together, not in the family as a separate entity.

This formulation places the therapist in the position of what Olson (34) calls an insider's view of relationships and is consistent with the emphasis given by Pinsof (Chapter 12) to the therapeutic alliance in studying process. On the other hand, this attention to the processes within the therapeutic system need not negate, but rather should complement, research in which family patterns outside therapy, before, during, and after contact with the family therapist, are studied, for example, in family interaction during videotaped problem-solving tasks. However, in assessing the family's functioning apart from therapy, the therapist's (and a "live" supervisor's) perspective about the family's problem should not be regarded as a valid *external* measure of family change that is relied upon *instead* of family self-report or an observer's view. A well-designed study of outcome should include but not rely exclusively on assessments by someone other than the therapist at baseline and at later points of follow-up.

The Researcher's Perspective

It is conceptually important to distinguish between participant family therapists and nonparticipant observers or researchers who help assess family intake and treatment. Research definitions of the problem under treatment often reflect the researcher's *re*formulation of what he or she thought the family and/or therapist reported as the presenting problem. It is my impression that reformulations of the presenting problem by both researchers and therapists often take place in ways that are not clearly specified, so that the amount of slippage from the family's perspective is difficult to document and is sometimes unrecognizable. It should be acknowledged that the researcher's own perspective is subtly, or not so subtly, conveyed in the choice of procedures for obtaining this information and, later, in organizing and analyzing the results.

Three kinds of procedures have been used by family therapy researchers in specifying family problems: (a) self-reports (preferably from the therapist as well as family members), either from case records or using specially designed forms (33, 35); (b) questions, summaries, or ratings (7) of statements by the family members and therapist during the initial sessions that are observed directly or on videotape, or heard on audiotape; or (c) conclusions reached from observation through a one-way window or from videotapes of the family members alone or with the therapist during discussion of a standardized question, such as "What would you like to see changed?" (3).

These methods are designed to provide a relatively standardized sample of lively family interactions about one or more of their problems as families. However, the ratings and coding systems that are applied to these samples of interaction assess general features of family functioning, such as clarity of communication and range of affect. They do not, I am dismayed to note, actually assess the specific problems for which the family is coming to the professional. *Family functioning, not family presenting problems, are evaluated.*

Further research on methods of systematically using the family's perspective of the presenting problems as a criterion of change is badly needed. As far as I know, only two unpublished methods have specifically addressed this issue. One is outlined in Chapter 4, where Auerswald has suggested a method for tracking such changes. A second unpublished method for assessing change in family presenting problems has been described by Feldman (15). He has proposed a procedure for eliciting individualized, quantifiable self-report data from family members regarding both family presenting problems and, in a distinct advance, family strengths. Feldman also has used a procedure in which these family members' self-reports are discussed in a brief interview intended to clarify the nature and strength of each problem and its perceived source. Scores for each problem and strength can be analyzed separately or combined into global and mean scores for each individual, family subgroups, and the total family.

Goal Attainment Scaling (GAS) has been the most commonly suggested method for assessing change in relation to goals flexibly targeted to fit the unique features in each case, but has not been applied to family therapy. (See Editor's Note 8 in Auerswald's Chapter 4 and Editor's Comment, 5, at the end of this volume for further discussion of GAS.) Despite difficulties in establishing reliability across cases, procedures for improving consistency across the reliability of GAS without losing its clinical integrity are being developed (see 32).

Societal Perspectives

Schools, courts, and community agencies are among the societal representatives most likely to refer families for treatment. Agency and family definitions of the presenting problem are likely to differ. Success in treatment programs, starting with referral agency definitions of problems, may be politically—but temporarily—advantageous for the family therapy field in gaining acceptance for work with such problems as schizophrenia, child abuse, family violence, substance abuse, and divorce. Although agencies often use formal psychiatric diagnoses in their records, the problems with which they are urgently concerned are quite different: Can a disturbed patient be hospitalized involuntarily? Is residential placement appropriate for a delinquent adolescent? What legal action and medical care should be provided for street-drug usage and alcoholism? How should a family court settle a dispute over parental visitation? From these societal perspectives of the "presenting problem," "corrective" or constraining actions are expected. It should be noted that such problems are usually labeled in terms of action, for example, "commitment to a state hospital," that is often far removed from the distress expressed by patients and families.

PROBLEM CHANGE OVER TIME

The seemingly straightforward recommendation that resolution of the presenting problem be a criterion for successful therapy outcome is complicated not only because of multiple perspectives across persons but also because the *timing* of problem definition affects what is regarded as the "presenting" problem. This issue is more forcefully and obviously apparent in family therapy than in pharmacologic treatment or individual therapy because more fluid, multiple contexts are involved in family therapy.

Furthermore, it is a well-established family treatment technique to reframe the presenting problem repeatedly over time as a way to induce change. When a therapist invites the whole family to come in for the first session, this act already frames the family context as relevant to the problem. And if the therapist refuses to see anyone in the family unless all members come, that message has a powerful, coercive impact that will influence whether or not the family is included in the research, and it will shape the quality of the therapeutic system that follows. In contrast, the problem is implicitly framed differently by the individual therapist who invites, or allows, only one family member to come. For example, a "patient" who may have defined himself or herself as ill because of symptoms of depression may, with symptom relief and/or therapeutic reframing, decide a month later that the central problem has become a marital, relational difficulty.

Gurman, Kniskern, and Pinsof (20) make a distinction between proximal and distal changes with therapy. Three kinds of proximal changes can take place in treatment goals:

1. *Evolving goals* involve the reframing of presenting problems by the therapists, as described above, most commonly early in family therapy.

2. *Emerging goals* "are any additional goals deemed worthy of therapeutic attention by any participants in therapy beyond those initially sought. Emerging goals, then, are different from evolving goals in that no new reframing of presenting problem occurs."

3. *Reordered goals* refer "to the reordering or reprioritizing of multiple initial goals."

As Gurman et al. (20) note, "None of these types of goal modification, so common in clinical practice, has yet been studied in family therapy research, despite their obvious salience in potentially understanding both the patterning and the process of therapeutic change" (p. 610).

RECOMMENDATIONS FOR STUDY OF PRESENTING PROBLEMS

The preceding discussion should dispel any assumptions that the presenting problem provides an easy, readily usable criterion for change with family therapy. But is the issue so complex that meaningful empirical research on family therapy is futile? I hope not, and think not. The following suggestions are not definitive solutions but may facilitate useful, interpretable research without provoking suicidal depression in the researcher.

1. *Build in data from multiple perspectives:* The researcher must forego search for, and belief in, a single "correct" perspective about presenting problems treated with family approaches. Rather, assessment of change from multiple perspectives should be built into therapy research designs. To be sure, this makes studies more complicated, but they will be conceptually sounder and more relevant to clinical practice.

2. *More comprehensive reporting about perspectives:* Minimally, the roles of all persons inside and outside the family whose perspective is used in the research should be specified and reported. Also, how and when the data about their perspectives have been obtained, and the content of each perspective, all should be described and reported (or available for review) in each study. Often it will be necessary to summarize such information in order to meet space limitations of journal publications, but far more detail can be reported than usually has been done. In the absence of description of whose perspectives are involved and how access to them has been obtained, generalizations and assumptions about presenting problems generate puzzlement about the meaning of negative findings and ungrounded reassurance when findings are positive.

3. The *family members' perspectives* about the initial presenting problem should be an invariant component of what is reported. The perspectives of individual family members, family subgroups, and the family consensus, if any, should be recorded separately. The family perspective will be fully understood only if data are included from all family members who participate in or impinge upon the therapeutic process. If data are not directly obtainable from some of these persons, the fact of the missing data should be recorded.

4. As with the family members, the perspectives of the *family therapist*, as well as cotherapist, team members, and supervisor, if any, should be individually recorded.

5. The perspective of the family and family therapist as a *therapeutic system*, including both splits in views and a consensus, when and if it occurs, can be regarded as the primary focus for, as Tomm (39) puts it, "a scientific explanation of family therapy" (p. 374).

6. The perspective of the *researcher* must be recognized as derivative from: (a) his or her values and implicit/explicit beliefs about family life, health, and illness, including assumptions about gender and age hierarchies, and about appropriate responsibilities for professionals, patients, and family members; and (b) the choice of assessment measures and data analysis methods, some of which will overlook and some of which will overemphasize aspects of the presenting problems as perceived by the family, the therapist, and society. Insofar as the researcher is able, his or her built-in biases should be reported and drawn to the attention of those reading and interpreting the research findings.

7. *"Societal"* perspectives, especially of referring agencies or clinicians, are pertinent in describing the kind of sample that has been assembled. If intake data from referral sources about the presenting problem are recorded in a systematic way across families, such information may be highly useful. For research, clinic telephone intakes need to be written down in detail; inquiry and record-keeping about the details of initial problem statements are usually obtained in a haphazard manner by clerical staff members who are not research-oriented or trained.

In a number of settings, the perspective and assessment of still other persons can and should be obtained, for example, nurses on an inpatient floor, aides in a residential treatment unit, and teachers, when the problem has been identified as academic or is manifested in a school setting. The perspective of physicians and other professionals is also relevant when there is a measurable somatic symptom such as blood pressure change or a question of intellectual impairment or a developmental disorder.

8. *Minimal data on problem perspectives:* Not all of these perspectives will be relevant to the purposes of any given study, nor feasibly obtained. However, if information about certain perspectives is omitted on the grounds of feasibility, even though it is clear that such information

would influence the interpretation of the study, then this important limitation surely should be openly acknowledged by the researcher and such acknowledgement should be expected by reviewers of grant applications and journal publications.

My recommendation is that information about at least three perspectives should be minimally included: (a) on clinical and ethical grounds, the perspectives of the family members; (b) on conceptual grounds, the consensus, or splits, reached by the therapeutic system (of family plus therapist); and (c) on methodologic grounds, the researcher's perspective, which may be most easily formulated with consistency in terminology and level of abstraction.

9. The *classification* of presenting problems in family therapy is a major issue that requires far more study. Some family therapists have objected to *any* form of classification because of an expectation that it would lead to inflexibly narrow treatment approaches shaped by classificatory pigeonholes. In medicine, diagnostic categories have, to be sure, led incompetent physicians to wear blinders about other significant difficulties. However, the systematic (and often systemic) review of *differential* diagnosis, both initially and later, is a tradition in medicine that nonphysicians may not understand or value. In family therapy teams, the review of alternative hypotheses is, in effect, a form of "differential diagnosis." On the other hand, there have been a number of ambitious efforts to classify families and their problems, dimensionally and typologically (16, 28, 42). Unfortunately, family researchers and therapists have not yet agreed upon a classificatory schema. A major reason for this failure of agreement has been the diversity of models of family therapy, each with distinctive problem interests and premises and differing ways of engaging with families. As Gurman (Chapter 10) and Epstein (Chapter 9) suggest, it may be appropriate at present to carry out research *within* specific models. The use of a common classificatory schema and the examination of common features across models would therefore be postponed. At this time, models that overlap can be incorporated into the same study. Also, a global health-pathology scale of family functioning, as proposed by Lewis, Beavers, Gossett, and Phillips (31), may be a useful index that can be used across models to assess changes in family competence levels over time.

A more qualitative start toward differentiating family therapy problems could begin with a simple but clinically useful classification proposed by Grunebaum (18): (a) families presenting with *relational problems*—marital conflict, family developmental transitions, child-parent issues, and so on; and (b) families with a *problem person*[3]—diagnosed as schizophrenic, anorexic, learning disabled, and so on.

---

3. See Editor's Comments, 1, at end of this volume for discussion of the term "problem person" as compared to "identified patient."

I suggest that Grunebaum's second group can be usefully divided: (a) families with a problem person who has received a professional's diagnosis that "punctuates" and serves as a external reference point in the family's perspective about the need for professional assistance; and (b) one or more family members seeking help because of the concern or burden for the family stemming from a family member's undiagnosed symptoms or problem behavior.

10. *Baselines for problem change:* The issue of problem change over time is indeed difficult to handle in family therapy research. As I have noted, with reframing, the problem definition held by the family may be steered toward a different view than initially presented by the family. Selecting baselines at different times during this process will clearly have distinctive consequences for what is studied and what outcomes are expected. I suggest that the complications generated by the many changes of problem definition over time may be manageable if family therapy researchers agree to focus upon *two primary baselines:* (a) *the family members' "initial" presenting problems*, individual or relational, agreed upon or not, and (b) *the relational problems later identified by consensus of family members and therapist.*[4]

THEORY-BASED FAMILY VARIABLES

Because family therapy theorists hypothesize that systems at different levels and in different areas are open but linked, it is reasonable that therapy research should examine hypotheses about the links between areas and levels of functioning. Also, systemic change is expected to emerge both between sessions and over an extended period after formal treatment ends. Therefore, measures of change should not be limited to intrasession data.[5]

Obviously, it is optimal to select and study at baseline those variables that will be interesting later during therapy and at follow-up. For example, if siblings of a diagnosed patient appear to benefit from family

---

4. This proposal for a dual punctuation of the starting point for family therapy research has some methodologic similarities to the use of multiple baselines in single-case research designs (24). In these approaches, multiple baselines are identified when treatment has been stopped and then is restarted, or, more feasibly in psychotherapy, when treatment can be assessed with different baselines for several aspects of family functioning or evaluated over time in relation to the same problem across several situations. Multiple baseline strategies are available for use in family therapy research but have rarely been implemented.

5. Stanton (Chapter 1) and Pinsof (Chapter 12) have discussed the importance and difficulties of assessing change that takes place outside of family therapy sessions.

therapy, it would be desirable that baseline data have been obtained about the siblings. With family therapy, in which the effects are often indirect and unexpected, hypotheses about change are especially difficult to formulate. Findings about such changes must be regarded as serendipitous, as part of discovery-oriented research. Relevant hypotheses and assessments can, of course, be incorporated into the next study.

In family therapy, the multiplicity of variables at several conceptual levels means that research is especially likely to produce piecemeal and noncumulative findings. Therefore, as a condition for supportable family therapy resarch, I propose that *at least one* (more, if possible) *theory-based family variable be built into the research design.* Therapeutic change in the targeted, presenting problems should be linked in specific hypotheses to change in these family variables.

As an example, let us take the now familiar hypotheses about how family variables relate to change in schizophrenic individuals who take part in family therapy. In current theories about the role of stressors and protective factors in relation to vulnerability to schizophrenia, it has been hypothesized that "simulus overload" will push the biologically and psychologically vulnerable individual into a clinically symptomatic schizophrenic state. Further, when family members are uninformed and perplexed about emerging symptoms, they are apt to become anxious and distressed and thereby add to the "stimulus-overload" effect. Under these circumstances of confused and uncertain family knowledge, it has been hypothesized that the family members may take on self-blame and guilt that heighten their emotional overinvolvement with the patient, which may become another form of overload for the patient. These forms of expressed emotion (30, 40) and affective style (10) have been hypothesized, and have been demonstrated within certain samples at least, to increase the likelihood of exacerbation or relapse of schizophrenic symptoms. Positive changes in these theory-based family variables have been explicitly studied as possible mediators of behavioral and symptomatic improvements in the schizophrenic patient, using psychoeducational and behavioral family approaches to family therapy (2, 9, 14, 17, 25).

This example illustrates that even when individually based disorders have been identified as the starting point for therapy, theory-based family variables can be incorporated into the research design. Another example can be found in the work of Stanton and Todd (37). They have formulated specific hypotheses linking a theory-based family variable (family addiction cycle) to individual dysfunction (substance abuse).

Other problems can be conceptualized from the beginning on a more strictly relational level, and theory-based family variables can more easily be included in the research design. For example, impending divorce, post-divorce custody disputes, abusing and battering families, sexual difficulties in marriage, as well as more vaguely defined relational syndromes such as "poor marital communication" can be regarded as involving "theory-based family variables" that quite "naturally" would be expected to change with marital or family therapy.

Nevertheless, the terminology in which family members present their relational problems is nearly always different from the jargon of theorists. Therefore, even when families present with a relational problem, their view of change in their terms needs to be explicitly identified and assessed at baseline and follow-up; but, *in addition*, there should be parallel assessment of one or more theory-based family variables. As emphasized by Reiss, Ryder, Pinsof, and others (see chapters 2, 3, and 12), family therapy research that simply demonstrates that a beneficial outcome takes place wastes the opportunity to gain invaluable conceptual understanding of those family processes that contribute to or enhance change.

There are several classes of theory-based family variables that can be incorporated into the approach recommended here. One set of theory-oriented variables involves *life events*, such as unexpected death or serious illness of a family member, divorce and remarriage, disruption of the home in environmental catastrophes such as floods, loss of employment, and so on. Here the strategy is to look at certain situations, hypothesize and evaluate how coping with these events may modify their impact upon individuals and families "at risk," and assess how family approaches improve coping skills as well as modify symptomatic responses to the crises.

A similar strategy relates to hypotheses about normative transitions, that is, expectable discontinuities in the *family life cycle*, for example, first pregnancy, the launching of adolescents, and retirement. Clinicians and family theorists have hypothesized that many family disorders and dysfunctions emerge at these transition points (21). High priority should be given to the comprehensive documentation of this hypothesis as an approach to a typology of family problems.

Still another approach to the family-level definition of problems involves a *dimensional approach*. One can look at the dimensions of the Circumplex Model, especially family cohesion and family adaptability (35), or at multiple dimensions such as those proposed in the McMaster Model of Family Functioning (13) and the Beavers Systems Model (3). One of the advantages of these dimensional approaches is that in principle *all* families can be assessed on these dimensions. Therefore, it should be possible to follow changes in functioning over time despite the reframing of the presenting problem. The dimensional approach can use both self-report instruments and assessments of direct interaction in experimental procedures or in the therapeutic situation itself. By arbitrarily defining cutting points along dimensions, typologies of family functioning have been delineated (4, 35).

It remains to be established whether these dimensions and typologies differentiate families in therapeutically relevant ways. Does the position of a family on these various dimensions, such as cohesion, relate to change in perceived problems or observable behaviors of the family as a unit or its members? If so, can dimensional change, problem change, and treatment interventions be linked? Further research is needed to confirm the hypothesis that the same family dimensions for studying changes with family therapy can be used to study changes in a community sample of families that share, for example, a common life event or diagnosed family member, but do not enter family therapy.

POLITICAL AND PRAGMATIC PRIORITIES

In the larger world, family therapy is not yet established as worth doing on as broad a basis as family therapists believe it deserves. In Chapter 3, Ryder warns that politically motivated research is not science. However, researchers and funders do not have the resources to carry out and support all studies with scientific integrity and merit. Therefore, it may be useful to consider, *after* scientific merit has been given first priority, how other priorities might be considered.

1. Does the problem or disorder have a *high incidence and prevalence?* One needs to document these factors not just in terms of DSM-III disorders, but also in terms of familial or marital problems, for example, the high frequency of divorce problems and post-divorce settlement difficulties.

2. Another priority consideration is the *severity* of distress, which obviously is high with schizophrenia, anorexia nervosa, incest, delinquency, substance abuse, and so on, all of which have been treated with a family approach. It would be valuable to know more about the severity of problems associated with transition points in the family life cycle.

3. *Costs* created by a problem or disorder should be compared to the benefits from treatment. For example, in the case of schizophrenia, Cardin, McGill, and Falloon (6) demonstrated that family management was more than twice as cost-efficient as traditional, individual-based management in achieving community care goals. Similarly, the enormous costs associated with substance abuse make efforts at more efficacious therapy especially valuable (37).

4. *Public visibility* of certain problems, such as substance abuse, pass into and out of phases of increased public attention. Despite the risks of public fickleness, situations of high public attention can be regarded by family therapists/researchers as opportunities to demonstrate visibly the efficacy of family approaches.

5. *Relative ineffectiveness of standard treatments:* If other considerations were equivalent, it would be sensible to give priority to studies of

family therapy dealing with problems that are unsatisfactorily treated with standard approaches. For example, after considerable debate, the conclusion has been reached that for marital problems "[t]here is *no* evidence, acceptable or otherwise, of the *efficacy* of individual marital therapy" (19, p. 59). Presumably, this should encourage researchers to document more convincingly the efficacy and processes of conjoint marital therapy. Similarly, the effectiveness of medication for the negative, deficit symptoms of schizophrenia has been disappointing. Psychosocial interventions, including family therapy, are relatively more valuable in the phase of deficit functioning than during acute, florid symptoms when medication is generally believed to be effective and necessary (14, 25).

6. *Treatment acceptability:* In order that referrals for family therapy take place and treatment compliance occurs, family therapy needs to be viewed as an acceptable and plausible approach for specific difficulties. If certain problems are regarded by referring persons and by the public as inherently unsuitable for marital or family treatment, then demonstration projects may be useful to improve treatment acceptability. For example, many battered-women programs regard family therapy as an approach that would return the battered woman to an untenable situation. Family therapists protest that this depends upon how the therapy is actually carried out. With regard to adolescent behavioral problems, family therapists believe that an integrated treatment program involving both the individual adolescent and the entire family is optimal to facilitate the maturation and differentiation of the adolescent and the other family members. However, there are respected individual therapists who believe that conjoint sessions in which the adolescent is brought into contact with the parents are antithetical to the adolescent's autonomous differentiation. These therapists regard family therapy as unacceptable. Hopefully such differences in starting-point acceptability by families and referral sources can be taken into account in research designs.

It should be recognized that it is not enough to have a scientifically sound design if families with specified problems are not actually accessible for family therapy. Collaboration of a research consortium may be necessary in order to pool samples from more than one center, and to disseminate data from work that is still in progress.

RECOMMENDATIONS

1. Studies of the efficacy of family therapy should routinely assess changes in the *family's view of the "presenting problem,"* that is, in their reasons for seeking therapy. The perspective includes the views of each

family member, including persons diagnosed as "ill," as well as the family consensus about the problems, how to go about changing them, and who should take part. The family's perspective should be obtained before therapy or at the beginning of therapy, and it should be periodically reassessed, especially at termination and after designated follow-up periods (for example, at three months, one year, and so on), or at the end of a consultation or contracting period. The family's initial views of the problem can be roughly classified as: 1) families presenting with *relational* problems and 2) families with a *problem person* either (a) carrying a psychiatric or medical diagnosis or (b) showing undiagnosed distress or problematic behavior.

2. The *therapist and/or supervisor's perspectives* about the problem are not useful as *external* measures of family change because therapist perspectives of what the problem is are necessarily intertwined with and changed by his or her interventions. However, in studies of *process within the therapeutic system*, the therapist's contributions are crucial. The perspectives of referral sources and other persons should be recorded and compared whenever possible, although the usefulness of such perspectives will vary from problem to problem.

3. The *researcher's definition* of the presenting problem will usually be one of the prime reference points for comparison studies of treatment across families because he or she should be expected to formulate the problem at a consistent level of abstraction. Researchers must examine their own contribution to shaping and selecting the therapeutic systems under study.

4. In family therapy, repeated *changes in problem definition* may result either from deliberate reframing as a treatment technique or be an emergent manifestation of therapeutic change, or both. Methodologic studies of problem reframing are needed. A dual baseline approach is proposed: the time when the problems of the family members are "initially" presented, and the time of their later consensus with the therapist.

5. Problem change should be targeted and linked in each study to specific, *theory-based family variables*. These family variables should be selected because of their relevance to hypotheses about how therapy with a given approach facilitates therapeutic change.

6. A partial list of *pragmatic considerations* relevant to research priorities in problem selection includes: high incidence and prevalence; high severity of distress or impairment; high health-care and community costs of the problem as presently managed; public visibility of certain problems; relative ineffectiveness of standard treatments; and reasonable public acceptability of a family treatment so as to generate a pool of families for research programs.

REFERENCES

1. Allman, L.R. The aesthetic preference: Overcoming the pragmatic error. *Family Process 21:* 43–56, 1972.
2. Anderson, C.M., Hogarty, G.E., & Reiss, D.J. Family treatment of adult schizophrenic patients: A psychoeducational approach. *Schizophrenia Bulletin 6:* 490–505, 1980.
3. Beavers, W.R. *The Beavers Systems Model for Family Assessment,* 1986. (Unpublished manuscript available from Southwest Family Institute, Dallas TX.)
4. _____, & Voeller, M.N. Family models: Comparing and contrasting the Olson Circumplex Model with Beavers Systems Model. *Family Process 22:* 85–98, 1983.
5. Bloch, D.A. Family systems medicine: The field and the journal. *Family Systems Medicine 1* (1) 3–11, 1983.
6. Cardin, V.A., McGill, C.W., & Falloon, I.R.H. An economic analysis: Costs, benefits, and effectiveness. In I.R.H. Falloon & Others (eds.), *Family management of schizophrenia: A study of clinical, social, family, and economic benefits.* Baltimore: Johns Hopkins University Press, 1985.
7. Carlson, C.I., & Grotevant, H.D. A comparative review of family rating scales: Guidelines for clinicians and researchers. *Journal of Family Psychology 1:* 23–47, 1987.
8. de Shazer, S. *Keys to solution in brief therapy.* New York: W.W. Norton, 1985.
9. Doane, J.A., Goldstein, M.J., Miklowitz, D.J., & Falloon, I.R.H. The impact of individual and family treatment on the affective climate of families of schizophrenics. *British Journal of Psychiatry 148:* 179–187, 1986.
10. _____, West, K.L., Goldstein, M.J., Rodnick, E.H., & Jones, J.E. Parental communication deviance and affective style: Predictors of subsequent schizophrenia spectrum disorders in vulnerable adolescents. *Archives of General Psychiatry 38:* 679–685, 1981.
11. Engel, G.L. The need for a new medical model: A challenge for biomedicine. *Science 196:* 129–136, 1977.
12. _____. The clinical application of the biopsychosocial model. *American Journal of Psychiatry 137:* 535–544, 1980.
13. Epstein, N., Baldwin, L.M., & Bishop, D.S. The McMaster Family Assessment Device. *Journal of Marriage and Family Therapy 9:* 171–180, 1983.
14. Falloon, I.R.H., Boyd, J.L., McGill, C.W., Strang, J.S., & Moss, H.B. Family management training in the community care of schizophrenia. In M.J. Goldstein (ed.), *New developments in interventions with families of schizophrenics.* San Francisco: Jossey-Bass, 1981.
15. Feldman, L.B. Assessment instruments for family therapy: Clinical and research applications. Unpublished manuscript, Chicago Family Institute, 1984.
16. Fisher, L. On the classification of families: A progress report. *Archives of General Psychiatry 34:* 424–433, 1977.
17. Goldstein, M.J. (ed.). *New developments in interventions with families of schizophrenics.* San Francisco: Jossey-Bass, 1981.
18. Grunebaum, H., personal communication, 1986.
19. _____, & Kniskern, D.P. Commentary: Individual marital therapy—Have reports of your death been somewhat exaggerated? *Family Process 25:* 51–62, 1986.

20. _____, Kniskern, D.P., & Pinsof, W.M. Research on the process and outcome of marital and family therapy. In S.L. Garfield & A.E. Bergin (eds.), *Handbook of psychotherapy and behavior change* (3rd ed.). New York: John Wiley & Sons, 1986.

21. Haley, J. *Uncommon therapy: The psychiatric techniques of Milton H. Erickson, M.D.* New York: Ballantine Books, 1973.

22. _____. *Problem-solving therapy: New strategies for effective family therapy.* San Francisco: Jossey-Bass, 1976.

23. Hatfield, A.B. What families want of family therapists. In W.R. McFarlane (ed.), *Family therapy in schizophrenia.* New York: Guilford Press, 1983.

24. Hersen, M., & Barlow, D.H. *Single case experimental designs: Strategies for studying behavior change.* New York: Pergamon Press, 1976.

25. Hogarty, G.E., Anderson, C.M., Reiss, D.J., Kornblith, S.J., Greenwald, D.P., Javna, C.D., Madonia, M.J., & Environmental/Personal Indicators in the Course of Schizophrenia Research Group. Family psychoeducation, social skills training, and maintenance chemotherapy in the aftercare treatment of schizophrenia. *Archives of General Psychiatry 43:* 633–642, 1986.

26. Holden, D.F., & Lewine, R.R.J. How families evaluate mental health professionals, resources, and effects of illness. *Schizophrenia Bulletin 8:* 626–633, 1982.

27. Keeney, B.F. *Aesthetics of change.* New York: Guilford Press, 1983.

28. Kinney, P., Ravich, R., Ford, F., & Vos, B. A typology of families: An interview with the Typology Task Force. *AFTA Newsletter No. 28:* 21–28, 1987.

29. Kniskern, D.P. Climbing out of the pit: Further guidelines for family therapy research. *Journal of Marital and Family Therapy 11:* 159–162, 1985.

30. Leff, J., & Vaughn, C. *Expressed emotion in families: Its significance for mental illness.* New York: Guilford Press, 1985.

31. Lewis, J.M., Beavers, W.R., Gossett, J.T., & Phillips, V.A. *No single thread: Psychological health in family systems.* New York: Brunner/Mazel, 1976.

32. Lewis, A.B., Spencer, J.H., Jr., Haas, G.L., & DiVittis, A. Goal Attainment Scaling: Relevance and replicability in follow-up of inpatients. *Journal of Nervous and Mental Disease 175:* 408–417, 1987.

33. Monteiro, M.J., Heiry, T.J., Beavers, W.R., Beavers, J., & Mohammed, Z. Dallas Self-Report Family Inventory, 1987. (Unpublished manuscript available from Southwest Family Institute, Dallas TX.)

34. Olson, D.H. Insiders' and outsiders' views of relationships: Research studies. In G. Levinger & H. Rausch (eds.), *Close relationships.* Amherst: University of Massachusetts Press, 1977.

35. _____, McCubbin, H.I., & Associates. *Families: What makes them work.* Beverly Hills CA: Sage Publications, 1983.

36. Prosky, P. The third eye. *AFTA Newsletter No. 23:* 32, 1986.

37. Stanton, M.D., Todd, T.C., & Associates. *The family therapy of drug abuse and addiction.* New York: Guilford Press, 1982.

38. Strupp, H.H., & Hadley, S.W. A tripartite model of mental health and therapeutic outcomes: With special reference to negative effects in psychotherapy. *American Psychologist 33:* 187–196, 1977.

39. Tomm, K. On incorporating the therapist in a scientific theory of family therapy. *Journal of Marital and Family Therapy 12:* 373–378, 1986.

40. Vaughn, C.E., & Leff, J.P. The influence of family and social factors on the course of psychiatric illness: A comparison of schizophrenic and depressed neurotic patients. *British Journal of Psychiatry 129:* 125–137, 1976.

41. Whitaker, C.A., & Keith, D.V. Symbolic-experiential family therapy. In A.S. Gurman & D.P. Kniskern (eds.), *Handbook of family therapy*. New York: Brunner/Mazel, 1981.

42. Wynne, L.C. A preliminary proposal for strengthening the multiaxial approach of DSM-III: Possible family-oriented revisions. In G.L. Tischler (ed.), *Diagnosis and classification in psychiatry: A critical appraisal of DSM-III*. New York: Cambridge University Press, in press.

43. _____. The family and marital therapies. In J.M. Lewis & G. Usdin (eds.), *Treatment planning in psychiatry*. Washington DC: American Psychiatric Association, 1982.

44. _____, McDaniel, S.H., & Weber, T.T. (eds.). *Systems consultation: A new perspective for family therapy*. New York: Guilford Press, 1986.

45. _____, McDaniel, S.H., & Weber, T.T. Professional politics and the concepts of family therapy, family consultation, and systems consultation. *Family Process 26:* 153–166, 1987.

8

PATIENT STATUS, FAMILY COMPOSITION, AND OTHER STRUCTURAL VARIABLES IN FAMILY THERAPY RESEARCH*

MICHAEL J. GOLDSTEIN

University of California
Los Angeles, California

CLINICAL WRITINGS on family therapy often imply that it is a broad-spectrum agent efficacious with many forms of psychological and psychophysiological disturbances. The family systems model is a broad theoretical schema that can be applied widely in clinical work, with a few adjustments in specific parameters of the model. A corollary of this assumption for research is that family therapy can be evaluated as a generic agent with few modifications related to the specific population addressed. In fact, a commonly assumed implication of the family systems model is that diagnoses of individual family members should be secondary to the diagnosis of the systemic dysfunction. If we follow this tenet to its logical conclusion, then the selection of families for efficacy research should be based on family-level diagnoses and not on diagnoses of index individual family members.

The notion that a family diagnostic system can be developed is an appealing one. For example, chaotic families and rigid families have been described as distinctively different and as posing different therapeutic issues. The baseline and outcome criteria to assess therapeutic change in such families may vary widely. Unfortunately, no accepted system for family diagnosis exists at present, and it does not appear to be feasible to select families for a controlled trial of the efficacy of family therapy solely on the basis of family dimensions.

As unpalatable as it may seem to the therapist who organizes clinical data on a family-system level, it is probably not practical to design family therapy research without considering the nature of the diagnosed disorder presented by an index family member. In all probability, the family

*Preparation of this chapter was made possible by a grant from the John D. and Catherine T. MacArthur Foundation for the UCLA Node of the Network on Risk and Protective Factors in the Major Mental Disorders. The author would like to express his deep appreciation to Eliot H. Rodnick who served as valued colleague and contributor to much of the research summarized here.

issues raised by a young adult schizophrenic offspring are quite different from those raised by an anorectic teenager, and their individual prognoses vary widely as well. So, it appears that efficacy studies of family therapy will have to select samples initially on the type and severity of the individual mental disorder in an index family member. A generic test of the efficacy of family therapy is not a feasible goal.[1]

Does this mean that we have to carry out a large series of studies on the efficacy of family therapy, one for each disorder? I don't think so. If we can carry out a series of well-designed studies evaluating family therapy that yield positive results for a few disorder groups, then a certain generalization about the potential efficacy of this form of intervention is possible by extrapolation. Consider the impact of the series of studies on focused, family-based intervention programs for families of recently discharged schizophrenics (3–6). The positive results of these studies have boosted enthusiasm about the role of combined pharmacological and psychosocial treatment of schizophrenia, and have increased the credibility of family therapy as a generic treatment modality, particularly among members of the mental health profession who have not been sympathetic to the role of psychosocial treatments with the major mental disorders.

---

1. *Editor's Note:* Goldstein argues that it is not practical to select families for research without knowledge of individual disorders, physical or mental, of family members. Most family therapy researchers probably will agree with this view whenever there is a family member with a delineated disorder that has altered, or threatens to alter, that family member's functioning and role in the family. This circumstance applies to most families seen in general psychiatric and medical inpatient and outpatient facilities. In contrast, many, if not most couples and families seen in clinics and private practice specializing in family and marriage therapy do not come because of an individual disorder or individual symptoms, but because of relationship difficulties. Even when a family member does meet DSM-III criteria for a mental disorder (beyond the vague category of Adjustment Disorder), the individual "mental disorder" is usually not the primary reason for referral to these clinics or family therapists and is not the primary focus for consultation and therapy in these settings. These relational difficulties include such serious presenting problems as impending divorce, custody and visitation disputes, incest, and family violence. Such relationship difficulties are relegated by DSM-III to the nonreimbursable nondisorders of the V codes, such as Marital Difficulty or Parent-Child Difficulty, despite their profound, enduring consequences for the mental health of the family members. Research criteria can focus selectively on specific forms of relationship difficulties but cannot and need not encompass *all* family "diagnoses" in DSM-III format for individual diagnoses. Therefore, Goldstein's view that "a generic test of the efficacy of family therapy is not a feasible goal" is undoubtedly correct. At the same time, the extensive research on marital therapy illustrates that it is not *always* necessary to "select samples initially on the type and severity of the individual mental disorder in an index family member." See chapters 7 and 17 for discussion of individual versus relational starting points for family and marital therapy.

The focus upon the clinical symptoms of an index family member as the criteria for the selection and participation of families in a study of family therapy efficacy does not preclude the use of family dynamics in designing the study. In fact, such information can be extremely useful in stratifying a sample along a dimension or dimensions likely to interact with treatment effectiveness. But it is not feasible to include all of the dimensions in a complex family diagnostic system because to do so would create an inordinate number of cells in the design. What is needed are some creative insights about what dimensions of the family system are likely to be relevant to the disorder selected for study and the therapeutic strategies to be investigated.

Consider, for example, the recent spate of studies cited above that dealt with family intervention programs for schizophrenics and their relatives. The design of most of these programs was predicated on prior empirical research demonstrating that the quality of affective communication (expressed emotion) was related to the probability of relapse after a schizophrenic returned home from the hospital. Thus, in these studies, only those families that were *high* in expressed emotion were selected on the grounds that the therapy was most likely to be effective with relapse-prone family environments. Although the positive results of these studies are encouraging, I believe that the failure to stratify on the full dimensions of the expressed emotion (EE) variable has limited the significance of the findings.

In the Falloon project, with which we have collaborated, schizophrenic patients considered to be at high risk for relapse were randomly assigned to either family or individual therapy. Both therapies followed a similar behavioral model that emphasized training in communication and problem solving. Each treatment was administered once a week for three months, once biweekly for the next three months, and monthly for the last three months of the program. In order to obtain evidence on the impact of the home-based family therapy as contrasted with a clinic-based individual therapy, a direct interaction task was repeated, once before, and again after three months of intensive outpatient treatment. These interactions were transcribed and then coded for parental expressions of affective style by using a coding system designed to capture the interpersonal manifestations of high EE attitudes (2). The task involved a confrontation in which family members dealt with an emotionally charged problem as defined by the family itself. The interaction was designed to sample the quality of affective communication that was the interpersonal analogue of the expressed emotion. Indeed, we found that the number of negative affective style (AS) statements was significantly less ($p < .0001$) in the family therapy group than in the individual therapy group at the posttherapy assessment (1, pp. 282–283).

Cases had been selected by Falloon as probably high EE on the basis of a preliminary nonresearch rating by a clinician of the Camberwell Family Interview (the instrument used to rate EE). However, when these interview tapes were later blindly and more definitively rated, a small number of low-EE families were found to have been included in each group. It turned out that when we grouped the families on a post-hoc basis on the EE variable, the largest and most consistent reductions in negative affective behaviors occurred in the *low*-EE families in the family therapy condition. The pattern for the high-EE families was in the same direction but more variable—some showed reduction while others did not, even after three months of intensive treatment. Had this sample been selected originally to permit equal entry into the study for both high- and low-EE families, it is likely that we would have been able to show a much larger effect of family therapy over a much shorter time period in the low-EE group compared to the high-EE families.

In order to understand more fully the mediating processes linked to long-term outcome, it may be invaluable to include standardized family interaction assessment procedures in the design of family therapy studies. For example, suppose that the direct interaction task data indicated that there were no differential reductions in the negative affective behaviors when the individual and family therapy groups were contrasted, yet relapse rates were significantly lower for the family therapy condition. What would this say about the effective process in family therapy? Clearly, it would suggest that the family therapy was efficacious through changing aspects of family functioning other than affective communication.[2]

HOMOGENEITY VERSUS HETEROGENEITY IN SAMPLE SELECTION

Although the criteria for selection of a sample may be based upon a specified disorder in an identified patient, there are other issues of sample homogeneity still to be addressed. For example, to take my favorite example, when the patient is schizophrenic, one has to decide

---

2. *Editor's Note:* By including the family variable of affective style in the study, and by not relying exclusively on outcome measures, an important step in understanding the affective component of the therapeutic process was taken. It is, furthermore, interesting to note that the family therapy was associated with a decrease in negative affect (not quite statistically significant). However, the larger, highly significant change was an increase in negative family affect in the individual treatment group. Thus, the family therapy may have prevented deterioration but not helped greatly in a positive way. It is through such stepwise exploration of hypotheses with theory-based process variables that a deepened, clinically relevant and cumulative grasp of therapy may develop. Goldstein's example well illustrates the point that the family variables included in therapy research should be theory-based (see Chapter 7).

whether the family intervention is best tested on first-break schizophrenics whose prognosis is sometimes good and whose experience with mental illness is short-term, or on chronic, poor-prognosis patients whose life course usually has been greatly changed by the illness. The situation becomes even more complex when other selection criteria are very broad. Consider the design of a recent multicenter study of the interaction between drug and family therapy for schizophrenic patients and their relatives. The selection criteria permit inclusion of patients who satisfy DSM-III criteria for schizophrenia and who range in age from 18 to 45. But, what if the sample at one or more sites contains a preponderance of 40-year-old, chronic schizophrenics who are still living with or in close contact with their parents? Is that sample likely to be helped by a family therapy approach? The heterogeneous age criteria that are intended to permit generalizable findings may limit the estimate of efficacy. Similar issues can be raised for studies involving other psychiatric disorders.

The question of heterogeneity of family structure is another important issue in the selection of a sample. Should we restrict the sample in a family therapy efficacy study to two-parent families? If we do, the study will be neat but questions about its generalizability can readily be raised. Family system theories are derived from and apply most readily to two-parent families. As Weiss (7) has pointed out, sharp generational boundaries, so highly valued in these families, may not be as functional for single-parent families in which the early assumption of adult roles by offspring often is essential. Similarly, with regard to outcome criteria, we are faced with the question of whether the impact of a family therapy approach should be evaluated with the same criteria for two-parent as for single-parent families.

If investigators choose to take all consecutive cases that satisfy the diagnostic criteria for the patient family member, they undoubtedly will aggregate a very heterogeneous sample of dual- and single-parent families. Even if the samples are stratified on family structure, there are problems in the analysis of pre- and posttherapy data. For example, how do you study relationship changes from pre- to posttherapy in families in which there are two parental data sources before therapy and one after therapy? Do you equate changes in mother-child interactions in single-parent families with those in dual-parent families? What do you do with the father-child and father-mother interaction data? These issues may be bypassed when the outcome measures are so general (family tension, adequacy of communication, and so on) that they can be applied to any family group independent of its composition or size.

Let me illustrate these issues more specifically with some other findings from an analysis of pre/post, 3-month measures of family interaction derived from the Falloon et al. study (3). Fortunately, this study was stratified so that half of the cases in each sample were single-parent and half two-parent families. We were interested in whether the family interaction data revealed comparable changes in dual- versus single-parent families. However, the number of cases in each treatment group was too small to test them as two separate samples for independent evaluation. Therefore, certain comparisons could be made only if they both could be placed on a comparable metric. We had to accept the fact that we could answer some questions in this way, but not others. We could not deal with the differentiation of therapy effects among mothers, fathers, and their offspring in dual-parent families when single-parent families were included on a common scale.

Our "solution" to this problem was quite simple. We assumed that in a single-parent family the parent has an equal opportunity to speak as both parents do in a two-parent family. Thus, a parental score for affective style (AS) statements was obtained in which the single parent's rate of these statements was considered equal to the sum of mother and father in the dual-parent families. The results of using this common metric can be seen in Figure 1. When treated with family therapy, both single- and dual-parent families show a notable and comparable reduction in negative affective statements directed at the patient. In contrast, when only the individual patient was in therapy, the single-parent families do not

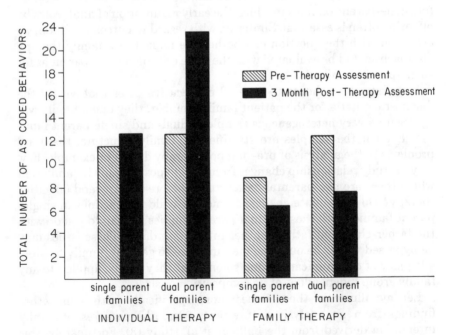

FIG. 1. Pre- and post-therapy changes in affective style (AS): family composition and individual therapy versus family therapy.

show reduced AS and the dual-parent families show a marked *increase* (deterioration) in this behavior.

Not only does this illustrate the virtue of considering family structure as an important stratification variable in outcome studies, but it also raises an interesting challenge to the assumption that without the support of a family-based therapeutic program, a single parent who is faced with the return of a mentally ill relative might be more likely to deteriorate than would a dual-parent family in which the two parents can help one another.

The single-parent/dual-parent distinction is but one of a class of structural factors that must be considered in evaluating the efficacy of family therapy. Other factors involve the comparison of families with wide variations in the number of offspring participating in the therapy, as well as the contrasting of families in which two versus three generations participate in the therapeutic process. The significance of these structural variables relates to the model of therapeutic efficacy. If one is interested only in the outcome of therapy for a specified, index family member, then these issues are less critical. If, on the other hand, one is concerned with the components and the processes of family therapy, then variations in the structural parameters of the family system are crucial.

REFERENCES

1. Doane, J.A., Goldstein, M.J., Miklowitz, D.J., & Falloon, I.R.H. The impact of individual and family treatment on the affective climate of families of schizophrenics. *British Journal of Psychiatry 148:* 279–287, 1986.
2. ————, West, K.L., Goldstein, M.J., Rodnick, E.H., & Jones, J.E. Parental communication deviance and affective style: Predictors of subsequent schizophrenia spectrum disorders in vulnerable adolescents. *Archives of General Psychiatry 38:* 679–685, 1981.
3. Falloon, I.R.H., Boyd, J.L., McGill, C.W., Razani, J., Moss, H.B., & Gilderman, A.M. Family management in the prevention of exacerbations of schizophrenia. *New England Journal of Medicine 306:* 1437–1440, 1982.
4. Goldstein, M.J., Rodnick, E.H., Evans, J.R., May, P.R.A., & Steinberg, M.R. Drug and family therapy in the aftercare of acute schizophrenics. *Archives of General Psychiatry 35:* 1169–1177, 1978.
5. Hogarty, G.E., Anderson, C.M., Reiss, D.J., Kornblith, S.J., Greenwald, D.P., Javna, C.D., & Madonia, M.J. Family psychoeducation, social skills training, and maintenance chemotherapy in the aftercare treatment of schizophrenia: I. One-year effects of a controlled study on relapse and expressed emotion. *Archives of General Psychiatry 43:* 633–642, 1986.
6. Leff, J.P., Kuipers, L., Berkowitz, E., Eberlein-Vries, R., & Sturgeon, D. A controlled trial of social intervention in the families of schizophrenic patients. *British Journal of Psychiatry 141:* 121–134, 1982.
7. Weiss, R.S. Growing up a little faster: The experience of growing up in a single parent household. *Journal of Social Issues 35:* 97–111, 1979.

PART III

DESIGN OF OUTCOME RESEARCH

9

DILEMMAS AND CHOICES IN THE DESIGN OF FAMILY THERAPY RESEARCH

NATHAN B. EPSTEIN

Brown University Medical School
Providence, Rhode Island

HIS BRIEF CHAPTER is an attempt to focus crisply on my recommendations for dealing with several basic issues in the specification of family therapy interventions.

Can Family Therapy Interventions Be Specified and Operationalized?

My answer is that it is both possible and desirable. The field of family therapy must attempt to specify family therapy interventions for *scientific* and *pragmatic* reasons. Some family therapists in the past have argued, and continue to do so, that family therapy is too "flexible, nonlinear, complex," and so on, to be specified in concrete, objective terms. Family therapy is certainly a highly complicated and complex phenomenon that is difficult to describe accurately and to operationalize. However, family therapy is no more complex than many other fields of science that have successfully quantified their constructs. These other fields, for example, endocrinology and neuroscience, have advanced their understanding of highly complex processes by starting at the simplest, most basic level, and then adding complexity as their knowledge base increases. I suggest that family therapy can be investigated in the same fashion, and I will elaborate some steps for doing so in the remainder of this chapter.

Pragmatically, the politics of third-party reimbursement, accountability, and federal funding suggest that if the family therapy field cannot specify the interventions and provide empirical evidence for their efficacy, we may find ourselves lumped with 1,000 other "therapies" with no firm scientific base and, in the future, no clinical reimbursement or research money. Despite the complexity of family therapy, therefore, we have to agree that specification of interventions is theoretically possible, scientifically useful, and pragmatically necessary.

What Is Family Therapy?

In the most generic sense, how do we define "family therapy"? Again, although no definition will please everyone or include all clinical possibilities, I suggest the following generic definition: *a therapeutic approach to working with the family unit as a system for the purpose of aiding the family members to achieve solutions to problems that interfere with their satisfactory functioning as individuals and as a family unit.* Ordinarily, the family therapy unit should involve all members living together under one roof and all others actively involved in any meaningful aspect of their lives.

At What Level of Detail Should Interventions Be Specified?

I recommend that family therapy interventions be specified according to their most basic, macro, larger-content stages and structures. Family therapy interventions can be described in terms of macro structures, content, and sequences, *or* they can be described in terms of the specific, micro, step-by-step interventions, interaction techniques, and strategies. Bishop and I (1) have previously described this distinction between macro and micro levels of intervention:

> We use the term *macro stages* to define the major stages of treatment. They are the large sequential blocks of the treatment process such as assessment, contracting, treatment and closure. Each incorporates a number of substages . . . Therapists make use of a variety of strategies and interventions in the course of leading a family through these macro stages. Here, "strategy" refers to the options and courses of action that may be taken to successfully complete a macro stage.
>
> We differentiate the macro stages and the strategies required to negotiate them from the *micro moves*, the specific intervention skills . . . These micro moves are the numerous interventions made by a therapist while carrying out the macro stages and include, for example, techniques for labeling, focusing, and clarifying.
>
> Neither the macro stages nor the micro moves should be confused with "style," which is based more on the personal qualities of the therapist . . . .
>
> [W]e would emphasize that the macro stages of therapy are the most important level of focus at this point in the development of research in family therapy. We are aware that intervention skills (the micro moves) are important . . . . In our experience, therapists vary in both their repertoire and number of such skills and we have no clear empirical data to indicate specifically which ones are required to negotiate most effectively given stages of the model. We feel, rather, that the wider the range of skills available to therapists, the more effectively and efficiently they will carry out treatment. [pp. 448–449]

In conceptualizing the difference between macro and micro levels of specification, I find the example of describing a piece of symphonic music a useful analogy. Any classical symphony has an almost infinite number of harmonic variations, rhythms, tempos, and sequences. However, there are only a few basic themes that are repeated throughout the complete symphony. The former components weave in and out of the central themes in rich variation and give the symphony its unique distinction and tonal qualities. Similarly, in all types of psychotherapy, there are only a few basic themes that run throughout a given therapy. On the other hand, all psychotherapies provide opportunities for the interplay of almost infinite patterns of variations in the basic themes that are unique to any given therapist/patient combination, and it is these that lend flavor and excitement to the therapy.

In summary, I believe that at the present stage of research we should focus on the larger, more macro stages of the family therapy intervention. There are several reasons for this recommendation. First, at our present state of knowledge, it is all we can do to specify and operationalize the most basic elements of treatment, let alone the more complex, detailed interactions and interventions. Second, following the footsteps of other disciplines and the law of parsimony, it makes sense to start with the simplest elements and then, after we understand those elements, to move on to an investigation of more complex processes. Third, it may be that operationalization of the basic steps of family therapy is sufficient to make progress in understanding the efficacy of family therapy at this time.

What Should Be the Focus of Research?

Should research focus on common or distinctive elements? *I believe that the most immediate priority is the development of rigorous, highly specific, and operationalized methods of family therapy.* Although identification of common therapeutic elements is clearly an important, long-range endeavor, I am concerned about premature emphasis in this direction for several reasons. First, I think the need to document rigorously and empirically the efficacy of family therapy is a more important priority for the field. This priority will be better served by concurrent development of family therapy interventions within specific approaches, rather than investigation of common elements.[1] Second, investigation of common elements across therapy types without a clear understanding of their nature is fraught with difficulty; I would be afraid of losing sight of the forest because of the trees. Third, it has always been easier to get people to devote time to their particular type of therapy rather than to someone else's. Therefore, I recommend encouragement of different types of specific family therapy interventions. In the future, when the field has several operationalized interventions that have demonstrated therapeutic efficacy, then investigation of common elements across types of treatments can be undertaken.

---

1. *Editor's Note:* In Chapter 10, Gurman agrees with Epstein's emphasis, but would give somewhat greater (though secondary) attention to the investigation of common elements across family therapy models.

Can (and Should) Treatment Manuals Be Developed?

To this question, I would give an unqualified "Yes!". As I have argued in the preceding pages, I think that the most important priority for the family therapy field is to specify and operationalize its interventions so that they can be evaluated in an empirical fashion. Development of treatment manuals has been an effective approach for the study of individual psychotherapy, and I see no reason why this same approach cannot be applied to family therapy interventions. Whereas others will continue to argue that family therapy interventions cannot be packaged in treatment manuals, I firmly believe that they are scientifically and politically necessary for the field and, further, that we can specify in manual form the "macro" or basic stages of particular family therapy interventions.[2]

Which Types of Family Therapies Should Be Investigated?

I recommend that those family therapy interventions and their proponents who have developed or are willing to develop highly specific, operationalized, manualized, and clinically sound interventions should be given research priority. For the reasons outlined previously, I believe that those models of family therapy intervention that cannot be operationalized should not be given research priority. Presently, I think that three models of family intervention appear to meet these criteria:

1. *Behavioral models* that have already produced several treatment manuals and demonstrated efficacy with several populations.

2. The *structural model* as defined by Minuchin and his colleagues (3, 4), with selected *strategic* components as defined by Stanton (5) and Haley (2), among others. (I personally have had difficulty distinguishing these two approaches from each other in my reading of the literature.) Although certainly not a unitary school, this general approach to family treatment appears sufficiently specifiable to have promise as a research intervention.

---

2. *Editor's Note:* The desirability and feasibility of using treatment manuals in family therapy research is controversial at present. For a negative view, see Stanton (Chapter 1); for a qualified positive view, see Jacobson (Chapter 11). If manuals are used as guidelines that are broadly compatible with the therapist's clinical judgment, then the research conference consensus seemed to be that manuals can facilitate research involving behavioral, psychoeducational, and problem-solving family therapy models. Irene Waskow of the NIMH staff noted that manuals do not need to be step-by-step instructions, but can describe general guidelines and strategies, supplemented by videotapes and supervision, as in good clinical training programs. In the NIMH collaborative study of the treatment of depression, an Interpersonal Psychotherapy Manual was used by psychodynamically oriented therapists who had a basically positive experience despite their initial qualms.

3. Our own *Problem-Centered Systems Therapy* of the family (1) has already been highly refined and defined operationally so that the development of a treatment manual would require only a relatively small amount of further work.[3]

Other methods of family treatment do not appear at this time to be good candidates for empirical evaluation.

What Level of Therapists Should Be Used in Outcome Studies?

I recommend that the most experienced, best trained therapists be used whenever possible. The use of such therapists will give family treatment its "best shot," and it will preclude an explanation of unsatisfactory outcomes as due to poorly trained or inexperienced therapists. Perhaps even more importantly, with inexperienced therapists, extensive effort must be given to empirically establishing a level of therapist competence through in-session rating scales or some other objective assessment measures.

Should Other Parameters of Family Therapy Intervention Be Specified?

Such parameters would include number of sessions, length and spacing of sessions, single therapist versus cotherapists, who is included in the family constellation, and so on. I recommend that these issues be specified in treatment manuals but otherwise left to the individual investigator's judgment. Whereas these variables may have significant effects, as long as they are specified, future research will evaluate their potential influence.

CONCLUSION

In summary, my recommendations about the specification of family therapy interventions are as follows:

1. We should agree that specification and operationalization of family treatment are feasible and desirable.

2. We should agree upon a common, generic definition of family treatment.

3. Family therapy interventions should be specified at the most basic or "macro" level.

---

3. *Editor's Note:* In Chapter 10, Gurman also encourages research on the three models regarded by Epstein as appropriate for current family therapy research, but he also takes a positive view of approaches for which research may not be currently feasible but which should be encouraged—such as, psychodynamic and Bowen family systems therapy. Psychoeducational family therapy has, of course, already been the subject of successful major research (Hogarty, Anderson, Reiss, et al., 1986).

4. Priority should be given to development and refinement of several different types of family treatments.

5. Treatment manuals should be developed for family therapy interventions.

6. Priority should be given to those types of family treatments that are most amenable to operationalization and development of specific treatment manuals.

7. The most experienced and best trained therapists should be used in initial outcome studies.

8. Other parameters of family therapy interventions should be specified in treatment manuals but should be left to the judgment of the individual investigators.

REFERENCES

1. Epstein, N.B., & Bishop, D.S. Problem-centered systems therapy of the family. In A.S. Gurman & D.P. Kniskern (eds.), *Handbook of family therapy*. New York: Brunner/Mazel, 1981.
2. Haley, J. *Problem-solving therapy: New strategies for effective family therapy*. San Francisco: Jossey-Bass, 1976.
3. Minuchin S. *Families & family therapy*. Cambridge: Harvard University Press, 1974.
4. _____, & Fishman, H.C. *Family therapy techniques*. Cambridge: Harvard University Press, 1981.
5. Stanton, M.D. Strategic approaches to family therapy. In A.S. Gurman & D.P. Kniskern (eds.), *Handbook of family therapy*. New York: Brunner/Mazel, 1981.

EDITOR'S REFERENCES

Hogarty, G.E., Anderson, C.M., Reiss, D.J., Kornblith, S.J., Greenwald, D.P., Javna, C.D., Madonia, B.A., & the EPICS Schizophrenia Research Group. Family psycho-education, social skills training and maintenance chemotherapy in the aftercare treatment of schizophrenia: I. One-year effects of a controlled study on relapse and expressed emotion. *Archives of General Psychiatry 43:* 633–642, 1986.

10

ISSUES IN THE SPECIFICATION OF FAMILY THERAPY INTERVENTIONS

ALAN S. GURMAN

University of Wisconsin Medical School
Madison, Wisconsin

B ECAUSE this volume on the state of the art in family therapy research is meant to punctuate and define this domain of inquiry, we must begin by asking a simple question that does not have a simple answer: "What is family therapy?" This question requires us simultaneously to consider complex conceptual matters and to define less esoteric operational terms clearly. It is difficult to study an "X" if one does not know (for epistemologists, read "decide" or "judge") what an "X" is. Before moving on to other important matters, we must address this basic question.

DEFINITIONS

I believe that there have been two dominant views of what constitutes the operational essence of family therapy:

1. At the broadest level, family therapy may be defined by *the conceptual "map"* in the mind of the therapist, such that if therapists regularly and systematically consider the family context, then they are doing family therapy irrespective of who is in the consultation room or how many people are present. For research, such conceptual maps, of course, need to include specification of the behavioral consequences (therapist actions) that are subject to empirical observation.

A related but more midrange definition would define family therapy by *the therapists' intent for the outcome.* That is, whom do they aim to influence—symptomatic or distressed persons only, the family as a whole, or all individuals, including nonfamily members, who are clinically relevant?

2. The most restrictive definition focuses only on those *persons who are present* in treatment sessions. By this criterion, face-to-face treatment of an individual would not be included in the definition of "family therapy," regardless of the therapist's conceptual map or outcome intent. Family therapy requires the presence and treatment of two or more related individuals.

These varying definitions are relevant in conceptualizing the enterprise called family therapy, in training family therapists, and in delimiting the boundaries of the field as seen by others, such as independent reviewers of therapy research reports. Thus, Gurman and Kniskern (23) employ a definition that focuses on "altering the interaction between or among family members" (p. 820), whether the family's presenting problems concern one symptomatic member or the interaction among family members, and, by implication, regardless of who is present during treatment (a version of definition 1 above). On the other hand, Wells and colleagues (43, 44) offer a definition that requires natural units of the family to be seen *together as a group over most of the duration of treatment with the goal of improving their functioning as a unit"* (44, p. 191; original emphasis). Dewitt's (11) definition requires a conjoint mode of intervention in which "all relevant members of the family must have been treated together as a unit for all or a major portion of the treatment" (p. 551).

Clearly, to begin to address more refined matters involving the specification of "family therapy" techniques, there must be an agreed-upon, operational (for epistemologists, admittedly arbitrary), and broadly conceived specification of what family therapy is. For the purposes of conducting training workshops, although it may be educationally important to adopt a definition more in keeping with the "conceptual" and "intentional" definitions noted above, these will not do for research purposes. For research purposes involving the specification of interventions and the testing and study of therapeutic methods, the nature of the therapist's thinking about therapy and outcome intentions are not relevant; what the therapist does is relevant. Of course, the therapist's thinking and intention may, themselves, be proper domains of empirical study, but they are surely not equivalent to, and cannot be construed as substitutes for what he or she does. For example, as has been repeatedly demonstrated in individual psychotherapy, there is an uncertain relationship between the stated therapeutic goals and values and the therapist's actual, in-session behavior, and between the therapist's *description* of his or her in-session behavior and his or her *actual* behavior (38).

For our immediate purposes of delimiting the field for research, I propose that "family therapy" be defined as any psychotherapeutic endeavor that (a) *explicitly focuses on altering the interactions between or among family members*—whether in same-generation (husband-wife, child-child) and/or cross-generation (parent-child-grandparent) relationships, regardless of who is symptomatic or distressed; and (b) *seeks to improve both the functioning of the family as a unit and the functioning of individual family members*, including but possibly not limited to the functioning of a symptomatic or distressed member of the family, if such a person is clearly identified (24).

This definition, it is important to note, quite intentionally does not exclude marital therapy (systemically oriented treatment of the husband-wife subsystem) or well-developed methods of intervention in family and marital interactions that are often viewed within the family therapy field as falling outside its boundaries—for example, the Couple Communication Program (42), Relationship Enhancement (18), and sex therapy.[1]

SPECIFICATION OF WHAT?

This conference occurs at a time in the evolution of the family therapy field that is both extraordinarily exciting and confusing, especially with regard to the development of "schools" and "methods" of intervention. Occurring simultaneously are (a) rapid changes in the refinement and elaboration of techniques within major schools of family therapy, for example, the several major variants of systemic and strategic family therapy (compare 14, 25, 30, 31, 39, 40), and (b) an increasing push for the development of integrative models that incorporate the thinking and techniques of apparently disparate views (see 13, 20, 32, 34, 36). Simultaneous movements toward within-school refinement and between-school integration are not unique phenomena in the field of psychotherapy (witness the last decade of developments in behavioral therapy), but they do appear to be occurring much more intensely in the family field.

These political and conceptual movements highlight a major policy dilemma for efficacy research. To what extent should relevant funding agencies and individual investigators be fostering research aimed at (a) the refinement of specific family therapy methods (for example, structural and strategic therapy) in order to enhance the efficacy of those methods and to support work in comparative outcome studies; and/or (b) the isolation of effective components of family intervention across

---

1. *Editor's Note:* At the 1984 NIMH/*Family Process* research conference, Gurman proposed, and Goldstein agreed, that a third component be included in a definition of family therapy for research purposes: "*works face-to-face with more than one family member* (albeit possibly in varying combinations and configurations over time) for a significant proportion of in-therapy time." This stipulation, Gurman went on to say, meant that "family therapy methods that involve the direct, face-to-face encounter between a therapist and only one person, no matter how philosophically compatible they are with multi-person, interactional methods, or how clinically appropriate and justifiable [see reference 10], fall outside this definition." In 1986, Gurman, Kniskern, and Pinsof (24) abandoned this component of the definition. See Chapter 17 for further discussion of the definition of family therapy.

schools of therapy in order to identify those common techniques crucial to change induction?

In responding to this dilemma, I believe that the central current issue in efficacy research is how to do research that will have a direct impact on clinical practice (4). Whereas my own clinical predilections are decidedly integrative (20) and oriented toward the common-elements strategy (17), I believe that the optimal strategy for research intended to influence practice will be to give a new priority to identifying the most specific and important components of the major, distinct treatment methods (21). It is widely acknowledged (21, 37) that psychotherapy research, especially that involving comparative outcome studies of alternative (competing) methods, has had and continues to have little impact on clinicians, even on those behavior therapists (see 4) who espouse a more empirical attitude in clinical work.[2]

It is in recognition of these considerations that I propose two major priorities for family therapy research: (a) the identification of the most potent change-inducing elements within the major methods of family therapy, and (b) the identification of the common elements across these methods that do *not* add measurably to the clinical effectiveness of each method. Such studies would necessarily include, yet go beyond, examination of techniques *qua* techniques to include studies of therapist characteristics, family characteristics, the patient-family-therapist relationship, treatment setting characteristics, and interactions among these domains of variables. In effect, this proposed line of research would be directed toward enhancing the power of *specific* family therapy methods with specific clinical populations.[3] Integrationism notwithstanding, there are, and will continue to be, numerous family therapists who practice only in terms of a single theoretical model. Component analyses, for example, by means of dismantling strategies, will help to refine the practices of given "schools" so that components accounting for meaningful amounts of variance can be emphasized both clinically and in training, while neutral or harmful elements can be avoided or minimized.

Second, and in concert with the emerging call for integration and rapprochement among family therapy methods, I propose as a research priority the identification of common ingredients in the various family

---

2. *Editor's Note:* See Editor's Comments, 6, for a discussion of the impact and relevance of therapy research for clinicians.

3. *Editor's Note:* In Chapter 9, Epstein also explicitly recommends that priority be given to study of family therapy interventions within specific approaches, a necessary step before the field will be ready for the important, longer-range endeavor of investigating common elements across approaches.

therapies. These two proposed directions for research on the specification of interventions are not contradictory, though they may appear to be
so. Just as Skynner (35) has quipped that we need "different thinks for
different shrinks" (p. 7), so too does the field need different research foci
for different clinician consumers.

THE AMENABILITY OF VARIOUS METHODS TO EMPIRICAL STUDY

In the context of the above proposal for more school-specific study, we
must consider which approaches to family therapy are presently most
amenable to such investigations. At the risk of offending numerous
colleagues, but for the purpose of stimulating discussion, I offer the
following comments on the major family therapy methods in terms of
their amenability to such research.

Structural Family Therapy

This is a highly teachable method that has been taught successfully to
both mental health professionals and nonprofessionals for years. Its
technical operations are clear and specific (see 41). For these reasons, and
because positive outcomes with structural therapy have been demonstrated with difficult-to-treat populations (3, 24), this approach should
probably rank as highly amenable to empirical study.

Strategic/Systemic Therapies

These quickly have become the applied "cutting edges" in the family
field. Although the assumptions and specific technical operations within
this group of methods vary from camp to camp, their combined impact on
the field has been impressive, and their effectiveness can be astounding
and dramatic. To date, there have been no well-designed comparative or
control-group studies of any of these strategic/systemic variations (24).
Because of their extraordinary impact on training and practice in the
field and their treatment-goal specificity, however, empirical study of
their overall efficacy and their therapeutic components should be given
high priority. While systemic (read, Milan-model) therapists refuse to
predict treatment outcome, demur on setting treatment goals apart from
those evolving out of the therapist-family interaction, and do not assume
(lineal) responsibility for achieving given outcome goals, traditional
methods of assessing outcome are still applicable to the study of the
Milan method and should not be forsaken because of prevailing epistemological arguments against the possibility of studying the effects of the
Milan method. One needs simply to be reminded that "outcome"
measurements represent a particular punctuation in a recursive series of
events (therapist-family interactions) at an arbitrary point in time.

Behavioral Therapy

Like structural therapy, this is highly teachable and replicable. Dozens of well-designed outcome studies already exist (see 24), especially in the area of behavioral marital therapy and parent-management training for conduct disorders. Although behavioral marital and family therapy began outside the mainstream of the family movement, increased attention to its methods are definitely needed.

Psychodynamic Therapy

This approach has had a long and significant influence on the family field since its beginnings (see 1). Although there are, in fact, relatively few prominent psychodynamic theorists or theories in the field, it is likely that psychodynamic thinking about clinical work with families presents the most unacknowledged yet pervasive conceptual footing for day-to-day practice.[4] The major existing pitfalls for efficacy research on psychodynamic family therapy is that there appear to be relatively few intervention techniques that are specific to these approaches (see 19, 20, 33), and these approaches technically seem to be the most eclectic in the field (19). One of the major justifications for efficacy research on dynamic family therapy certainly is its generalizability to the practices of large numbers of clinicians. Even though only a handful of controlled or component studies of psychodynamic marital and family therapy have been published to date (see 24), evidence of their effectiveness exceeds that which exists for most methods of marital/family therapy. Continued empirical study of the efficacy of psychodynamic methods, therefore, is to be encouraged, with particular emphasis on disentangling those components of psychodynamic treatment that contribute unique variance to treatment outcomes, above and beyond what is attributable to techniques often held in common with alternative family treatment methods.

Symbolic-Experiential Therapy

This approach (for example, 45), is one that seems to have achieved prominence in the field almost exclusively because of the charismatic qualities of its creator, Carl Whitaker. To date, no empirical study of this method has appeared (see 24). Moreover, there are few family clinicians who have been thoroughly trained in this approach. Many of the stated propositions about its change-inducing mechanisms may be untestable.

---

4. *Editor's Note:* In Chapter 4, Auerswald takes a much dimmer view of psychodynamic approaches and regards a psychodynamic paradigm as having been "largely abandoned by family therapists" during the last decades. In terms of numbers of actual practitioners, as contrasted with theorists, Gurman probably is correct in his view of the continuing importance of this framework.

In addition, because of the particular therapist "style" called for, it is unlikely that a systematic sequencing of interventions and prescription of therapist behaviors can be established; further, many of its methods may be unteachable. For these reasons, this approach is probably not currently amenable to systematic empirical research.

Bowen Family Systems Therapy

This therapy has occupied a central, historical role in the evolution of family therapy (see 7). To date, only a small number of studies has appeared that have tested any of its central constructs (see 19), and none has involved the evaluation of its outcomes (see 24). The major pitfall in empirical study of the method is, as Kerr (28), a prominent representative of this school, has written: "There are no specific steps to follow other than the general one of being in better contact with parents, siblings, and the larger extended system. *The theory is the guide*" (p. 257). Nonetheless, predictable patterns of therapist intervention certainly do occur in Bowen therapy and, like the Milan method (which has been considered as unresearchable by traditional methods), it is also testable.

Psychoeducational Family Therapy

This method (see 2) has been the subject of a major research project (27) that, to date, has provided some of the most compelling evidence of the efficacy of psychosocial treatment methods (in combination with neuroleptics) in the context of major psychopathology (for example, schizophrenia). The various forms of psychoeducational treatment need continued study in order to specify further which are the most appropriate at different stages of the illness.

Problem-Centered Systems Therapy of the Family

This approach (see 12) was originally developed at McMaster University in Canada. It is unusually explicit in its methods and is readily teachable even to those who are not mental health professionals, for example, primary care physicians. Several outcome studies are under way, and systematic research on its assessment devices has been done. Though not a widely known or practiced method, it has many characteristics that make it highly amenable to research.

Other Methods

These do not appear to be particularly promising for large-scale research, either because they are in limited use in the field, though having a promising empirical base, for example, functional family therapy (5), or because of the lack of technical specificity of some models that, contrariwise, are widely known, for example, contextual family therapy (6).

Criteria for Assessing Amenability of Family Therapy Models to Efficacy Research

As may have been implicit in the above comments, the major criteria for the assessment of the amenability of family therapy models to efficacy research are:

- the degree of technical specificity, replicability, and, hence, learnability
- the relative amount and quality of existing research on outcome evaluation and/or testing of basic propositions (for example, pathological interaction processes)
- the apparent extent of influence in the family therapy field, gauged partly by estimates of the numbers of its practitioners
- other considerations such as the historical significance of the methods (for example, psychodynamic family therapy) and their pervasive influences on practices in the field, even in the absence of identifiable major theorists or training centers

THE STUDY OF COMMON CHANGE-INDUCING MECHANISMS

Although there are perhaps a handful of psychotherapeutic methods that are clearly superior to alternative methods in the treatment of specific psychological disorders, in general it has been the approximate, overall equivalence of outcomes of the major psychotherapeutic methods that has been most strikingly and consistently found (16). Data such as these have led many (see, for example, 15, 17) to lobby for the study of common ingredients in psychotherapeutic change, including not only the mechanisms of change inhering in the apparently diverse techniques, but also the critical components in the therapist-patient relationship. As noted earlier, there is a strong movement afoot in the family therapy field toward integration and rapprochement, notwithstanding critics of such a movement (for example, 29). Many possibilities may be identified for studying these common ingredients in family therapy techniques, of which a few illustrations are:

- induction in the family of a set of perceptions (beliefs, attributions) about their presenting problem that differs from that which they initially showed
- transformation of the family's view of their problem (where clinically appropriate) from individualistic to interactional or systemic
- modification of the permeability of channels available for the exchange of information (communication)
- creation of alternative modes of problem solving, whether through "direct" or "indirect" intervention

- modification of symptom-related, affective arousal
- modification of generational boundaries and other forms of hierarchical incongruities
- modification of rates and relative proportion of social and aversive interpersonal behaviors

I would encourage the reader at this point to think divergently about the variety of specific, well-known techniques of different schools of family therapy that, in each case, might provide the technical vehicle for the activation of each of these possible, "common" change-inducing strategies and mechanisms.

Family Therapy and Intervention "Packages"

Quite beyond the study of the techniques of family therapy as a method of psychosocial treatment, it is essential to keep in mind that the conceptual underpinnings of all family therapies are systemic. One important practical implication of this position is that, to be true to their systemic stance, family therapists often intervene in levels of biopsychosocial organization that extend well beyond the family as a unit of social interaction. Certainly, in institutional treatment settings, appropriate systemic intervention frequently necessitates a clinical combination of family therapy as well as, for example, the use of psychotropic medication, and contact and collaboration with members of the legal, educational, and other nonpsychiatric medical communities.

Such a requisite disposition to intervene in systems both larger (for example, educational) and smaller (for example, biochemical) than the family renders the study of family therapy, as it is frequently practiced, problematic from a design point of view. Family therapy often involves (a) intervention at multiple levels of social organization (the individual, marital dyad, nuclear family, extended family, social agencies); (b) multiple dimensions of individual functioning (physiological, behavioral); and (c) varying combinations of system-level interventions in different phases of treatment (drugs plus hospitalization as a first phase in the treatment of a psychotic family member, followed by outpatient drug maintenance plus family therapy plus peer group therapy—as in the treatment of anorexia).

Thus, in outcome studies of the treatment of certain disorders known to require complex packages of intervention that extend well beyond family therapy (in the usual or typical, conjoint sense), differentiating the relative independent contributions to outcome variance of each package component and of their interactive contributions to outcome variance would be complex indeed. Moreover, organizing and administering family (systemic) treatment that requires multifaceted packages would seem to require a level of fiscal support, project personnel, and so on, that might render such studies unfeasible at the present time, despite the obvious, potential importance of such studies. The unfortunate alternative to such complex research projects in the field most often seems to have resulted in careful control and monitoring of the family therapy component in the treatment package (for example, structural therapy of anorexia), with questionable parallel monitoring and/or control (and rare reporting in the literature) of concurrent interventions (antidepressant medications, peer therapy groups, individual therapy, behavioral contingency management procedures, and so on).

For these reasons, a research strategy that may offer an optimal match to the complexity of such treatment packages is the use of multiple baseline designs (26) that allow the systematic introduction and withdrawal, single or in combination, of treatment components. Under these conditions, studies using multiple baseline designs within cases, and accumulating a series of cases of a given type, may be much more currently practical than efforts to mount large-scale, group-design studies.

RECOMMENDED PRIORITIES FOR FAMILY THERAPY RESEARCH

As I have stated, I believe that the major, overriding research priority in the field of family therapy is to enhance both the quality and amount of investigative activity that is likely to have perceptible impact on practicing family clinicians. Indeed, I believe that this aim subsumes the two other major aims articulated at this conference, that is, improving our scientific understanding of the mechanisms of therapeutic change, and generating data relevant to various public policy issues in the broad field of psychosocial intervention.

To these ends, I have recommended above that priority be given to:

1. *The study of common elements and mechanisms of change in effective family therapies.*

2. *The specification of effective ingredients within each of the major family therapy approaches.*

In addition, I also recommend that special research attention be given to:

3. *The study of "family therapy-as-usual,"* meaning the practice of family therapy as a major component in naturalistic treatment "packages," for example, in combination (sequentially and/or simultaneously) with drug interventions or other psychotherapy interventions.

4. *The study of the factors associated with deterioration or "negative effects."* Except for one major article on this topic (22), there has been virtually no empirical study in this domain. A book on the topic (8) includes a major conceptual treatise on the analysis of family therapy failures (9).

5. *Intensive study of expert family therapists* representative of the major family therapy schools. Family therapy needs to be studied under conditions in which there is maximum likelihood of achieving positive outcomes.

6. *The study of the family treatment of specific disorders or relational problems.* Because family therapists regularly treat couples and families in which no family member carries a primary DSM-III diagnosis, or in which individual psychopathology is not the focus of treatment (for example, family violence, remarriage, divorce), the study of family therapy with primary relational disorders is necessary.[5] Studies of family treatment that focus on individual disorders should emphasize two parameters: (a) the study of disorders for which there is conceptual warrant for predicting that family therapy may be the treatment of choice (for example, in anorexia), and (b) the study of disorders for which there already is substantial evidence that effective nonfamily treatments exist (for example, cognitive therapy of depression, exposure therapy of phobias).[6]

7. *The use and study of multidimensional assessment of family treatment outcomes*, including both multiple perspectives (for example, therapist, family, judges, extended family) on change, multiple units of change (symptomatic patient, marital relationship, parent-child relationship), and multiple levels of change (self-report, behavioral observation, unobtrusive records).

8. *Explication of the implications of systems thinking for the assessment of nonfamily therapy intervention outcome studies*, for example, effects of individual therapy on patients' marriages, on patients' relation-

---

5. *Editor's Note:* For the pragmatic reason of improving the credibility of family therapy, Anderson and Goldstein recommended during the research conference that priority be given to studies in which well-defined individual disorders are under treatment.

6. *Editor's Note:* At the NIMH/*Family Process* conference, Goldstein argued the reverse, namely, that priority be given to the study of disorders that have had only moderate or limited success with nonfamily treatments. In contrast, he argued that there would be relatively little interest in family therapy research on problems for which the results of current treatments are regarded as reasonably satisfactory, for example, in the treatment of mania, given the efficacy of lithium for that disorder. Except for clinicians already committed to family therapy, there would be little motivation for colleagues to participate in such research (see Editor's Comments, 6, at the end of this volume); they might even raise ethical questions about withholding a successful standard treatment in favor of an untried family approach. For similar reasons, the case for funding such research would be more difficult to make. If family therapy were to be combined with another treatment approach with a relatively low success rate, the advantages of adding the family approach would more easily be demonstrated.

ships with their children, and on family interactions between other family members.

REFERENCES

1. Ackerman, N.W. *The psychodynamics of family life: Diagnosis and treatment of family relationships.* New York: Basic Books, 1958.
2. Anderson, C.M., Reiss, D.J., & Hogarty, G.E. *Schizophrenia in the family: A practitioner's guide to psychoeducation and management.* New York: Guilford Press, 1986.
3. Aponte, H.J., & VanDeusen, J.M. Structural family therapy. In A.S. Gurman & D.P. Kniskern (eds.), *Handbook of family therapy.* New York: Brunner/Mazel, 1981.
4. Barlow, D. On the relation of clinical research to clinical practice: Current issues, new directions. *Journal of Consulting and Clinical Psychology 49:* 147–155, 1981.
5. Barton, C., & Alexander, J.F. Functional family therapy. In A.S. Gurman & D.P. Kniskern (eds.), *Handbook of Family Therapy.* New York: Brunner/Mazel, 1981.
6. Boszormenyi-Nagy, I., & Ulrich, D.N. Contextual family therapy. In A.S. Gurman & D.P. Kniskern (eds.), *Handbook of family therapy.* New York: Brunner/Mazel, 1981.
7. Bowen, M. *Family therapy in clinical practice.* New York: Jason Aronson, 1978.
8. Coleman, S.B. (ed.). *Failures in family therapy.* New York: Guilford Press, 1985.
9. _____, & Gurman, A.S. An analysis of family therapy failures. In S.B. Coleman (ed.), *Failures in family therapy.* New York: Guilford Press, 1985.
10. de Shazer, S., & Berg, I. A part is not apart: Working with only one of the partners present. In A.S. Gurman (ed.), *Casebook of marital therapy.* New York: Guilford Press, 1985.
11. DeWitt, K.N. The effectiveness of family therapy: A review of outcome research. *Archives of General Psychiatry 35:* 549–561, 1978.
12. Epstein, N.B., & Bishop, D.S. Problem-centered systems therapy of the family. In A. S. Gurman & D.P. Kniskern (eds.), *Handbook of family therapy.* New York: Guilford Press, 1981.
13. Feldman, L.B. Dysfunctional marital conflict: An integrative interpersonal-intrapsychic model. *Journal of Marital and Family Therapy 8:* 417–428, 1982.
14. Fisch, R., Weakland, J.H., & Segal, L. *The tactics of change: Doing therapy briefly.* San Francisco: Jossey-Bass, 1982.
15. Frank, J.D. The present status of outcome studies. *Journal of Consulting and Clinical Psychology 47:* 310–316, 1979.
16. Garfield, S.L., & Bergin, A.E. *Handbook of psychotherapy and behavior change: An empirical analysis* (2nd ed.). New York: John Wiley & Sons, 1978.
17. Goldfield, M. Toward the delineation of therapeutic change principles. *American Psychologist 35:* 991–999, 1980.
18. Guerney, B.G. *Relationship enhancement.* San Francisco: Jossey-Bass, 1977.
19. Gurman, A.S. Contemporary marital therapies: A critique and comparative

analysis of psychoanalytic, behavioral and systems theory approaches. In T.J. Paolino & B.S. McCrady (eds.), *Marriage and marital therapy: Psychoanalytic, behavioral and systems theory perspectives.* New York: Brunner/Mazel, 1978.

20. _____. Integrative marital therapy: Toward the development of an interpersonal approach. In S. Budman (ed.), *Forms of brief therapy.* New York: Guilford Press, 1981.

21. _____. Psychotherapy research and the practice of psychotherapy. Presidential Address, Society for Psychotherapy Research, Sheffield, England, July, 1983.

22. _____, & Kniskern, D.P. Deterioration in marital and family therapy: Empirical, clinical, and conceptual issues. *Family Process 17:* 3–20, 1978.

23. _____, & Kniskern, D.P. Research on marital and family therapy: Progress, perspective, and prospect. In S.L. Garfield & A.E. Bergin (eds.), *Handbook of psychotherapy and behavior change: An empirical analysis* (2nd ed.). New York: John Wiley & Sons, 1978.

24. _____, Kniskern, D.P., & Pinsof, W.M. Research on the process and outcome of marital and family therapy. In S.L. Garfield & A.E. Bergin (eds.), *Handbook of psychotherapy and behavior change: An empirical analysis* (3rd ed.). New York: John Wiley & Sons, 1986.

25. Haley, J. *Leaving home: The therapy of disturbed young people.* New York: McGraw-Hill, 1980.

26. Hersen, M., & Barlow, D.H. *Single case experimental designs: Strategies for studying behavior change.* New York: Pergamon Press, 1976.

27. Hogarty, G.E., Anderson, C.M., Reiss, D.J., Kornblith, S.J., Greenwald, D.P., Javna, C.D., Madonia, B.A., & the EPICS Schizophrenia Research Group. Family psycho-education, social skills training and maintenance chemotherapy in the aftercare treatment of schizophrenia: I. One-year effects of a controlled study on relapse and expressed emotion. *Archives of General Psychiatry 43:* 633–642, 1986.

28. Kerr, M.E. Family systems theory and therapy. In A.S. Gurman & D.P. Kniskern (eds.), *Handbook of family therapy.* New York: Brunner/Mazel, 1981.

29. Liddle, H.A. On the problem of eclecticism: A call for epistemologic clarification and human-scale theories. *Family Process 21:* 243–250, 1982.

30. Madanes, C. *Strategic family therapy.* San Francisco: Jossey-Bass, 1981.

31. Papp, P. *The process of change.* New York: Guilford Press, 1983.

32. Pinsof, W.B. Integrative problem-centered therapy: Toward the synthesis of family and individual psychotherapies. *Journal of Marital and Family Therapy 9:* 19–35, 1983.

33. Sager, C J. *Marriage contracts and couple therapy: Hidden forces in intimate relationships.* New York: Brunner/Mazel, 1976.

34. Segraves, R.T. *Marital therapy: A combined psychodynamic-behavioral approach.* New York: Plenum Press, 1982.

35. Skynner, A.C.R. Comment. *The Family Therapy News 12* (5): 7, 1979.

36. Stanton, M.D. An integrated structural/strategic approach to family therapy. *Journal of Marital and Family Therapy 7:* 427–439, 1981.

37. Strupp, H.H. Clinical research, practice, and the crisis of confidence. *Journal of Consulting and Clinical Psychology 49:* 216–219, 1981.

38. Sundland, D.M. Theoretical orientations of psychotherapists. In A.S. Gurman & A.M. Razin (eds.), *Effective psychotherapy: A handbook of research.* New York: Pergamon Press, 1977.

39. Tomm, K. One perspective on the Milan systemic approach: Part I. Overview

of development, theory and practice. *Journal of Marital and Family Therapy 10:* 113–125, 1984.

40. _____. One perspective on the Milan systemic approach: Part II. Description of session format, interviewing style and interventions. *Journal of Marital and Family Therapy 10:* 253–271, 1984.

41. Umbarger, C.C. *Structural family therapy.* New York: Grune & Stratton, 1983.

42. Wampler, R.S. The effectiveness of the Minnesota Couple Communication Program: A review of research. *Journal of Marital and Family Therapy 8:* 345–356, 1982.

43. Wells, R.A., & Dezen, A.E. The results of family therapy revisited: The nonbehavioral methods. *Family Process 17:* 251–274, 1978.

44. _____, Dilkes, T.C., & Trivelli, N. The results of family therapy: A critical review of the literature. *Family Process 11:* 189–207, 1972.

45. Whitaker, C.A., & Keith, D.V. Symbolic-experiential family therapy. In A.S. Gurman & D.P. Kniskern (eds.), *Handbook of family therapy.* New York: Brunner/Mazel, 1981.

11

GUIDELINES FOR THE DESIGN OF FAMILY THERAPY OUTCOME RESEARCH*

NEIL S. JACOBSON

University of Washington
Seattle, Washington

T HERE ARE encouraging signs that outcome research is becoming a growing concern among participants in the family therapy movement. This trend is encouraging because claims for the efficacy of family therapy, until recently, were based largely on speculation and anecdote (see 8). The family therapy movement has created a true revolution in the field of psychotherapy along with an enthusiastic cadre of adherents and advocates. This zeal makes the delay in generating evidence regarding treatment efficacy even more striking. Controlled outcome research can serve a number of important purposes in the development of psychotherapy techniques by shedding light on limitations and contraindications and, thereby, serving as a vehicle for technique development and innovation. Any trend that suggests a greater emphasis on controlled invesigations is welcome.

As the family therapy field embarks upon a scientific exploration of its efficacy, a set of conventions for designing research investigations will inevitably evolve. The field has little to gain by uncritically adopting the conventions used to explore the efficacy of individual psychotherapy. By capitalizing on the benefits of hindsight, it is possible to criticize a number of the conventions that have evolved in individual psychotherapy research. This seems an opportune time to reexamine these conventions and try to improve upon them in the design of family therapy outcome studies.

In this chapter, I will raise issues that need to be resolved in those areas in which adopted conventions do not seem adequate. Although my purpose is to raise rather than resolve these issues, in some instances I suggest directions that I believe would facilitate their resolution. The

---

*This chapter is based on an article published in the *Journal of Marital and Family Therapy 11:* 149–158, 1985, entitled "Family Therapy Outcome Research: Potential Pitfalls and Prospects," portions of which had been presented at the 1984 NIMH/*Family Process* Conference on Family Therapy Research.

areas of focus include: clinical relevance, comparative outcome studies, internal validity, standardized versus flexible treatments, choice of therapists, and the primary criterion for inferring change.

CLINICAL RELEVANCE

In the field of clinical research, academicians have lamented the lack of influence that clinical research has on clinical practice (1). Although recent developments in the family therapy field, such as research on psychoeducational approaches to schizophrenia, indicate that this lament may not apply to the family therapy field as much as it does to traditional psychotherapy, in general, the gulf between research and family practice appears wide indeed (for example, see 5). To the extent that clinicians find research irrelevant to their day-to-day activities as therapists, part of the problem may be that results of outcome studies are not reported in ways that are clinically meaningful (1, 4, 7, 9, 13). When a clinician reads a research report that includes no descriptive statistics other than group means and standard deviations, it is impossible to determine the likelihood that a particular client will respond favorably to treatment. In other words, often there is little discussion of variability in outcome within a sample. Such a discussion requires some statistics reflecting the proportion of clients who improve. Although these statistics are sometimes reported in outcome studies, the criteria for classifying clients as improved are usually derived post hoc, and they are therefore typically haphazard and often arbitrary.

Clinical relevance is also compromised when treatment efficacy is determined solely by tests of statistical significance. Statistical significance bears no necessary relationship to clinical significance. Two treatment groups may differ significantly in a statistical sense, but the magnitude of the differences may not be large enough to make a difference from the point of view of a clinician; or the differences between two treatments may be statistically significant but families in both treatments remain dysfunctional after therapy; finally, the differences may be enormous but fail to reach significance because of factors that have nothing to do with the power of the treatment, such as small samples or heterogeneity within the subject population. The first two kinds of problems frequently occur in marital therapy research in which control group couples rarely improve and often deteriorate while on the waiting list (10). Thus, almost any reliable improvement in couples receiving treatment—no matter how small in magnitude—will show up as a statistically significant treatment effect. Yet to argue that the marital therapy is effective, based on clinically insignificant but statistically significant treatment effects, is quite problematic.

One helpful supplement to tests of statistical significance involves the use of descriptive statistics that reflect the magnitude of the treatment effect, such as the effect-size statistic (22). Certainly, any statistic that provides information about the magnitude of the treatment effect constitutes an improvement over the exclusive reliance on tests of statistical significance. Unfortunately, statistics reflecting effect size bear no necessary relationship to clinical relevance because magnitude of change is determined relative to a control group rather than to some clinically relevant criterion; even when the effect size is large, the superior treatment may fail to yield outcomes that are of practical importance.[1] For example, a strategic treatment for obesity may lead to a mean weight loss of 20 pounds in a sample of clients who average 300 pounds at pretest. If no one in the control group loses any weight, and the variability of the sample prior to therapy is low to moderate, the resultant effect size would be quite large, even though the outcome—obese clients who now average 280 pounds rather than 300—would have little practical importance.

Jacobson, Follette, and Revenstorf (9) recommended that the proportion of clients who improve become a standardized, descriptive statistic in outcome research. In order for such a statistic to be meaningful, conventions must be adopted establishing improvement criteria that are standardized and widely applicable. These criteria must be both psychometrically sound and clinically meaningful. In short, by reporting the proportion of clients who improve to a clinically significant degree, the data from family therapy outcome research will be much more useful to family therapists than it will if researchers limit their reports to group means and tests of statistical significance. The problematic aspect of this recommendation lies in the establishment of conventions for classifying clients as improved.

Jacobson et al. (9) recommend a two-fold criterion; a client (or family) is improved (a) if the posttherapy status places that client outside the distribution of dysfunctional clients (or families) and/or within the limits of a functional distribution of clients; and (b) if the amount of change during the course of therapy exceeds chance expectations (as assessed by the reliable change index, to be described below).[2]

---

1. *Editor's Note:* In Chapter 2, Reiss similarly expressed reservations about relying on the effect-size statistic to reach clinically meaningful conclusions. However, Rosenthal (1983) has recommended that effect-size data be routinely reported in treatment research in order "to give us more useful and realistic assessments of how well we are doing in research in psychotherapy" (p. 12).

2. *Editor's Note:* Jacobson, Follette, and Revenstorf (9) provide a critique of five other criteria for assessing statistically reliable improvement. Of these alternatives, single-subject experimental designs are viewed by Jacobson et al. as the most viable, but those authors are concerned about practical difficulties in establishing stable baselines prior to intervention, especially in outpatient, clinical outcome studies.

The first criterion means that the client has to change for the better, and that he or she has to end up outside the dysfunctional range and/or within the functional range on measures of interest. As long as the measures used in the study possess adequate psychometric properties, the cutoff points for clinically significant change can be established (see 9). To determine whether or not the client has left the dysfunctional range (or entered the functional range) on a variable of interest, a cutoff point can be established that places the client at equal likelihood of being a member of dysfunctional or functional populations. In order to calculate this cutoff point, normative data are required for both functional and dysfunctional clients on the variable of interest. If the client ends up crossing the cutoff point during the course of therapy, one can infer that the client is no longer dysfunctional. Even when norms are not available on functional clients, the cutoff point can be estimated from data on the sample treated in the study by using a conservative criterion of two standard deviations from the mean of the dysfunctional group.[3]

Jacobson et al. (9) also require, as a second criterion, that the magnitude of change during the course of therapy be sufficiently large ($p < .05$) so as to rule out the possibility that it could be attributable to measurement error. A statistic, known as the *reliable change index* (RC), is used to make this determination. I recommend that the recent modification of this index, suggested by Christensen and Mendoza (3), be used rather than the formula initially proposed by Jacobson et al. (9).[4]

---

3. *Editor's Note:* Wampold and Jenson (1986) have engaged in a thought-provoking dialogue with Jacobson, Follette, and Revenstorf (1986) on the question of how to study clinical significance. Wampold and Jenson are concerned that the assessment of clinical significance proposed by Jacobson et al. calls for the assumption of two distinct distributions, whereas most clinical conditions exist on a continuum from functional to dysfunctional—for example, in the continuum of depressive symptoms. Jacobson et al. note that their proposal is related to whether or not persons are treated, and not to the distribution of symptoms. In treatment research, there are two distinct groups of interest: those who seek (or need) help for a particular clinical disorder, and those who do not.

4. *Editor's Note:* Christensen and Mendoza (3) recommend an index of what they call "significant change" (SC), which is measured by dividing the difference between pre- and posttest scores by the standard error of the difference between the two test scores. If the scores have a normal distribution, an SC larger than 1.96 indicates that "the pre- to posttest change is (probably) not due to measurement error alone but is a real change in the true score due to the experimental treatment" (p. 307). A difficulty with either the reliable change index or the significant change index is in selecting and obtaining measures that are relevant to the treatments being assessed. Jacobson, Follette, and Revenstorf (1986) note that the use of multiple measures in most psychotherapy studies creates interpretive ambiguity when clients meet criteria for clinically significant change on some measures but not on others. Nevertheless, I believe it is probably

The overall point of these two criteria of change is that if the cutoff point separating functional from dysfunctional populations is crossed, and if the magnitude of change during the course of therapy is sufficient to rule out measurement error as the explanation for the change, we can infer that the change is not an artifact of an unreliable assessment instrument and that it is clinically significant because the client (or family) has recovered.

A final word about the importance of standardization of outcome criteria. Kniskern (17), in a reply to the article on which this chapter is based, argued that standardization is unrealistic.[5] I strongly disagree with this pessimistic assessment, and would argue that even if it is true in the absolute sense, the clinical relevance issue is so important that the effort to achieve conventional, standardized criteria is essential even if it ultimately fails. Standardized criteria for clinically significant change are feasible because change in any clinical problem implies criteria inherent in the statistics proposed by Jacobson et al. (9). All consumers expect and all clinicians aspire toward recovery in their clients; and all expect the change to be nonartifactual. Standardized criteria are necessary because of the way conventions are adopted in our field. If criteria remain idiosyncratic or disorder-specific, there is no basis for comparison between one study and another. This is the problem with current, nonstandardized criteria. Many authors report proportions of recovered clients, but cumulative knowledge integrating these various findings is impossible because the criteria are relatively arbitrary and highly variable from one study to another.[6] Consequently, the results never attain the standardized status of group means, F tests, and p values, and are usually presented as supplementary data, almost as an afterthought. Standardized conventions would do for clinical significance what they have been doing for statistical significance. Without such conventions, clinical significance will always remain subordinate to statistical signifi-

---

a mistake to rely upon simple or single indices of change; multifaceted change processes should be recognized as part of clinical "reality" and must be tackled methodologically despite their complexity.

5. *Editor's Note:* Kniskern (17) appears to think that standardized improvement criteria are especially unrealistic for the "systemic therapies" because of "the possible non-quantifiability of many systemic 'problems'." Kniskern goes on to suggest that it is "not important that each clinician/researcher use the same convention to determine functionality, if he/she defines *a priori* what a 'good outcome' would be for a family" (p. 160). Jacobson's response here to these concerns seems cogent.

6. *Editor's Note:* Jacobson's point about the need for cumulative knowledge from research deserves to be underscored. If knowledge remains fragmentary and noncumulative, a tendency to be nihilistic about what has been learned—and what can be taught—is almost inevitable.

cance in research reports. And clinicians will continue to yawn and/or cancel their journal subscriptions!

If family therapy outcome research is going to be more than an academic exercise, data should be reported in a way that has meaning for the primary consumer of this literature. With clinicians as the consumers, the lesson to be learned from psychotherapy outcome literature is that summary group statistics and significance tests are non sequiturs.

COMPARATIVE OUTCOME STUDIES

Psychotherapy outcome research has tended to follow a specified sequence initially involving a comparison between treatment and no-treatment control groups, followed by a comparison with a nonspecific or placebo group, and then branching off in a number of possible directions. For example, the treatment package may be dismantled in order to isolate its active ingredients; new components may be added onto the treatment package in order to enhance its effectiveness; various parameters of the treatment may be varied in order to find the optimal format for maximizing treatment efficacy; or the treatment package may be compared to a theoretically distinct treatment package in the so-called comparative outcome study (15). Comparative outcome studies have received a great deal of attention in the literature during the past decade. Two recent examples are (a) the ongoing NIMH-sponsored Collaborative Depression Study in which cognitive therapy (2), interpersonal psychotherapy (16), and pharmacological treatments are being compared, and (b) the Sloane, Staples, Cristal, et al. (21) study that compared psychoanalytic and behavior therapy.

Comparative outcome studies address themselves to practical questions that seem to be of fundamental importance to the field of psychotherapy; few family therapists would be uninterested in a controlled study comparing strategic and Bowenian approaches to family therapy, for example. Such studies are encouraged by funding agencies, they arouse excitement and interest in the field, and they seem like the most direct ways to get concrete information about the effects of family therapy. Unfortunately, there are significant deterrents to conducting useful comparative outcome studies. The problems resulting from these deterrents are serious enough to suggest either that such studies be deemphasized or that the field at least alter its expectations of them (see 15).

The most obvious observation to be abstracted from the comparative outcome literature in individual psychotherapy is that significant differences are rarely found between two bona fide treatments and, when they are, that they are seldom consistently replicable. From these null findings, the erroneous conclusion is often drawn that there are no differences in the effectiveness of the treatments. The rules of statistical inference do not allow us to accept null hypotheses; the best we can do is consider the null hypothesis as one plausible interpretation of null findings, to be weighed against the several competing explanations: insufficiently powerful experimental designs, invalid or insensitive measures of therapy outcome, inadequately executed treatments, and many more.

The search for main treatment effects in a comparative outcome study may be fruitless because there may be few such effects in nature. Remember that in a comparative outcome study the experimenter is looking for general, overall differences between two multifaceted treatments typically sharing a number of overlapping features, differences that are sufficiently robust to manifest themselves across a population of heterogeneous clients and therapists, and relatively small sample sizes. In psychological experiments, main effects are seldom found unless other sources of variance can be kept to a minimum. Yet in psychotherapy research, the other major sources of outcome variance—especially individual differences in therapist and client characteristics—may have a greater impact on outcome than treatment differences. Not only is it extremely difficult to suppress such powerful sources of variance, but, even if it could be done, one would end up with a study of highly questionable generalizability.

In short, it may be that the differences in effectiveness between models of therapy that are statistically reliable as well as clinically meaningful can be found only in complex two-way and three-way interactions involving the therapist and client variables. It is also conceivable that the sample sizes necessary to ferret out such complex interactions would make adequate statistical tests prohibitive.

Consider the lengths to which principal investigators are often willing to go in order to overcome some of these problems. One obvious and often suggested solution is to run studies with large sample sizes. Even when an investigator has the necessary resources to do so, exactly what is gained when a sample size is increased in order to produce differences that are statistically significant? Neither the magnitude of the effect nor its clinical importance is being altered, simply the p value. By manipulating our sample size in order to influence the p value, we are increasing the likelihood that the scientific community will perceive our results as credible.

In fact, however, confidence in a set of findings should not be influenced by a p value, and the fact that it is suggests widespread misunderstanding of what a p value is. A p value is often interpreted as if it reflected the probability that the null hypothesis was true, although, of course, it has nothing to do with that probability, which is in fact unknown. Nor does a p value reflect the probability of a given set of results being replicable; one cannot infer that there is a 95% chance of successfully replicating a group difference when $p = .05$. A p value is nothing more than the probability that a given set of results would have been obtained if the null hypothesis were true, that is, if there were actually no differences in effectiveness between treatments. As the p value changes, so does the plausibility of the argument that there are differences between the two treatments. But a p value does not vary according to either the size or the clinical meaningfulness of the effect. Nor does it vary according to the reproducibility of the effect. Therefore, it makes little sense to run expensive studies with enormous samples simply to increase the "power" of our statistical tests.[7] Instead of being captivated by p values, family therapy researchers should resolve to pay adequate attention to effect size, clinical significance, and replications. This theme will be reintroduced below as part of a proposal for changing our expectations of comparative outcome studies.

The other major deterrent to powerful comparative outcome designs is the preponderance of outcome variance accounted for by client characteristics. Investigators from individual psychotherapy outcome studies have attempted to cope with client heterogeneity by studying extremely homogeneous samples, a policy that is enforced by invoking multiple exclusionary criteria. As an example, a hypothetical set of exclusionary criteria in a study investigating the effects of marital therapy in the treatment of depression may result in the exclusion of subjects who are psychotic, melancholic, suicidal, brain damaged, currently abusing alcohol and narcotics, bipolar, younger than 20, older than 60, or schizophrenic. Consider the proportion of depressed people you have seen who would survive all of these exclusionary criteria. Consider the price that one pays in terms of generalizability by studying such restricted samples. The irony is that these tactics usually do not work anyway because significant group differences are seldom found.

All of these problems plague comparative outcome research more than do within-model comparisons because the former typically constitute relatively "weak" manipulations. In clinical practice, the technical overlap between models of therapy is extensive; moreover, the areas of divergence may be relatively trivial compared to the common elements, despite the selective focus on the former by advocates of various "schools." Once again, when investigators engage in "good research" by creating rules for what clinicians can and cannot do in each condition in order to minimize this overlap, they may be strengthening the manipula-

---

7. *Editor's Note:* The erroneous belief that large samples of subjects are necessary for meaningful research has discouraged many therapists from considering how treatment research could be carried out in their settings.

tion, but they are also removing the treatment farther from clinical practice.

Thus, if comparative, between-model outcome studies are to continue in family therapy research, our expectations of them should change. Rather than looking for statistically significant differences between treatments, the evaluation should focus on the relative effect sizes, clinical significance, and demonstrable replicability. For example, in comparing a behavioral to a strategic treatment for distressed couples, the study may be conducted twice (in different cities, at different times, by different therapists, and so on), and an advance decision could be made regarding what would constitute a clinically meaningful difference.[8] Perhaps the threshold would be a 10% difference in the proportion of families that improve to a clinically significant degree. If that threshold is consistently crossed in both studies, perhaps tests of statistical significance would be expendable.

Moreover, family therapy treatment models can be compared on dimensions other than efficacy. Examples would be comparative process studies in which common and divergent elements in two or more treatments are identified through the intensive analysis of therapist-client interaction (see 19).

Of course, an alternative would be to emphasize intra-model comparisons using constructive, parametric, and dismantling strategies to study the components of complex treatment packages (14). If the family therapy field could agree on outcome measures, criteria for classifying families as improved, and rigorous standards for specifying client populations, such studies could accumulate in a way that would provide a basis for comparing models.

Despite these caveats, I am not suggesting that comparative outcome studies be abandoned. In particular, studies comparing family-oriented approaches to a particular clinical problem with a more traditional monadic approach (for example, psychoanalysis or behavior therapy) would be extremely interesting. However, such studies should focus on

---

8. *Editor's Note:* The idea of using a research consortium, with investigators from different settings agreeing to collaborate, has been implemented in NIMH-sponsored studies, particularly in the NIMH Treatment of Depression Collaborative Research Program, and in the more recent Treatment Strategies of Schizophrenia Cooperative Agreement Program involving the integrated use of drugs and family therapy. Less ambitious, well-focused collaborative research should be carefully considered by like-minded family therapists, each of whom might have access to a relatively small sample of families treated in a particular way. Such potential collaboration was one of the motives for instigating the meetings of family therapy researchers that led to the NIMH/*Family Process* conference from which this book derives.

the magnitude of change in each condition, the clinical significance of those changes, their applicability, and the process mechanisms associated with outcome. The search for statistically significant treatment effects is not only doomed to failure, but is a relatively uninteresting search anyway.

INTERNAL VALIDITY: THE BOTTOM LINE

An ideal research design for a family therapy outcome investigation—or for that matter any outcome investigation—strikes the optimal balance between experimental precision and relevance to clinical practice. There are two aspects of research design that are generally considered necessary without much debate: the use of random assignment and the inclusion of a control group.[9] However, there are experimental questions that can be answered without either; these kinds of questions are typically reserved for the later stages of research.

During the early stages of a research program designed to investigate the efficacy of a particular form of therapy, there is no substitute for random assignment of families to treatment conditions. Without random assignment, group differences are uninterpretable; the study is not worth conducting. Even when matching is used, once blocks have been formed, assignment to groups must be determined randomly. Without random assignment, subject selection factors cannot be ruled out as explanations for any group differences that are found. As elementary as this point is, it needs to be made because this requirement provides one of the most powerful deterrents to conducting research in many clinical settings. Family therapy researchers must not yield to the temptation to compromise on this issue. Instead, mental health bureaucracies must be educated. After all, random assignment provides as rational a basis for assigning clients to treatments as those that are used in many clinical settings, particularly if "rational" is equated with "supported by empirical evidence."

There is a stage in an outcome research program when random assignment not only can but must be dispensed with. At some point, the investigator needs to determine whether or not outcome can be enhanced by tailoring the treatment to fit the needs of individual clients. To put it another way, the treatment package must be made more flexible so that its generalizability to conditions that mirror clinical practice can be evaluated. In such studies, the treatment is altered according to clinical indication rather than altered randomly, and the outcomes are compared

---

9. *Editor's Note:* In Chapter 12, Pinsof sharply challenges the necessity and even the desirability of adhering to these two traditional features of research design, at least at this stage of the development of the field of family therapy research.

to those obtained under standardized conditions in which a relatively invariant treatment is applied to all families assigned to it, regardless of clinical indication. In a way, this kind of study compares a treatment under "research" and "no-research" conditions. Ideally, random assignment would still be used to determine whether families are assigned to structured or flexible treatments, but the variations within the flexible treatment would be determined by state-of-the-art clinical wisdom.

One reasonable alternative to a waiting list or no-treatment control group during the early stages of a research program is a standard, already established treatment. For example, Rush, Beck, Kovacs, et al. (20) compared cognitive therapy for depression with a standard pharmacological treatment whose effectiveness was well-specified and clearly established. Provided that the investigator can demonstrate the fidelity of the standard treatment, this kind of comparison group offers several advantages. First, it circumvents the ethical problem of denying needy families immediate treatment; second, it provides more information because such a study tells us not only whether the treatment is better than nothing, but also how it compares to a well-established treatment; third, in an age of informed consent, the pool of willing participants will inevitably increase if potential volunteers do not have to worry about being assigned to a no-treatment control group; fourth, differential drop-out rate is less likely to be a problem; and fifth, agencies are more likely to refer families to the study.

Unfortunately, in the family therapy literature there are few treatments that have received enough empirical support to be considered standard. Two possible candidates are parent-training approaches with preadolescent, aggressive boys (18), and behavioral marital therapy (11). Both have been evaluated in a number of well-controlled studies, and their effects as well as their limitations are well-established (see 10).

Another alternative to a control group is a well-established "spontaneous remission" rate for a clearly specified population (15). As outcome studies accumulate for a particular population of families, and the rate of change in the absence of treament becomes specified, eventually it may be possible to compare such untreated norms to an experimental treatment. However, if a comparison were to be undertaken, the burden of proof would be on the experimenter to demonstrate sufficient similarity between subject populations so as to lend credibility to such a comparison. Of course, strictly speaking, such comparisons would be useless in the absence of random assignment. Yet, if past studies under similar conditions consistently produced the same rates of change in a control group, and subject selection procedures remained the same across these studies, these quasi-experimental designs can serve as compelling alternatives to the use of a control group as the research program becomes more focused on other issues.

STANDARDIZED VERSUS FLEXIBLE TREATMENTS

In the previous section, a comparison between standardized and flexible treatments was mentioned as an instance in which randomization procedures could be modified. This kind of comparison has rarely been attempted, but it has important implications. A current belief is that experimenters should write standardized treatment manuals to guide the therapist in executing the treatment in question.[10] Thus, for the sake of experimental precision, constraints that do not exist in clinical practice are placed on therapists. Many have assumed that these constraints detract from the efficacy of therapy, and that outcome research therefore provides a conservative test of treatment efficacy (15). This is indeed possible and should be investigated.

It is also possible, however, that these constraints are balanced by other factors that actually enhance the quality of therapy conducted in a research setting relative to standard clinical practice. These factors include: the greater amount of time and attention devoted to each case in a clinical research setting; the fact that therapists are observed and sessions are often taped in an outcome study; the multiple perspectives that are available when difficult cases are discussed; and the group support that typically exists in a clinical research setting. Moreover, the reduction in options that exists under research constraints makes the job of a clinician easier in some ways; flexibility implies ambiguity and a minimum of decision rules. It is an empirical question whether the advantages of clear-cut decision rules are outweighed by the research constraints. As clinicians, we may feel desperately in need of maximal flexibility; but to the extent that outcome variance is accounted for by nonspecific therapist and client characteristics, the technical flexibility available outside a research setting may be unimportant and, therefore, outweighed by the advantages of simplification inherent in the research structure. If one were to find that outcomes are equivalent under "research-structured" and "clinical-flexible" conditions, the advantages of the former in terms of greater ease in teaching and wider dissemination would make a compelling case for altering clinical settings so as to resemble those of a research setting. What is viewed as a constraint today may be clinically indicated tomorrow.

WHO SHOULD THE THERAPISTS BE?

A much neglected and complex issue in outcome research pertains to the question of who the therapists should be. This issue is particularly important in family therapy because the abundance of charismatic school

---

10. *Editor's Note:* Two views on the controversial issue of treatment manuals are given by Stanton (Chapter 1) and Epstein (Chapter 9).

leaders increases the risk of confounding therapist with type of therapy. For example, did Milton Erickson discover a powerful method of therapy that can be highly effective in the hands of adequately trained disciples, or was he a magician therapist whose extrapolation of a disseminable method was little more than an academic exercise? Questions like this lend themselves to outcome research, but the selection of therapists becomes elevated to an issue of major importance.

Two particularly important design issues related to the selection of therapists are the optimal level of experience and the extent to which therapists should be treated as an independent variable in the overall design. Conventional wisdom dictates that family therapy should be evaluated when highly experienced clinicians serve as therapists. Although it would be nice if clinical experience were directly related to positive outcomes, it is an important but unsettled empirical question that can only be answered by directly comparing experienced and inexperienced therapists in the same studies. As one who has trained numerous therapists at all levels of clinical experience and watched the transition process by which a therapist gradually becomes more experienced, I am not at all convinced that experienced therapists produce better outcomes in marital therapy. Experienced therapists do indeed look more like our preconceived notions of what a good therapist should look like. But whether or not they produce better outcomes is another matter.

In the marital therapy literature, what scant evidence there is does not support the hypothesis that experienced therapists produce better outcomes (12). Not enough is actually known about the effects of family therapists to make this assumption. It is entirely possible that level of experience interacts in theoretically interesting ways with other variables to influence family therapy outcomes. For example, perhaps the importance of clinical experience is inversely related to the degree of standardization or structure in the treatment package. In addition to the theoretical importance of therapist experience as an independent variable, some kinds of outcome research will be considerably more feasible if inexperienced therapists can be substituted with no deleterious impact on outcome. Rather than insisting on experienced family therapists when family therapy is to be evaluated, funding agencies should be open to the examination of the role of therapist experience.[11]

Should each treatment condition in a comparative study be executed by a different group of therapists? Or should each therapist treat families in all conditions as determined by random assignment so that the effects of therapy can be separated from the effects of therapists? A standard methodological convention is to assign families randomly to treatments

---

11. *Editor's Note:* Epstein (Chapter 9) takes an opposing view.

and to therapists; without crossing therapists and treatments, the two
factors are hopelessly confounded. In addition, by reducing error variance attributable to variation in therapist characteristics, one is providing a more sensitive test of treatment effects.

Despite these standards and conventions, it is interesting that there is
a current trend to have different therapists conducting each treatment.
This new tradition has attained prominence within a *Zeitgeist* emphasiz-
ing comparative outcome research. In an inter-model comparative study,
it is argued that therapists usually prefer (and are more competent in)
one model, and that it is therefore self-defeating to cross therapists with
treatments. It is also argued that the conditions will be more distinct if
therapists concentrate on only one model. The expectation that therapists keep each condition pure is viewed as naive. Thus, from this vantage
point, the experimental manipulation is viewed as actually stronger if
each therapist specializes in one and only one treatment.

Although the above arguments are persuasive, they do not address or
counter the justifications for treating "therapist" as a randomized factor.
I have no solution to this dilemma except to caution family therapy
researchers against reaching premature closure or institutionalizing
conventional wisdom without adequately dealing with its disadvantages.
It may be that the decision should depend on the conditions of the study.
That is, therapists may be treated as a randomized factor when the
eligible therapists are not committed to the treatment models being
tested and when the distinctions between the models are relatively
clear-cut and easy to maintain; conversely, perhaps when the available
therapists are committed to one model and the distinctions between
models are subtle and difficult to maintain, therapists should confine
their activities to one model. Generally, intra-model comparisons and
studies conducted with relatively inexperienced therapists may lend
themselves to assigning therapists randomly, while inter-model comparisons with seasoned therapists may require different therapists for each
treatment.

THE PRESENTING PROBLEM: PRIMARY CRITERION
FOR SUCCESS

Finally, although the major focus of this chapter has been on "independent variables," I cannot resist the temptation to address briefly the
question of how to measure outcome in family therapy research. Currently, there is considerable debate in the field about the pros and cons of
various kinds of measures. All popular modalities have advantages and
disadvantages; none is inherently superior. Self-report measures are
subjective, highly susceptible to demand characteristics, and prone to a
variety of biases. On the other hand, observational measures are susceptible to other kinds of bias, and are not always more directly reflective of
the presenting problem.

Family therapists are interested in changing family interaction as well as producing change in a family member who is a diagnosed patient. Outcome investigations of family therapy are bound to use multiple measures in order to tap all of the domains that are influenced by the treatment process. When multiple measures are used, decisions have to be made about how to deal with inconsistencies across measures. It is here that family therapists must not let their clinical predilections interfere with their scientific objectivity. As Haley (6) reminds us, the primary criterion for successful therapy is whether or not the family "got what they came for." Thus, the primary outcome measure is the most direct possible measure of the presenting problem or problems. It is, of course, conceivable that new problems will emerge as treatment proceeds; thus, it is not always clear what the problems are during pretreatment assessment (5). Ultimately, however, a successful outcome means that the presenting (or emergent) problems have been eliminated.

Changes in family interaction are often the hypothesized means whereby a family therapist proposes to solve the problems that brought the family in. But this is only a hypothesis. The vindication of a model bent on changing family interaction is whether or not such change leads to elimination of the presenting problem(s). Except in those instances in which dysfunctional family interaction is the presenting problem, measures of family interaction are, at best, indirect measures of treatment outcome.[12] They can be likened to manipulation checks that can be used to document the success or failure of therapy at changing family interaction. Ultimately, however, the value of altering family interaction will depend on whether or not these changes do, in fact, facilitate the

---

12. *Editor's Note:* In commenting on this view of Jacobson, Kniskern (17) objected that these views "seem inappropriate guides for research in a field that is defined by its focus on interactions between and among family members" (p. 161). Jacobson and Kniskern agreed that multidimensional assessment of family therapy is necessary and that the presenting problems should not be the *sole* criterion for determining efficacy. However, Jacobson (1985) viewed as "extremely problematic" Kniskern's recommendation that family interaction measures be thought of as "primary." Jacobson continued his response as follows: "To adopt Kniskern's recommendation is to presuppose the validity of the family systems perspective. If the family failed to obtain relief from the problem which brought them to therapy, it would be unacceptable to view the case as a success even if family interaction patterns were altered in a way viewed as desirable by the therapist or researcher. In contrast, if the family 'got what they came for' but family interaction patterns were left unaltered, most people in the community (perhaps everyone except family systems theorists) would view the case as a success and it would be family systems theory rather than the efficacy of the therapy that would be called into question" (p. 164). In the Introduction and chapters 7 and 17, Wynne has discussed related issues about the presenting problem and family interaction variables as alternative focal points in family therapy research designs.

resolution of the kinds of problems in living that lead people to seek therapeutic assistance.

SUMMARY

This chapter raises and attempts to resolve some significant, controversial issues in the design of family therapy outcome studies. First, the issue of clinical relevance is addressed. Much of psychotherapy research has little relevance for practicing clinicians, and I have discussed some partial explanations and proposed some changes that would have a salutary effect on the way data are reported. Second, inter-model comparative outcome studies are critiqued. Third, the necessary preconditions for internally valid outcome studies are delineated, along with conditions in which randomization and the use of control groups can be abandoned. Fourth, there is a discussion of a research strategy that examines the generalizability of treatment effects found in research settings to conditions that come close to resembling clinical practice. Fifth, questions about the selection of therapists for family therapy outcome research are addressed, including the issue of optimal level of therapist experience and the question of whether or not "therapists" should be treated as a randomized factor in the overall design. Finally, there is a brief discussion of outcome criteria, with a fairly clear-cut and straightforward recommendation for determining whether or not a family therapy has had a desired and desirable effect.

REFERENCES

1. Barlow, D.H. On the relation of clinical research to clinical practice: Current issues, new directions. *Journal of Consulting and Clinical Psychology 49:* 147–155, 1981.
2. Beck, A.T., Rush, A.J., Shaw, B.R., & Emery, G. *Cognitive therapy of depression.* New York: Guilford Press, 1979.
3. Christensen, L.C., & Mendoza, J. A method of assessing change in single subject designs: An alteration of the RC index. *Behavior Therapy 17:* 305–308, 1986.
4. Garfield, S.L. Evaluating the psychotherapies. *Behavior Therapy 12:* 295–307, 1981.
5. Gurman, A.S., & Kniskern, D.P. Family therapy outcome research: Knowns and unknowns. In A.S. Gurman & D.P. Kniskern (eds.), *Handbook of family therapy.* New York: Brunner/Mazel, 1981.
6. Haley, J. *Problem-solving therapy: New strategies for effective family therapy.* San Francisco: Jossey-Bass, 1976.
7. Hugdahl, K., & Ost, L. On the difference between statistical and clinical significance. *Behavioral Assessment 3:* 289–295, 1981.
8. Jacobson, N.S., & Bussod, N. Marital and family therapy. In M. Hersen, A.E. Kazdin, & A.S. Bellack (eds.), *The clinical psychology handbook.* London: Pergamon Press, 1983.
9. _____, Follette, W.C., & Revenstorf, D. Psychotherapy outcome research:

Methods for reporting variability and evaluating clinical significance. *Behavior Therapy 15:* 336–352, 1984.

10. _____, Follette, W.C., Revenstorf, D., Baucom, D.H., Hahlweg, K., & Margolin, G. Variability in outcome and clinical significance of behavioral marital therapy: A reanalysis of outcome data. *Journal of Clinical Psychology 52:* 497–504, 1984.

11. _____, & Margolin, G. *Marital therapy: Strategies based on social learning and behavior exchange principles.* New York: Brunner/Mazel, 1979.

12. _____, Schmaling, K., Katt, J.L., Wood, L.W., Holtzworth- Munroe, A., & Follette, V. Structured versus flexible versions of cognitive behavioral marital therapy, 1986. (Unpublished manuscript available from first author, Department of Psychology, University of Washington, Seattle WA 98195.)

13. Kazdin, A.E. Assessing the clinical or applied importance of behavior change through social validation. *Behavior Modification 1:* 427–452, 1977.

14. _____. *Research design in clinical psychology.* New York: Harper & Row, 1979.

15. _____, & Wilson, G.T. *Evaluation of behavior therapy: Issues, evidence, and research strategy.* Cambridge MA: Ballinger, 1978.

16. Klerman, G.L., & Weissman, M. Interpersonal psychotherapy: Theory and research. In A.J. Rush (ed.), *Short-term psychotherapies for depression.* New York: Guilford Press, 1982.

17. Kniskern, D.P. Climbing out of the pit: Further guidelines for family therapy research. *Journal of Marital and Family Therapy 11:* 159–162, 1985.

18. Patterson, G.R. Interventions for boys with conduct problems: Multiple settings, treatments, and criteria. *Journal of Consulting and Clinical Psychology 42:* 471–181, 1974.

19. Pinsof, W.M. Family therapy process research. In A.S. Gurman & D.P. Kniskern (eds.), *Handbook of family therapy.* New York: Brunner/Mazel, 1981.

20. Rush, A., Beck, A., Kovacs, M., & Hollon, S. Comparative efficacy of cognitive therapy and pharmacotherapy in the treatment of depressed outpatients. *Cognitive Therapy and Research 1:* 17–37, 1977.

21. Sloane, R.F., Staples, F.R., Cristal, A.H., Yorkston, N.J., & Whipple K. Short-term analytically oriented psychotherapy versus behavior therapy. *American Journal of Psychiatry 132:* 373–377, 1975.

22. Smith, M.L., Glass, G.V., & Miller, T.I. *The benefits of psychotherapy.* Baltimore: Johns Hopkins University Press, 1980.

EDITOR'S REFERENCES

Jacobson, N.S. Toward a nonsectarian blueprint for the empirical study of family therapies. *Journal of Marital and Family Therapy 11:* 163–165, 1985.

_____, Follette, W.C., & Revenstorf, D. Toward a standard definition of clinically significant change. *Behavior Therapy 17:* 308–311, 1986.

Rosenthal, R. Assessing the statistical and social importance of the effects of psychotherapy. *Journal of Consulting and Clinical Psychology 51:* 4–13, 1983.

Wampold, B.E., & Jenson, W.R. Clinical significance revisited. *Behavior Therapy 17:* 302–305, 1986.

PART IV

APPROACHES TO
FAMILY THERAPY PROCESS

12

STRATEGIES FOR THE STUDY OF FAMILY THERAPY PROCESS

WILLIAM M. PINSOF

Center for Family Studies
The Family Institute of Chicago
Chicago, Illinois

THIS CHAPTER embodies a series of recommendations to the National Institute of Mental Health and the field of family therapy research. The recommendations concern strategies and measures that can be used to facilitate the development of the field of family therapy research. My recommendations focus on the link between the process and outcome of family therapy.

DEFINITION OF FAMILY THERAPY

The first question that must be addressed is what is family therapy. Family therapy, according to Gurman, Kniskern, and Pinsof (12), is

> any psychotherapeutic endeavor that explicitly focuses on altering the interactions between or among family members and seeks to improve the functioning of the family as a unit, or its subsystems, and/or the functioning of individual members of the family. This is the goal regardless of whether or not an individual is identified as "the patient." Family therapy typically involves face-to-face work with more than one family member[,] . . . although it may involve only a single family member for the entire course of treatment . . ." [pp. 565–566].[1]

---

1. *Editor's Note:* This definition, which is essentially the same as that provided by Gurman in Chapter 10, represents a predominant view of the contributors to this volume, though there is not quite a unanimous consensus. The misgivings are pragmatic. It would be convenient to adopt an operational definition for family therapy in terms of the persons present in the session and to study separately, in comparison samples, cases treated with a family orientation but with only a single family member present. It is a matter of practical interest, even to ecosystemic therapists, who is or is not actually participant in the therapeutic system. Indeed, later in the chapter from which this definition is taken, Gurman, Kniskern, and Pinsof (12) state: "Process research is complicated enough without recognizing the need to consider members of the patient system not directly involved in therapy. The methodologic problems involved in studying their contribution to the process of therapy are formidable. At a minimum, however, they need to be put on process researchers' maps of the terrain to be studied. Ideally, process research will go further than this minimum" (p. 611).

Family therapy attempts to change the "natural" interpersonal context in which psychiatric and psychological problems occur. This means that family therapy is not concerned with just the family, but with all of the relevant natural systems that comprise a person's or family's psychological "world." For instance, for children who have school problems, working directly with the school may be as or more important in certain cases than working directly with the family.

Individual or intrapsychic change may or may not be an additional goal of family therapy. This definition is not tied to the number of people directly involved in treatment at any one time, but focuses primarily on the goals and conceptual framework of the therapy. Marital therapy is considered a subclass of family therapy.

THE DEFINITION OF PROCESS RESEARCH

In the introductory chapter to our book on process research (9), Greenberg and I presented a new definition of process research that incorporates a variety of new ideas about process research and psychotherapy research that have been emerging over the last 10 to 15 years:

> Process research is the study of the interaction between the patient and therapist systems. The goal of process research is to identify the change processes in the interaction between these systems. Process research covers all of the behaviors and experiences of these systems, within and outside of the treatment sessions, which pertain to the process of change. [p. 18][2]

Historically, process research has been defined as pertaining primarily, if not solely, to phenomena that occur within the spatio-temporal confines of the therapy session. More recently, as the definition presented above reveals, the concept of process research has expanded to include both within-session and out-of-session phenomena that occur over the course of a therapy.

A certain degree of intentional ambiguity is implicit in this new definition in that the end of "a therapy" can seldom if ever be definitively identified. The process of change ideally continues within the client or

---

2. The terms "patient system" or "client system" refer to all the human systems that are or may be involved in the maintenance or resolution of the presenting problem. "Client" can be used interchangeably with "patient." The patient or client system typically consists of at least the person(s) identified as client(s), other nuclear and extended family members, and members of the other social systems that interact with the client and the family. The whole client system is seldom if ever directly involved in therapy. The "therapist system" consists of all the identified therapists and associated personnel involved in providing "treatment" to the client system. Together, the clients and therapist comprise the "therapy system" or "therapeutic system."

patient system after the therapy has formally terminated, and such posttermination change processes should be an important target of process research.

This definition of process research also attempts irrevocably to link process and outcome research. Substantive (content-oriented) process research is meaningless without an immediate or remote link to outcome. Linking process to outcome makes process research the study of the process of therapy. Its primary task is elucidating the mechanisms and processes of change. Process research ultimately attempts to reveal how therapy works (or fails).

These statements should not be construed as deprecating methodologically oriented process research that is not linked to some kind of outcome or change process. Methodological research is necessary for the development and evaluation of instruments and procedures that eventually will be used to test substantive hypotheses about change processes. For instance, establishing the discriminant validity of a process measure like Pinsof and Catherall's (23) Family Therapy Alliance Scale, is a crucial developmental step even though the specific studies involved may not focus on outcome or change processes. However, any process instrument and the methodological studies involved in its development must ultimately be aimed at the process-outcome link or their relevance and value will be limited.

Another important change in the new definition is the shift away from process measures that solely target overt behavior. The new definition says that the participants' experience of therapy, their thoughts and feelings, are as legitimate a target of process research as their observable actions. The primary methodological implication of this assertion is that self-report methods should be considered as legitimate and valuable as are observational methods. A comprehensive process analysis requires both (20). In regard to certain biases favoring observational methods as compared to self-report methods (see 26), it is important to note that neither methodology has the corner on the systemic market. Both methodologies, if properly used, can be consistent with a systemic perspective.

Perhaps the most important shift in the new definition, particularly from the perspective of family therapy, is the addition of a "systemic perspective." Kiesler (14), in his classic work on process research, began elaborating a "communications model" of therapy process. Greenberg and I (9) have extended Kiesler's initial efforts by fully and formally introducing key systemic concepts into our definition of process research. In our definition, therapy is viewed as "the interaction between client and therapist systems" (p. 18). Implicit in this definition is the concept of circular interaction between two systems, not just between two individuals. Linearity or the direction of influence is not specified; thus, the bidirectionablity of the influence process is formally acknowledged. The therapist system impacts the client system and vice versa in an ongoing, "circular" pattern over the course of therapy. With this new definition, all types of therapy (individual, family, group, and so on) are viewed with a systemic perspective in terms of the units involved and the nature of the interaction between them.

Another systemic concept implicit in the new definition is the notion of "punctuation" (28, p. 59). What is defined as "a process" and "an outcome" is arbitrary and a function of the viewer's interests and perspective. An outcome can cover everything from the immediate or proximal (20) outcome of an intervention within a session to the status of the family at termination or follow-up. A process similarly can refer to everything from a specific act performed by a therapist in a session to the nature of the change process going on at home in the intervals between sessions. In fact, it is even possible to define a therapist's intervention within a session as the outcome of the family's behavior since the last session. Eventually we may have to replace the terms "process" and "outcome" with a new terminology that is less dichotomous and rigid. However, for continuity's sake we will continue to use them, remembering that they are somewhat arbitrary distinctions that only take on meaning within specific contexts defined by the researcher and the project.

The Importance of Process Research

Outcome research, without process research, is minimally informative (20). It can only tell us whether families that received a particular treatment did better, as a group, than families that received no treatment or an alternative treatment. Without process research, we cannot know what actually occurred in the therapy and what processes were associated with the success (or failure) of the treatment.

Clinical researchers consistently lament the fact that clinicians do not seem interested in therapy research. Process research can help to remedy that problem because it provides clinicians and therapy trainers with information that can have an impact on their own behavior. To know that the process of joining a particular type of family system in a particular way (for example, being active and directive) results in a better therapeutic alliance than joining a similar family system in a different way (being more reflective and passive) is directly meaningful to practitioners and trainers (4). In contrast, knowing that the outcome of behavioral marital therapy is slightly better than psychodynamic marital therapy with conflictual couples (a hypothetical result) is not a clinically translatable finding. The result may be viewed as meaningful by administrators; but, without knowing what factors in each treatment were associated with improvement and deterioration for which couples within each group, such findings lack clinical relevance and meaning.

CURRENT STRATEGIES FOR PROCESS-OUTCOME RESEARCH

Developmentally, family therapy research is emerging from infancy and entering early childhood. Process research (in terms of both the old and new definitions) has just begun and has yet to produce any conclusive evidence about the specific effects of any clinical intervention (12, 20). By and large, family therapy researchers have not availed themselves of the conceptual and methodological advances that have occurred within the area of individual therapy process research (8, 9, 14, 20, 24). With a few exceptions, family therapy researchers consider the knowledge and expertise developed within the domain of individual therapy research to be "nonsystemic" and, therefore, not relevant to or appropriate for family therapy research. This atavistic and narrow-minded stance has kept most attempts at family therapy process research at a fairly primitive and uninformative level. Family therapy researchers must know about and use the newest conceptual and methodological advances within the general field of psychotherapy research in order for our field to progress scientifically.

At this time, there is no empirical or even quasi-scientific foundation for generating hypotheses about the processes or mechanisms of change in family therapy. Clinical researchers are left with family therapy *theory* as a base for generating process-outcome hypotheses. Unfortunately, most family therapy theory has been articulated at such a level of abstraction and generality that formulating specific process-outcome hypotheses becomes problematic (20; see also Chapter 2, this volume). The family field is desperately in need of specific micro-theories that can be used to generate and test specific hypotheses about change processes in family therapy.

This situation calls for discovery-oriented (in contrast to confirmatory) research strategies and policies dedicated to developing an empirical foundation for process-outcome research. Discovery-oriented research[3] not only has the potential to develop an empirical foundation for subsequent research, but also has the capacity to facilitate the development of specific micro-theories about the family therapy change process. There is a feedback loop between family therapy theory and discovery-

---

3. Discovery-oriented research, as I am defining it, refers to the systematic application of a quantitative, empirical methodology to discover significant relationships between two or more variables.

oriented research, the activation of which facilitates the development of both.

If we follow a clinical-trial research methodology predicated upon a confirmatory research strategy (such as that commonly used in drug and medical research), we are in the same position as a parent trying to teach a three-month-old infant to walk. Developmentally, the science of family therapy research is not ready for clinical-trial research, which needs an empirical foundation from which to proceed. It is most productive only after preliminary research has pulled together enough evidence to suggest potentially fruitful hypotheses.

For instance, in drug research, a clinical trial comparing two drugs and a placebo in the treatment of a particular disorder is predicated upon the assumption that we know the ingredients of the drug, that we can know the amounts administered and possibly even absorbed by the patients, and that the patients are all suffering from a relatively uniform and specific disorder. Described analogically, in the field of family therapy research we have not adequately identified our drugs, the amounts of the drugs administered and/or absorbed, or specific and uniform disorders. We also lack an empirical foundation and scientific history that would clearly suggest the suitability of certain treatments (drugs or therapies) for certain disorders.

An emergent exception to this position is the work on the psychoeducational treatment of schizophrenia (see chapters 6 and 8). However, this work, although promising, is crude from the new perspective of process research. We are still in the dark as to the processes and mechanisms of change in the psychoeducational treatment of schizophrenia and other severe disorders. This area of research is greatly in need of more discovery-oriented research. Most psychoeducational research has been cast in the confirmatory (and political) mode of finding the best treatment, rather than determining which families and patient systems with which types of disorders are helped or hurt by the psychoeducational approach.

Discovery-Oriented Research Strategies

Discovery-oriented research is not predicated upon random assignment to different groups and the analysis of between-group variance.[4] It uncovers relationships between variables and accounts for within-group

---

4. *Editor's Note:* In Chapter 11, Jacobson takes a strong stand, recommending randomization as optimal. Although this difference represents a genuine controversy, it should be noted that Jacobson was discussing *outcome* research, which is most meaningful *after* discovery-oriented and methodologic research has identified variables and constructed variables worthy of incorporation into studies with randomized samples.

variance. Correlational or naturalistic research strategies fit the discovery paradigm. Discovery-oriented research involves identifying or discovering linkages between process and outcome variables. There are several strategies for discovering these linkages. These strategies are not mutually exclusive and can be used to complement each other.

None of the strategies mentioned below use control groups. Typically, control groups are an essential component of confirmatory research, and many researchers have asserted that their exclusion from psychotherapy studies greatly diminishes their worth.[5] I do not think that the use of control groups is scientifically worthwhile or meaningful at this time in the field of psychotherapy research. (This is not to say that they are not of political value within the current mental health field.) Control groups are used either to demonstrate that a therapy or intervention is better than no treatment at all (a no-treatment control) or that one treatment is better than another (the control condition). In regard to the use of no-treatment control groups, I think that most, if not all treatments or interventions will help some patients and harm or not affect others. The critical question is not whether a treatment is better than no treatment, but who is helped and who is hurt by that treatment.

In studies with control or comparison treatments, the primary issue is not which treatment is better (who has the fastest horse), but which treatment for which patient or family. Our task as psychotherapy researchers is to determine who is best helped and who is likely to be hurt by a particular treatment or intervention. At this point in the development of the family therapy research field, the time, money, and energy spent in the use of control or comparison groups would be better spent in the implementation of one of the discovery-oriented strategies identified below.

The Success-Failure Strategy

The first strategy, giving recognition to the difficulty of uncovering process-outcome links, maximizes the chances of discovery through the use of an extreme-group or condition analysis. This is the most basic discovery strategy and "loads the dice" in favor of uncovering process-outcome relationships. It involves taking a group of families and rank-ordering them on an outcome variable at some significant evaluation point (midtherapy, termination, follow-up, and so on). Subsequently, the cases at the low end of the distribution (clear failures) are compared on a process variable with the cases at the high end of the distribution (clear successes). This strategy or design creates extreme groups from a single

---

5. *Editor's Note:* In Chapter 11, Jacobson strongly recommends the use of control groups, but notes that a reasonable alternative "during the early stages of a research program is a standard, already established treatment."

group of cases exposed to some kind of treatment. Typically, researchers using this strategy will focus on the cases in the bottom and top thirds or quarters of the distribution.

Ideally, the cases in the whole group should be as similar as possible demographically and diagnostically. Homogeneity is particularly important in regard to presenting problems, interpersonal context (intact family, divorced couple, single parent, and so on), and the developmental stage of the family. Such homogeneity decreases the extent to which sampling variables, and increases the extent to which process variables, are likely to account for outcome variance. The same holds true for therapists treating the families in such a study. They should be as similar in training, orientation, and expertise as possible. Further, it is important that cases are randomly assigned to therapists in order to control for selection/assignment bias.[6]

As well as maximizing the likelihood of finding process-outcome links, this extreme-group, success/failure strategy also maximizes the extent to which nonlinear process-outcome relationships are likely to be found. Nonlinear relationships would be obscured in a conventional correlational analysis that included all cases in the group. The extreme-group design would also elucidate linear process-outcome findings, but would not definitively identify them as such.

The Multivariate Correlational Strategy

This strategy involves taking all the cases in a group and examining relationships between outcome variables and process variables. This strategy is ideal for identifying linear relationships and involves all cases in the treated group, not just the clear successes and failures. This strategy tests the extent to which process variables can be used as predictors of outcome. A major asset of this strategy is that multiple regression can be used to evaluate the extent to which combinations of variables (client/therapist and process), as opposed to single variables, predict outcome.

This strategy or design is more rigorous and demanding than the extreme-group design. By including the midrange cases, the likelihood of finding clear process-outcome relationships diminishes. Additionally, as mentioned above, a correlational analysis is not designed to elucidate nonlinear relationships, and it may lead to the erroneous conclusion that no relationship exists between the process and outcome variables when

---

6. *Editor's Note:* It is important to distinguish (a) random assignment of cases to therapists (as recommended by Pinsof), (b) random assignment of cases to experimental versus control groups (not recommended by Pinsof), and (c) random assignment of therapists to treatment approaches, a dubious procedure in psychotherapy research (see Chapter 3, Note 4, and Chapter 11).

that relationship does not take a linear form. Ideally, the extreme-group and correlational strategies can be used to complement each other within the same project. Together, they are not likely to miss process-outcome links within the data set.

The Episode or Small-Chunk Strategy

This discovery strategy has only recently emerged as a central design in the field of individual therapy process research (24). It involves targeting smaller chunks of therapy or therapeutic episodes. Conventional outcome or process-outcome research focuses almost exclusively on the whole course of therapy and attempts to find links between the "final" outcome or "Big O" and some dimensions of the process at some point in treatment. Not surprisingly, such research has failed to identify any consistent process-outcome patterns and has led some researchers to conclude (erroneously, I believe) that process is not a critical determinant of outcome.

Within the field of psychotherapy research, it is increasingly apparent that we have been too ambitious and naive in our attempts to find process-outcome links. The likelihood of finding a statistically significant relationship between either an aspect of process at some point in treatment or an aspect of process that spans the whole course of treatment and the final outcome (at termination or follow-up) is not very great. What occurs in the first five sessions is not likely to have much relationship to the outcome of treatment after 50 sessions. A therapy could easily have a wonderful beginning phase and fall apart in midphase, leading to the erroneous conclusion that what occurred in the first phase was associated with poor outcome.[7]

Similarly, attempting to find a summary (mean or average) measure of a process variable spanning the whole course of treatment that will relate to the "Big O" is probably impossible. The expectable vicissitudes of most process variables (for example, empathy, activity level, warmth, confrontation, and so on) over the entire course of therapy would not be adequately represented in a mean summary score. In fact, studies of process patterns within a therapy (10) or even within a session (22) suggest that there is substantial and meaningful variation that would be washed out with the use of a summary statistic. Research on the Experiencing Scale (15) suggests that peak experiencing levels are more predictve of outcome in individual therapy than are mean scores.

The solution to this problem is "smaller is better"—a focus on smaller units of therapy (9). The rationale of this strategy is to reduce the interval of time and experience between the process and outcome

---

7. *Editor's Note:* Alexander's approach in Chapter 13 to differentiating the phases of family therapy process is highly relevant to Pinsof's point here.

measurements. The smallest process-outcome unit is the episode within a session. One can meaningfully discuss the outcome of an episode. For instance, if the therapist is attempting to get a family to focus on a problem within a session, one can ask whether that goal or outcome was achieved. This kind of outcome has been called a "proximal" as opposed to a "distal" outcome (20). Rice and Saperia (25) and Greenberg (7) have developed a promising methodology called Task Analysis, which focuses on intra-session episodes that involve a therapeutic "operation" in the context of a client "marker."

The next largest unit is the session. After focusing a session on the intimacy problems of a couple, did the couple experience less conflict and more intimacy during the interval before their next session? The session provides a natural, easily defined process unit, and the intersession interval similarly provides a natural, easily identified outcome unit. Individual therapy researchers have begun to focus increasingly on these two spatially and temporally defined units in the quest for process-outcome links. Family therapy researchers have only recently begun to focus on the session as a unit (22).

Beyond the session, the researcher can focus on a series of sessions. For instance, within our research project at the Center for Family Studies/ The Family Institute of Chicago, we have focused on eight-session blocks. We examine the process and the outcome within each eight-session block by using both the extreme-group and multivariate correlational strategies. The data analysis strategy we use is like a "moving window" (17) that traverses the course of therapy and focuses on successive eight-session blocks. Ultimately, the block findings can be related to each other (two- and three-block outcomes) and to the outcome of treatment at termination and follow-up.[8]

All of these episode or small-chunk strategies focus on "small-o" outcomes. They are predicated on several assumptions. The first is that process-outcome linkages are best discovered in smaller units that do not obscure the phases or vicissitudes of therapy. The second assumption is that such small-chunk results are meaningful and valuable. It would be worthwhile to discover that the best way to help a united-front or pseudomutual couple to deal with a delinquent adolescent early in therapy is to ignore the couple's relationship and to focus on co-parental as opposed to marital issues. Such a conclusion would offer clinicians a research finding that they can translate directly into their practice. By itself, such a finding will not tell a therapist how to conduct an entire therapy, but it will provide a useful guide during the initial phase of therapy.

---

8. *Editor's Note:* It will be important to try to adapt this strategy for use in research on brief family therapy, which typically lasts only three to six sessions.

Strategy Summary

These discovery-oriented strategies are based on three primary recommendations for the immediate future of family therapy research. The first is that we need to focus on the analysis of within-group as opposed to between-group variance. We need to identify those families that deteriorate or improve, and then attempt to determine the process variables that account for that variance. Second, we need to focus on smaller process-outcome units that reduce the time and experience interval between measurement points. These units can be selected on the basis of temporal or clinical criteria. The last recommendation is that family therapy researchers should focus less on summary measures of process variables and more on patterns of process variables within sessions and over the course of therapy. Research that combines these three approaches stands the greatest chance of producing scientifically reliable and clinically meaningful results.

PROCESS DIMENSIONS

This last section identifies three process dimensions that family therapy researchers can usefully address. The first concerns the therapeutic or working alliance between the family and the therapist over the course of therapy. The second dimension concerns the specific behaviors of the therapists and families within the session. The third concerns the quality and quantity of out-of-session change that occurs during the course of therapy.

The Therapeutic Alliance

Individual therapy process researchers within the last ten years have begun to focus on the concept of the therapeutic or working alliance (3). A number of distinct research groups have developed measures for studying the alliance in individual therapy and have found significant and positive relationships between the alliance and outcome (13, 18). Increasingly, the alliance between the therapist and the client is becoming a core, organizing dimension in the study of individual therapy process (8, 9). The robustness of the alliance-outcome link across different research settings with different research groups using different instruments for measuring the alliance has been particularly impressive in a field with so few, consistent process-outcome findings.

Family therapy theorists have addressed issues related to the alliance in family therapy, such as "joining" (16), establishing "useful rapport" (1), and managing the "coalitionary process" (27). However, they have not explicitly cast their theories about therapy in terms of an alliance between the family and therapist. Only recently have clinical theorists and clinical researchers begun to develop an explicit theory about the therapeutic alliance in marital therapy (5, 6, 11). Catherall and I (23) have been among the first to develop a formal theory about the therapeutic alliance in family therapy and the implications of a systemically based alliance theory for the study and conduct of individual therapy. Along with the theory, we have also developed three separate client self-report instruments to measure the alliance in family, couple, and individual therapy.

Transporting the concept of the alliance from individual therapy to the domain of family therapy complicates the concept. The addition of multiple clients to the therapeutic situation introduces many possible alliance configurations that do not exist in the same way in the individual therapy situation:

> On the lowest level, the family therapist has an alliance with each family member—*the individual alliance*. On the highest level, the therapist has an alliance with the whole family system . . .—*the whole system alliance*. On an intermediate level, the therapist has an alliance with each of the multi-person subsystems (parents, children, etc.) within the family—*the subsystem alliance*. The alliance the therapist has with one or two family members impacts the alliance with other family members in a circular, reciprocal fashion. [23, pp. 138–139]

The family therapist can have a "split" or "intact" alliance with the whole family system (23). An intact alliance is one in which the family therapist has a positive alliance with all of the subsystems and individuals in the family system. In a split alliance, the therapist has a positive alliance with certain subsystems and a negative alliance with others. We believe that "with a split alliance, the therapist must have a positive alliance with the most powerful subsystem in order to maintain an alliance with the whole system that is sufficient to keep the family working in therapy" (23, p. 139).

We also believe that similar alliance configurations exist in individual therapy, but are less apparent. For instance, even though a patient's spouse may not be directly involved in therapy, his or her feelings about the therapy and therapist represent a kind of alliance that can hinder or facilitate the therapy. In other words, regardless of the therapeutic context, the therapist has an alliance with the entire client or family system as well as related but distinct alliances with the different interpersonal subsystems and individual system members.

Family therapy theory and research would greatly benefit from concerted conceptual and empirical work on the alliance dimension in family therapy. New alliance concepts need to be articulated and additional measures developed to study the alliance from different perspectives (observer report, therapist report, and so on). Not only would such work enrich the family field, but it would also be a step toward linking family therapy and individual therapy theory and research. This would bring the field of psychotherapy research closer to a comprehensive psychotherapy theory incorporating family and individual dimensions.

Behavior/Act Dimension

The second process dimension that warrants further development is the specific behavior or act dimension. This dimension addresses the actual and specific behaviors of the therapy participants. My 1981 review chapter (20) addressed many of the major theoretical and methodological concerns with this dimension in family therapy resarch. This dimension was also the primary focus for process researchers during the early years of the field's development (14).

I recently published a chapter (22) detailing the history of my attempt, over the past 13 years, to elucidate this dimension of family therapy. My recent research in this area has used the Family Therapist Coding System (19) to study the verbal behavior of the therapist. That chapter also reported my recent efforts to identify within-session patterns of therapist behavior that differentiate beginning and advanced family therapists.

One striking finding was that at the McMaster University Department of Psychiatry in the mid-1970s, advanced therapists conducting live supervision of initial interviews, and neophyte family therapists conducting initial interviews produced similar amounts of disagree/disapprove (DD) behaviors in the first third of the session. However, in the middle third, the advanced therapists produced ten times more DD behaviors. In the last third, both groups returned to similar midrange levels. Both groups of therapists also increased the number of supportive interventions over the session as a whole. These results suggest that although the advanced therapists were increasing their supportiveness, they were also increasing the extent to which they confronted the family, in contrast to beginners who decreased direct confrontations. Although interesting theoretically and methodologically, these results still need to be linked to some kind of outcome to become truly meaningful.

In terms of defining specific client or family acts, Benjamin, Foster, Roberto, and Estroff's (2) Structural Analysis of Social Behavior (SASB) holds great promise. It has been widely and productively applied to the study of family interaction outside of therapy, and a number of individual therapy researchers have started to use it to study individual therapy process.

Much more work needs to be done in the study of both client or family and therapist behavior. Current systems need to be validated and applied more broadly, and systems need to be developed to tap nonverbal and paralinguistic behavior. Data analysis procedures for pattern and sequence analysis need to be refined and applied more extensively.

Lastly, the "act" dimension needs to be studied in relation to the alliance. Any therapist with even minimal experience knows that similar or identical acts, such as confrontations, will have a different meaning and impact depending on the alliance context in which they occur. If our research model can begin to push clinical theorists to articulate an act/alliance theory, the field will also progress theoretically. If we can tap both dimensions in our research, our findings will also have more relevance to clinicians.

The "Small-o" Dimension

The last dimension concerns how to measure small outcomes (the "small o"). For our research project in Chicago, I have developed an instrument called the Intersession Report (21). It consists of eight scales that each tap a different aspect of the family system. Before each session, each family member rates the amount and direction of change, since the last session, in each area (for example, self, relations with partner, relations with children). The Intersession Report is designed to provide a brief snapshot of family change between sessions. Intersession change can be used as an outcome criterion for a session. It can also be used to identify the process of change—when and where in which kind of therapies improvement or deterioration occurs.

Much work still needs to be done in the area of change-process research. We have only begun to tap proximal outcomes and our measures of process are still crude. Linking process and outcome measures in more than a simple linear fashion is still in the future. Patterns of change have yet to be identified, and the circularity of the therapeutic process (process to outcome to process to outcome, and so on) has only begun to be addressed empirically. Promising leads exist. They must be pursued.

CONCLUSION

This chapter embodies a number of recommendations that are summarized below:

1. Family therapy outcome studies should include process variables if they are to be clinically relevant and have an impact on the actual practice of family therapy.

2. Governmental and institutional support for a research program that gives primacy to confirmatory research based on a controlled clinical-trial methodology is premature and possibly even wasteful at this stage of the field's development.

3. Greater institutional and monetary support should be given to discovery-oriented research that emphasizes the analysis of within-group variance and that focuses process-outcome analyses on smaller chunks or episodes of therapy.

4. Family therapy theorists and researchers should focus their theories and investigations on three major process dimensions: (a) the therapeutic alliance, (b) the specific acts and behavior patterns of the therapist and family systems (the therapy participants), and (c) the delineation of proximal or "small-o" outcome. These three dimensions need to be linked theoretically and empirically. In focusing their work on these dimensions, family therapy researchers should avail themselves of the knowledge and expertise that have accumulated in studies of these broad dimensions within individual therapy reseach.

5. My last recommendation is specifically to the NIMH. I think that it is imperative that the family or systems perspective be more fully represented on senior-staff levels within NIMH as well as on grant-review committees. Family therapy researchers need to be more actively involved with the development, evaluation, and funding of psychother-apy research. Family therapy researchers are not only relevant in terms of family therapy studies, but they also provide an important perspective that enriches individual and group therapy studies. They can actively contribute to the development of a comprehensive body of knowledge about psychotherapy that incorporates interpersonal as well as individ-ual dimensions.

REFERENCES

1. Ackerman, N.W. *Treating the troubled family.* New York: Basic Books, 1966.
2. Benjamin, L.S., Foster, S.W., Roberto, L.G., & Estroff, S.E. Breaking the family code: Analysis of videotapes of family interactions by Structural Analysis of Social Behavior (SASB). In L. Greenberg & W. Pinsof (eds.), *The psychotherapeutic process: A research handbook.* New York: Guilford Press, 1986.
3. Bordin, E.S. The generalizability of the psychoanalytic concept of the working alliance. *Psychotherapy: Theory, Research and Practice 16:* 252–260, 1979.
4. Davatz, U. Establishing a therapeutic alliance in family systems therapy. In A.S. Gurman (ed.), *Questions and answers in the practice of family therapy.* New York: Brunner/Mazel, 1981.
5. Dryden, W., & Hunt, P. Therapeutic alliances in marital therapy: I. Pre-therapy influences. In W. Dryden (ed.), *Marital therapy in Britain. Vol. 1: Context and therapeutic approaches.* London: Harper & Row, 1985.
6. _____, & Hunt, P. Therapeutic alliances in marital therapy: II. Process issues. In W. Dryden (ed.), *Marital therapy in Britain. Vol. 1: Context and therapeutic approaches.* London: Harper & Row, 1985.
7. Greenberg, L.S. Task analysis: The general approach. In L.N. Rice & L.S. Greenberg (eds.), *Patterns of change: Intensive analysis of psychotherapy process.* New York: Guilford Press, 1984.
8. _____, & Pinsof, W.M. (eds.). *The psychotherapeutic process: A research handbook.* New York: Guilford Press, 1986.
9. _____, & Pinsof, W.M. Process research: Current trends and future

perspectives. In L.S. Greenberg & W.M. Pinsof (eds.), *The psychotherapeutic process: A research handbook.* New York: Guilford Press, 1986.
10. Gurman, A.S. Instability of therapeutic conditions in psychotherapy. *Journal of Counseling Psychology 20:* 48–58, 1973.
11. _____. Creating a therapeutic alliance in marital therapy. In A. Gurman (ed.), *Questions and answers in the practice of family therapy. Vol. II.* New York: Brunner/Mazel, 1982.
12. _____, Kniskern, D.P., & Pinsof, W.M. Research on the process and outcome of marital and family therapy. In S. Garfield & A. Bergin (eds.), *Handbook of psychotherapy and behavior change* (3rd ed.). New York: John Wiley & Sons, 1986.
13. Horvath, A., & Greenberg, L.S. The development of the Working Alliance Inventory (WAI). In L. Greenberg & W. Pinsof (eds.), *The psychotherapeutic process: A research handbook.* New York: Guilford Press, 1986.
14. Kiesler, D.J. *The process of psychotherapy: Empirical foundations and systems of analysis.* Chicago: Aldine, 1973.
15. Klein, M., Mathieu-Coughlin, P., & Kiesler, D.J. The experiencing scales. In L. Greenberg and W. Pinsof (eds.), *The psychotherapeutic process: A research handbook.* New York: Guilford Press, 1986.
16. Minuchin, S. *Families & family therapy.* Cambridge: Harvard University Press, 1974.
17. Mishler, E.G., & Waxler, N.S. The sequential patterning of interaction in normal and schizophrenic families. *Family Process 14:* 17–50, 1975.
18. Morgan, R., Luborsky, L., Crits-Christoph, P., Curtis, H., & Solomon, J. Predicting the outcomes of psychotherapy by the Penn Helping Alliance Rating Method. *Archives of General Psychiatry 39:* 397–402, 1982.
19. Pinsof, W.M. *The Family Therapist Coding System (FTCS) manual.* Chicago: The Family Institute of Chicago, 1980.
20. _____. Family therapy process research. In A.S. Gurman & D.P. Kniskern (eds.), *Handbook of family therapy.* New York: Brunner/Mazel, 1981.
21. _____. The Intersession Report, 1982. (Unpublished manuscript available from author, Center for Family Studies/ Family Institute of Chicago, 666 N. Lake Shore Drive, Suite 1530, Chicago IL 60611.)
22. _____. The process of family therapy: The development of the Family Therapist Coding System. In L. Greenberg & W. Pinsof (eds.), *The psychotherapeutic process: A research handbook.* New York: Guilford Press, 1986.
23. _____, & Catherall, D.R. The integrative psychotherapy alliance: Family, couple and individual therapy scales. *Journal of Marital and Family Therapy 12:* 137–151, 1986.
24. Rice, L.N., & Greenberg, L.S. (eds.). *Patterns of change: Intensive analysis of psychotherapy process.* New York: Guilford Press, 1984.
25. _____, & Saperia, E.P. Task analysis of the resolution of problematic reactions. In L. Rice & L.S. Greenberg (eds.), *Patterns of change: Intensive analysis of psychotherapy process.* New York: Guilford Press, 1984.
26. Rogers, L.E., Millar, F.E., & Bavelas, J.B. Methods for analyzing marital conflict discourse. *Family Process 24:* 175–187, 1985.
27. Sluzki, C.E. The coalitionary process in initiating family therapy. *Family Process 14:* 67–77, 1975.
28. Watzlawick, P., Beavin, J.H., & Jackson, D.D. *Pragmatics of human communication: A study of interactional patterns, pathologies, and paradoxes.* New York: W.W. Norton, 1967.

13

PHASES OF FAMILY THERAPY PROCESS:
A Framework for Clinicians and Researchers

JAMES F. ALEXANDER

University of Utah
Salt Lake City, Utah

EARLY PROPONENTS of family therapy needed to meet three major goals in order to establish its legitimacy as a viable treatment modality. First, to attract potential practitioners, the early writers needed to present popular, conceptually viable and persuasive models for changing problematic family situations. Second, to develop support among consumers and other potential funding sources, proponents needed to demonstrate empirically the effectiveness of family-based treatment. Third, so that new generations of therapists could be trained, theorists and researchers needed to identify, articulate, and examine critically the various elements that were hypothesized to be important in the intervention process with families.

The first goal, clinical popularity, clearly has been attained, but we have not been so successful in meeting the second and third goals. Clinical popularity far exceeds the degree of research support, and journals continue to reflect discussions and controversy about basic conceptual issues. One needs only to note the spate of recent discussions about epistemological issues (for example, 23) and criticisms of the adequacy of the theoretical substratum of family therapy (for example, 14, 15).

Certainly, there is sufficient empirical evidence to justify continued confidence in and development of mini-models of family therapy. However, with the emergence of several new and popular intervention approaches (for example, cognitive-behavioral therapy with individuals) as well as the resurgence of biologically based treatments, family therapy must redouble its efforts to develop empirical support in order to remain a viable treatment modality.

Unfortunately, several problems face the family therapy researcher, including the fact that the "ultimate outcome"[1] of family therapy remains difficult to identify. Both conceptually and operationally, dif-

---

1. *Editor's Note:* See discussion of this concept by Olson (Chapter 5).

ferent family therapy models differ as to goals or desired outcomes of intervention, be they the cessation of problematic behaviors, the individuation of family members, the modification of relationship structures (for example, enmeshment), the absence of symptoms for a period of time after termination, a "positive" divorce process, and so on. As long as different models of family therapy coexist, the variable nature of outcome definitions will continue to be a source of confusion for researchers and occasionally outright contention among adherents of certain models. To add complexity, it appears that outcome often becomes an issue of punctuation. That is, clinicians often see an early positive outcome as merely getting family members to attend a session together. Other "positive outcomes" include having family members express themselves in certain ways, continue to attend sessions, commit themselves to attempting changes, maintain changes without direct therapist support, and so on. Each of these "outcomes," of course, can also be seen as "process" measures that relate to or at least predict a successful "ultimate outcome."

Thus, family therapy can no longer be considered a homogeneous process that has a unitary and consensually validated outcome at a particular point in time. Instead, family therapy involves a series of steps, each of which involves a set of processes, yet each of which could be seen as representing an outcome in its own right. For example, whether or not families return for a second session could be regarded as an outcome measure of first-session processes. Similarly, the degree to which family members adhere to therapeutic directives in the third session can be regarded as one outcome measure of the degree of success of earlier joining. Viewed in this way, the concepts of process and outcome appear to be somewhat arbitrary; this situation is problematic for traditional "linear-cause" thinkers but not at all inconsistent with the basic assumptions of systems-based family therapies—not inconsistent, but nevertheless complex.

For both the clinician and researcher, solutions to these complexities lie in conceptual, methodological, and statistical developments. At the conceptual level, we must continue to develop clear theoretical and operational articulations of basic concepts, goals, and intervention processes. At the methodological and statistical level, theorists and researchers must work together to apply new research methodologies and statistical techniques to subtle clinical phenomena (5, 12).

As one step in working together, in this chapter I offer a framework, designed to be useful to both clinicians and researchers, for articulating the basic processes in family therapy. In doing so, I will not discuss specific family therapy models in detail, nor describe the new methodological and statistical tools available. Such discussions exist elsewhere. Instead, I will adopt a broader perspective and describe the generic features of family intervention that I believe exist in most if not all family therapy models.

THE PHASES OF INTERVENTION

Although different family models derive from divergent theoretical assumptions and emphasize different assessment and change techniques, at a generic level, all family therapies must deal with certain major tasks: 1) initiating the process of intervention (getting acquainted, joining, and so on); 2) assessing salient issues and variables and creating intervention strategies; 3) modifying negative or otherwise unproductive cognitive, emotional, and motivational processes; 4) changing overt problem behaviors and developing adaptive, long-term interaction patterns; and 5) terminating the therapy in such a way that the family can go it alone. In different family therapy models, these tasks and strategies to deal with them receive varying degrees of emphasis. Different models deal with these tasks in different sequences; they may repeat them and/or they may deal with them simultaneously—but these tasks all occur. They have been analyzed in the Anatomy of Intervention Model (AIM), which is described below and in greater detail in Alexander, Barton, Waldron, and Mas (2) and Warburton and Alexander (27).

An additional task, that of deciding if family therapy is to occur at all, also must be faced. However, this review will not consider this issue for two reasons. First, it has been raised and dealt with eloquently by Wynne and his associates (29, 30); second, because we are particularly interested in linking process with outcome, I will focus on family therapy only in the context where it occurs. The process of deciding whether family therapy should or should not occur may require both a different conceptual approach and different research tools.

Table 1 describes the major tasks of intervention[2] that have been organized into phases of activity, each with distinctive goals and a requisite set of therapist skills necessary to carry out appropriate activities. For example, the goals and techniques of the Assessment/ Understanding Phase center on understanding the family. These goals and techniques are different from the goals and techniques of the Induction/Motivation Phase, which are designed to develop a positive therapeutic relationship, to enhance motivation for change, to modify negative attributions, and to deal with early indices of resistance. While

---

2. Table 1 and the related discussion were presented at the NIMH/*Family Process* conference and were distilled in large part from the chapter by Warburton and Alexander in L'Abate's edited, two-volume *Handbook of Family Psychology and Therapy*, 1985 (27). Several significant modifications have been made, particularly in terminology. These modifications have been suggested by Lyman Wynne, to whom I am indebted.

TABLE 1

Anatomy of Intervention Model

Components of Intervention

Therapist Dimensions	Introduction/ Impression	Assessment/ Understanding	Induction/ Motivation	Behavior Change	Generalization & Termination
Goals	Maximize family initial expectation of positive change.	Understand family parameters and potential for change.	Create motivational context for long-term change.	Institute individual & interactive change programs.	Maintain change & facilitate independence.
Central Tasks	Appear appropriate & credible to family members.	Elicit, structure, & analyze information, develop plans.	Use interpersonal sensitivity to impact negativity.	Structure & monitor performance in/ outside sessions.	Facilitate generalization of change into future.
Attributes & Skills	Superficial qualities that reflect expertise	Intelligence, perceptiveness, & conceptual model	Relationship/ interpersonal skills	Structuring/ teaching skills	Blend of all skills used in other components
Representative Activities	If possible, present stimulus qualities that family will see as appropriate, e.g., type & location of treatment center, clothing, office trappings, therapist appearance.	Identify extra- & intrafamily context & function of problematic & adaptive patterns, including stressors, support, constraints, & family value systems. Evaluate resistance & cooperative responses.	Modify adverse reactions to therapist. Provide rationale for treatment techniques. Change meaning & attributions, usually emphasizing the positive (e.g., reframe & relabel).	Provide directives & apply behavior change techniques (e.g., communication training, relaxation tasks). Modify antecedents & consequences, describe & model appropriate interactive behaviors.	Insure attainment of spontaneous & adaptive family processes, problem-solving styles, & problem cessation. Anticipate future & extrafamily stresses & intervene if necessary.

performing assessment and treatment planning, therapists need strong analytic/conceptual skills, whereas in developing a therapeutic relationship, therapists have a greater need for relationship/interpersonal skills. Fortunately, some therapists have the range of skills to be effective in all the tasks of intervention, but some have none, and some have only a select few (1). Researchers and clinicians need to consider each of these skills and the tasks for which they are appropriate if we are to be successful in therapy training and in researching the intervention process.

The Introduction Phase of Intervention

Families and therapists come together at a first session with a number of expectations about what will happen. Some time ago, Frank (10) identified the importance of the "credible ritual" as an important component of psychotherapeutic healing. A major part of establishing a credible ritual is the presentation of the person who will perform the ritual, the family therapist. Thus, for the initial contact to be as productive as possible, the therapist must appear credible as a helper to the family. The best therapist will fail at the task of moving a family toward its desired goals during subsequent phases of treatment if the family finds the therapist unconvincing as a change agent.

As the shorter-term marital and family therapies become highly used as modes of treatment, the initial client and therapist biases and expectations about stimulus characteristics increase in importance (6, 7, 13, 22). Because stimulus characteristics of the therapist and the setting are superficially observable, they are different from therapeutic skills that must be demonstrated over time as the therapist engages in the therapy process itself. A number of attributes generate credibility, especially overt characteristics such as gender, race, physical size, age, dress, and office equipment, all of which have been noted in the literature (24, 28) as having some effect on initial impressions and on the interactions that follow. Different families and family members, of course, view these factors in different ways. To use a personal example, twenty years ago the author (being relatively young) was seen as credible by delinquents; but, at the beginning of the first session, parents of those delinquents often were somewhat dubious about a therapist who was clearly too young to have adolescent children. Now, of course, parents see me as obviously credible, but the delinquents are initially dubious that, given my age, I can understand their perspective.

With regard to credibility, a number of tactics have been used to influence clients' perceptions positively. These include matching client and therapist characteristics, joining in obvious mannerisms and self-disclosures, and using the family's stereotypes (see 17). As a matter of fact, the popular community-psychology emphasis on community-based crisis clinics and the use of indigenous paraprofessionals[3] (19) reflect the potential importance of therapist characteristics. Of course, therapist characteristics often cannot be easily changed or matched to each family. In this case, therapists must deal with initial, nonproductive reactions in subsequent phases, as described below.

The Assessment/Understanding Phase

Beyond establishing credibility in the first session, the therapist must collect enough information about a family to begin to make sense of the subtleties and complexities of its interactions. Intelligence, perceptiveness, and use of a clear conceptual model allow the therapist enough objectivity and distance to understand a family member's behavior within the context of the family, as opposed to being engaged by it. Obviously, the therapeutic goal of understanding a family requires considerable cognitive skill because only occasionally, and only through luck, can we change something we do not understand. The therapist must be able to create a context in which the family will provide the information relevant to the family's potential for change, and be capable of generating meaningful hypotheses about what the information means. In turn, this will lead to the development of therapeutic solutions firmly based on the integration of assessment information.

The assessment phase is probably one of the least understood and researched phases of therapy in terms of therapist characteristics or skills. Assessment skills have not had entire models of intervention built around them like the relationship skills of the Induction/Motivation Phase (for example, in the client-centered model) and the structuring or technical skills of the Behavior-Change Phase (for example, in behavioral models). The importance of cognitive and intellectual skills essential to the understanding of a family are thus underrepresented in the literature.

An additional problem derives from the relative lack of technical aids to assess families, in contrast to individual therapy in which numerous assessment and psychometric devices have been used to assist the practitioner. Whereas psychometric devices such as behavioral observation, checklists, supervision, and consultation have assisted both individual and family practitioners' assessment of individual members, few useful tools have been devised for the assessment of relationships (9). Certainly, none have achieved the popularity and widespread use of individual assessment tools such as the MMPI and the WAIS.

To make things even more difficult, in the Assessment phase the

---

3. *Editor's Note:* In Chapter 1, Stanton recommends research on the specific point of how or whether academic degrees make any difference in the ways in which family therapists actually function.

therapist must *be* competent; in the Introduction Phase the therapist simply had *to appear* competent. There seems to be considerable literature to indicate that experience helps at this point (16). The seasoned clinician is more likely to be skilled at deciphering the vast amounts of information presented in initial sessions than is the novice. Much of the extraneous noise may be automatically screened out by the more experienced therapist, allowing attention to be focused on the relevant behavior. Unfortunately for the researcher, this makes it difficult to tease out the overt and covert processes that the therapist is using. For the less experienced therapist, it is the Assessment/Understanding Phase that requires a clear conceptual model of therapy. Without a clear conceptual model as a guide, therapists may quickly find themselves mired in confusion.

An additional problem is the fact that while therapists are assessing the family, they are simultaneously having an impact upon the family. Therefore, assessment becomes a dual process of evaluating what the family is like "on its own," and assessing how it is responding to the therapist's stimulus characteristics and interpersonal maneuvers. If these reactions are nonproductive, it may require that two phases of intervention be conducted *simultaneously*. During the assessment phase, problems of considerable resistance must be handled if they occur. Therapists may have to use the relationship skills associated with the Induction/Motivation Phase (see below). In this case, the therapist must remember that relational skills are used *in addition to* (not instead of) cognitive skills. Assessment is also a phase frequently returned to in later stages of the intervention when the therapist questions previous assumptions or needs to gain new information. This creates a complex situation for the therapist, but an even more difficult one for the researcher. Once again, however, at least acknowledging this situation will allow researchers to begin to tease apart conceptually (if not operationally) the variables operating at this and other stages of intervention.

The Induction/Motivation Phase

This is the phase of intervention that creates the climate in which families are willing to change and have the motivation to do so. It is assumed that it is the therapist's, not the family's, responsibility to move the clients through this phase of treatment. Family therapists in particular use such techniques as relabelling (3, 4) or reframing (17) to influence family members' cognition and affect. These techniques are contingent upon the family because they react to and depend upon what family members say, do, and feel. Relabeling and reframing will not be successful if they do not "make sense" to the phenomenological reality of the family, and if they are not acceptable (18). Thus, therapists need *relational skills* and *interpersonal sensitivity*, skills variously described in the literature as affect-behavior integration, humor, and nonblaming (1), as empathy, genuineness, and nonpossessive warmth (20, 25), and as interpersonal manner (21). These skills are necessary in order to provide a motivational climate conducive to the application of techniques for behavior change, and are necessary early in the process of intervention (3).

Relational skills appear to be a necessary but not sufficient ingredient for change (21). It is this "necessary but not sufficient" phrase that can be the nemesis of the family therapist. Because the therapist works hard to create the context for change, to get the family reframed or relabeled, to overcome resistance, and to establish likability, the temptation to remain in this phase of treatment is seductive. There are in fact schools of therapy that imply that the application of relationship skills alone is enough to accomplish successfully all of the intervention. However, the majority of family therapy models maintain that specific techniques designed to change behavior directly must also be applied.

The Behavior-Change Phase

The therapist's goal in most marriage and family therapy approaches is to produce change in patterns of interaction by using specific techniques that focus on specific aspects of behavior, feelings, and thoughts or beliefs. The class of therapist attributes necessary to produce actual change are *structuring* skills. Because the therapist must instruct the family how to do things differently, the therapist must present these techniques in a clear, direct, and understandable way. Negotiation skills, communication skills, time out, relaxation techniques, techniques for behavioral contracting are examples of these techniques, and the specific techniques depend on the therapist's treatment model. If the therapist's structuring skills are not sufficiently developed at this phase, the family may fail to comply because they have not understood the directions. Thus, for example, a behavioral contract between a teenage child and the parents may not have been sufficiently specific in terms of expectations and sanctions. This would reflect a therapist *skill* problem. On the other hand, if the therapist reviews the contract and perceives that the degree of specificity was adequate and that both teenager and parents understood the contract, the family resistance would alert the therapist (through a sensitivity to performance) that earlier assessments and assumptions about the family were erroneous, and additional assessment is necessary to determine why.

Generalization/Termination Phase

The goal of most families and therapists is a positive change in the family system that will be maintained after the therapist ceases involvement. Just as therapists need to assess their impact on a system as they begin treatment, so they must be cognizant of the effect that their leaving will create. Although most models of therapy make reference to the importance of termination, few models of therapy operationalize criteria for decision-making about termination. It is generally assumed that some combination of problem cessation, changes in family structure, behavior generalization, and/or the attainment of problem-solving skills and adaptive attitudes constitute indications to the therapist that the family is ready for termination (2). However, if the family has not understood or benefited sufficiently from the Behavior-Change Phase of intervention, or if assessment was inaccurate, generalization and maintenance of new patterns of behavior cannot be expected.

Further, if positive changes are dependent on continued therapist involvement, the therapist must help the family learn to function independently. This stage of intervention often takes on an "as-if" quality because the therapist must guess how the family will behave without him or her, and also guess about future contexts. This contrasts with other phases in which scanning is almost exclusively on the "here-and-now" process.

Therapists in this phase of treatment need to rely on a combination of skills because termination contains a microcosm or condensation of the entire therapeutic experience and repertoire. In order to answer the question of appropriateness of termination, a therapist must summarize the entirety of the intervention process, mentally reviewing each phase in order to understand the current situation. This summary then provides clues as to whether there is likely to be a successful termination. This phase rarely represents a focus for research, yet it may have a great deal to do with the maintenance of positive treatment effects.

IMPLICATIONS FOR FAMILY THERAPY RESEARCH

In family therapy research that links process and outcome measures, it is essential to differentiate the phases of intervention and the distinctive therapist skills required in each. Otherwise, different studies that tap different phases will produce different findings, and measures linking process to outcome will tend to be correlated at only a modest level, if at all. As we have seen, therapist relationship skills, such as warmth, are relatively more important in some phases (for example, Induction) than in others (for example, Assessment). Studies linking therapist warmth with outcome will lead to different findings if this warmth is measured when some therapists are performing assessment techniques, others are performing induction, and others applying a structured communication technique.

Identifying the phases of intervention also underlines the point that process and outcome represent arbitrary distinctions. For example, in a recent study we looked at the impact of therapist gender on the expression of defensive and supportive communications between mothers and therapists and fathers and therapists (28). In this study, therapist gender represented the independent variable, and supportiveness/defensiveness in the first session represented the outcome of interest (the dependent variable). In another study, therapist supportiveness/defensiveness represented the independent (process) variable, and posttreatment marital adjustment scores represented the outcome (dependent) variable (26). Finally, another study examined how well marital adjustment scores (independent variable) could predict marital interactions as an outcome (dependent) variable. In other words, the "process" measures in one study represented another study's "outcome" measures. Family therapy research, particularly that which uses newer data-analytic models such as structural equations (8, 11; see also chapters 14 and 16), will proceed more coherently and effectively if process and outcome are seen by researchers as merely "punctuations" in a complex, ongoing phenomenon.

This framework also forces family therapy researchers and theorists to *unconfound* goals and techniques. Even those family theorists who have argued that behavior has meaning only in its context have often tended to behave as though techniques exist independently of the context. As one example, some writers have recommended that in order to "join" the family, the therapist should use a language system similar to the family's (3). In most circumstances this technique does help meet the goal of joining the family. However, some families interpret such therapist behavior as demeaning or otherwise inappropriate. In such a case, the goal of joining the family would not be accomplished—in fact, the opposite result may occur. The AIM framework helps us to understand that the specific activities undertaken by a therapist may take a variety of forms, and it reminds us that certain goals do not necessarily always imply certain techniques.

Another important contribution of this framework is a separation of generic versus specific components. Researchers have struggled with this issue for quite some time, and will continue to do so. The AIM framework reminds researchers to separate the generic elements of intervention, which are present in *all* family therapies, from the specific applications that are unique to one or a few models.[4] For example, we all attempt to motivate clients, but some do it by focusing on symptoms, some by switching the focus to relationships rather than symptoms, some by using prompts such as family games, and so on. Although it does not solve the

---

4. *Editor's Note:* See the discussion by Epstein (Chapter 9) and Gurman (Chapter 10) concerning priorities for research attention to elements of specific treatment models versus common elements.

problem of developing measures for both generic and specific levels, the framework helps to clarify the difference.

Finally, the AIM framework emphasizes the role of the therapist in therapy research. Many research projects attempt to evaluate specific techniques or models as if these techniques or models existed independent of therapists. An earlier review of 265 family and individual therapy studies in five major journals uncovered only one article formally addressing the issues of therapist characteristics (2). This shortcoming is astonishing because the myriad techniques we use must, with very few exceptions, be performed by a therapist. AIM reminds us that in order to perform the techniques, therapists require specific skills—skills that differ from technique to technique, from phase to phase of intervention, and maybe from model to model.

In conclusion, I recommend that investigators who attempt to link the processes of therapy to outcome carefully articulate the phase(s) of intervention that represent the focus of the research.[5] The investigators also should take care to articulate the hypothesized relationship between the measures during that phase and the outcome measure(s) being used. Finally, the investigators should discuss how they are dealing with additional variables that may operate during that phase, as well as those variables operating during other phases that may confound the process-outcome relationship being studied.

REFERENCES

1. Alexander, J.F., Barton, C., Schiavo, R.S., & Parsons, B.V. Behavioral intervention with families of delinquents: Therapist characteristics and outcome. *Journal of Consulting and Clinical Psychology 44:* 656–664, 1976.
2. _____, Barton C., Waldron, H., & Mas, C.H. Beyond the technology of family therapy: The anatomy of intervention model. In K.D. Craig & R.J. McMahon (eds.), *Advances in clinical behavior therapy.* New York: Brunner/Mazel, 1983.
3. _____, & Parsons, B.V. *Functional and family therapy: Principles and procedures.* Monterey CA: Brooks/Cole, 1982.
4. Barton, C., & Alexander, J.F. Functional family therapy. In A.S. Gurman &

---

5. *Editor's Note:* Some problems and illnesses, such as grieving and schizophrenia, have well-defined phases through which they characteristically pass. This means that there are two kinds of phases—phases of crisis resolution or illness and phases of intervention—that need to be related to one another. More broadly, a similar point can be made about phases of individual and family development in the life cycle. Consideration of the appropriateness with which phase of intervention and phase of illness/life cycle are matched is a clinical and research issue of great importance—and great neglect. Alexander's delineation of the phases of family therapy process is a major contribution.

D.P. Kniskern (eds.), *Handbook of family therapy*. New York: Brunner/
Mazel, 1981.

5. _____, Alexander, J.F., & Sanders, J.D. Research and family therapy. In
L. L'Abate (ed.), *The handbook of family psychology and therapy*.
Homewood IL: Dorsey Press, 1985.

6. Brodsky, A.M., & Hare-Mustin, R.T. (eds.). *Women and psychotherapy: An
assessment of research and practice*. New York: Guilford Press, 1980.

7. Collins, A.M., & Sedlack, W.E. Counselor ratings of male and female clients.
*Journal of National Association for Women Deans, Administrators and
Counselors 37:* 128–132, 1974.

8. Dwyer, J.H. *Statistical models for the social and behavioral sciences*. New
York: Oxford University Press, 1983.

9. Fisher, L. Transactional theories but individual assessment: A frequent
discrepancy in family research. *Family Process 21:* 313–320, 1982.

10. Frank, J.D. *Persuasion & healing: A comparative study of psychotherapy*.
Baltimore: Johns Hopkins University Press, 1961.

11. Freedman, D.A. *Structural equation models: A case study* (Technical
Report No. 22). Berkeley: University of California, Department of Statistics, 1983.

12. Gottman, J.M. Temporal form: Toward a new language for describing
relationships. *Journal of Marriage and the Family 44:* 943–962, 1982.

13. Gurman, A.S., & Klein, M.H. Marital and family conflicts. In A.M. Brodsky
& R.T. Hare-Mustin (eds.), *Women and psychotherapy: An assessment of
research and practice*. New York: Guilford Press, 1980.

14. Howard, G.S. The roles of values in the science of psychology. *American
Psychologist 40:* 255–265, 1985.

15. L'Abate, L., & Colondier, G. The emperor has no clothes! Long live the
emperor! A critique of family systems thinking and a reductionistic
proposal. *American Journal of Family Therapy 15:* 19–33, 1987.

16. Luborsky, L., Bachrach, H., Graff, H., Pulver, S., & Christoph, P. Predicting
the outcome of psychotherapy: Findings of the Penn Psychotherapy
Project. *Archives of General Psychiatry 37:* 371–381, 1980.

17. Minuchin, S. *Families & family therapy*. Cambridge: Harvard University
Press, 1974.

18. Morris, S., Alexander, J.F., & Waldron, H. Functional family therapy: Issues
in clinical practice. In I.R.H. Falloon (ed.), *Handbook of behavioral family
therapy*. New York: Guilford Press, in press.

19. Reiff, R., & Reissman, F. *The indigenous non-professional*. New York:
Behavioral Publications, 1965.

20. Rogers, C.R. The necessary and sufficient conditions of therapeutic personality change. *Journal of Consulting Psychology 21:* 95–103, 1957.

21. Schaffer, N.D. Multi-dimensional measures of therapist behavior as predictors of outcome. *Psychological Bulletin 92:* 670–682, 1982.

22. Seiden, A.M. Overview: Research on the psychology of women. II. Women in
families, work, and psychotherapy. *American Journal of Psychiatry 133:*
1111–1123, 1976.

23. Shields, C.G. Critiquing the new epistemologies: Toward minimum requirements for a scientific theory of family therapy. *Journal of Marital and
Family Therapy 12:* 359–372, 1986.

24. Strong, S.R. Social psychological approach to psychotherapy research. In
S.L. Garfield & A.E. Bergin (eds.), *Handbook of psychotherapy and
behavior change: An empirical analysis* (2nd ed.). New York: John Wiley
& Sons, 1978.

25. Truax, C.B., & Mitchell, K.M. Research on certain therapist interpersonal skills in relation to process and outcome. In A.E. Bergin & S.L. Garfield (eds.), *Handbook of psychotherapy and behavior change: An empirical analysis.* New York: John Wiley & Sons, 1971.
26. Waldron, H., Turner, C., Barton, C., Alexander, J.F., & Szykula, S. The contribution of therapist defensiveness to marital therapy process and outcome: A path analytic approach. Poster session presented at the Annual Meeting of the Association for the Advancement of Behavior Therapy, Philadelphia, November, 1984.
27. Warburton, J.R., & Alexander, J.F. The family therapist: What does one do? In L. L'Abate (ed.), *The handbook of family psychology and therapy.* Homewood IL: Dorsey Press, 1985.
28. _____, Alexander, J.F., & Barton, C. Sex of client and sex of therapist: Variables in family process study. Paper presented at the Annual Convention of the American Psychological Association, Montreal, August, 1980.
29. Wynne, L.C., McDaniel, S.H., & Weber, T.T. (eds.). *Systems consultation: A new perspective for family therapy.* New York: Guilford Press, 1986.
30. _____, McDaniel, S.H., & Weber, T.T. Professional politics and the concepts of family therapy, family consultation, and systems consultation. *Family Process 26:* 153–166, 1987.

14

TREATMENT PROCESS:
A Problem at Three Levels*

GERALD R. PATTERSON
PATRICIA CHAMBERLAIN
Oregon Social Learning Center
Eugene, Oregon

THE DEVELOPMENT of more powerful theories of treatment must await the development of more adequate models for empirically investigating treatment process variables. Empirical studies of treatment process require a satisfactory answer to a sequence of questions at three levels: Does behavior change? Why does the behavior change? Why is it that not everyone changes to the same degree? Stated in a more technical form, these questions are: 1) Do random-assignment comparison designs demonstrate that the intervention is effective when measures of change are used that are not reactive to the measurement process? 2) Does the treatment model specify the variables that produce the changes in the problem behavior, and do these variables account for the majority of the variance available in the criterion measures of the problem behavior? 3) What are the variables in the dyad or system that regulate how much these determining variables will be changed? The

*The two years of support for this project were provided by the National Institute of Mental Health, Grant No. MH38730. The authors wish to acknowledge the contributions of J. Reid, M. Forgatch, and K. Kavanagh to the general formulation about noncooperation, and J. Ray for her unremitting labors in analyzing these data.
Editor's Note: The present volume was intended to be an assemblage of viewpoints and recommendations about the state of the art in family therapy research, not a literature review or a series of research reports. At the NIMH/ *Family Process* conference, Patterson described examples of his research that illuminated principles and issues of concern to all the participants. As editor of this volume, I believe that some of its recommendations will become more vivid with this inclusion of a detailed example of Patterson's research, which is carried out at the cutting edge of theory and methodology. Readers should not be intimidated by the sophistication and complexity of this research; they should not believe that anything less is not worth doing or that research differing in style, conceptualization, or method cannot be another aspect of the "state of the art." The volume as a whole reveals a great many controversial and unclarified issues in family therapy research waiting to be studied.

present report addresses these three issues in the context of parent-training therapy for families of antisocial children.

Level 1: Does Behavior Change?

The first requirement for finding out empirically what does and does not work is the use of nonreactive criterion measures of outcome.[1] For example, when studying outcome in the treatment of antisocial children, observation data may be used to study what is occurring in the home. The relative nonreactivity of this measure compared to parent global reports will be explored in a later section. In studying generalization to other settings, it should be possible to use community records about, for example, court offenses or discipline contacts at school. It may also be that defining the criterion by multiple methods and agents could provide a sensitive and relatively nonreactive score. That possibility is explored in the current report. For each criterion, normative data should be obtained; this, in turn, would make it possible to specify the number of clinical cases functioning within the normal range at treatment termination and at follow-up.[2]

We believe that using the reactive measures ordinarily employed in outcome studies for antisocial children constitutes a reinforcement trap. This means that individual therapists, and treatment theories as well, remain frozen in place; everything, and nothing, works. For example, the most widely applied measures for treatment outcome for antisocial children rely on parent self-report data. Such criterion measures are highly reactive. The studies to be reviewed in a later section suggest that no matter what kind of treatment is employed for antisocial children, a significant number of parents will report that the problem child has shown "some" improvement. Such ratings are found in placebo and failed-intervention procedures even when the home observation data show no change in or a worsening of problem behaviors (5, 16, 41). Such a reactive criterion measure creates a reinforcement trap for therapists. No

---

1. *Editor's Note:* Family systems theorists are greatly concerned about "circular" effects in which those who observe family processes are expected to be "reactively" influenced by the observation process and by those who are observed. Indeed, in systems theory, reactivity is anticipated as a norm. However, this abstract assumption neglects a fact that is important for research—that there are *degrees* of reactivity. Patterson and Chamberlain are keenly aware of this issue and, as they describe later in their chapter, have extensively studied the effects on home observers of child behavior when potentially biasing factors were deliberately introduced. Apparently, certain kinds of observational methods are so minimally reactive, in relation to observed behavior, that they can be regarded, pragmatically, as "nonreactive."

2. *Editor's Note:* This criterion of change is similar to that recommended by Jacobson (Chapter 11) for ascertaining whether change is clinically significant.

matter what their treatment approach is, they will "know" they have positive outcomes. Parent gratitude and a munificent salary also insure little change in therapist behavior, hence the term *reinforcement trap.*

The second requirement for measuring change includes replicated, random-assignment comparison designs. It is necessary to do this in order to demonstrate that the outcome is specific to the treatment process and not brought about by placebo effects that may arise from merely interacting with a professional or coming to a clinic.[3] Treatments that do not survive this first level of analyses would not be candidates for the more complex studies required at Levels 2 and 3.

Level 2: What Determines the Change?

A demonstration that the treatment is effective in changing behavior sets the stage for the next question: What are the specific components in the treatment that produce the changes? Many of the major theories of treatment have failed to specify clearly the necessary and sufficient components in treatment that produce change. Those that have made some effort to delineate such components as warmth, shifts in family structure, or reframing, have not been successful in specifying the means by which these components are to be measured. These omissions plus the employment of inadequate criteria for evaluating outcome have created something of a stalemate in treatment research.

One reason for such a stalemate lies in the inability to specify whether the treatment components were actually introduced. Pre- and posttreatment comparison of the scores for the critical components would provide some estimate of how well the treatment was carried out. Having such measures may also enable theorists to rid themselves of a good deal of excess baggage in their notions about what causes families to change. For example, if many families show significant changes in problem behaviors but no shift in the pre- to posttreatment comparisons for the component scores, then obviously that component is not a necessary condition. If, on the other hand, there are a significant number of families that show pre- to posttreatment shifts in the component scores, but no shift in the problem behavior, then that component is not a sufficient condition for change.

The present report introduces the concepts of family-management

---

3. *Editor's Note:* Interacting with a professional or coming to a clinic will have unspecified effects. Nonspecific effects may be substantially different (better or worse!) than the effects of a placebo, that is, a nontreatment such as an inert drug that the recipient thinks is a treatment. A waiting-list control assignment is not a placebo because the clients do not believe that they are being treated. True placebos are not possible in psychotherapy research. The comparison in this report, of a specific treatment with nonspecific professional interaction, is more clinically relevant than a hypothetical placebo would be anyway.

skills as the components in family treatment that are necessary and sufficient conditions for producing changes in antisocial child behavior. As shown in Figure 1, the impact of the interpersonal exchanges between therapist and parents on child problem behaviors is thought to be mediated by the impact of those exchanges on parenting skills. Families that demonstrate significant improvements in monitoring and discipline skills will produce significant decreases in criterion measures of antisocial behavior. Those that do not demonstrate improvements in parent skills will not show improvements in child problem behaviors.[4]

Reviews of the literature repeatedly demonstrate that antisocial children are also lacking in the social skills related to work and to peers (22). Expectably, the majority of the chronically antisocial children tend to be rejected by peers and also fail in school (40). It is hypothesized that improvement in parent reinforcement and problem-solving skills will produce increases in children's academic skills and in the social skills needed for coping with their peer group. If these parental patterns do not change, then there will be no changes in anti- or prosocial behaviors of the target child.

One of the key concepts in the current study is that treatment may be used as an experimental manipulation. Pre- and posttreatment measures for all the indicators defining the constructs in the parenting models are the first prerequisites. The second requirement is that one has an intervention that will produce significant changes in a major portion of treated cases. In the present study, treated cases are classified as successes or failures based on a comparison of baseline, termination, and follow-up scores for TAB (observed child total aversive behavior). The initial step in the conversion of significant path coefficients or bivariate correlations into statistically causal status requires that the scores for a family-management variable, such as monitoring, show significant improvements for successful cases and no change, or worsening status, for failure cases.

Level 3: Why Do Some Change More Than Others?

Given that the findings show treatment changes in the child's antisocial behavior and that the termination measures of family-management practices account for substantial variance in the termination criterion scores, then one is in a position to raise the even more interesting third question: What determines the individual differences among families in their responsiveness to treatment, and why do some families change a great deal and others only slightly, or even get worse?

---

4. *Editor's Note:* The study of variables mediating behavioral change makes this an investigation of process/outcome in the sense recommended by Pinsof (Chapter 12) and others in this volume.

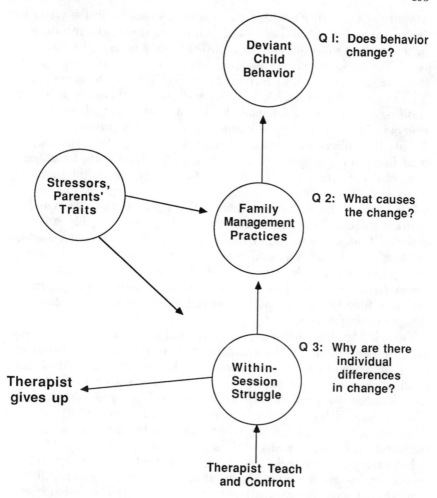

FIG. 1. Struggle and change.

The pivotal concept here is thought to be *within-session struggle*. Our prior studies showed that therapist efforts to teach parents (social learning procedures) were likely to elicit immediate increases in parent noncooperation (31). As used here, the notion of noncooperation is synonymous with the idea of struggle ("I can't do what the therapist asks") and conflict among family members as well as noncompliance ("I won't do what the therapist asks").

The paradox is that if the therapist does not try to teach, there will presumably be no change in family-management practices and no improvement in antisocial problems. However, the teaching and confronting (for failure to carry out homework assignments) increase the intensity of the struggle within the sessions. As shown in the study by Chamberlain, Patterson, Reid, et al. (8), novice therapists encountered higher levels of within-session struggle than did experienced staff therapists.[5] For experienced and inexperienced therapists alike, one of the effects of this struggle is to decrease therapist liking for the clients. This is also related to increasing risk for a change in therapist behavior, resulting in two possible outcomes: letting the case fail, or letting the case drop out of treatment. The assumption in this parent-training approach is that all families can change, but the rate of change for some may be exceedingly slow (several weeks for some and several years for others). One problem in therapy with antisocial families is to keep the therapist involved.

It is assumed, then, that high rates of therapist efforts to teach and to confront will correlate with greater changes in parenting skills. It is also expected that measures of within-session struggle will covary significantly with such changes, as will measures of how cooperative the parents are in carrying out their homework assignments. These assumptions are summarized in Figure 1, where the measures of family-management practices function as mediators between within-session struggles and changes in the problem child.

There is a set of confounding variables built into this model, and these variables serve as family disrupters. Outside stressors such as unemployment, prolonged illness, the daily round of hassles, marital conflict, and psychiatric illness all serve to disrupt family-management procedures, as shown in the empirical studies by Patterson, Reid, and Dishion (32). These same variables play a dual role in disrupting the therapy process. They not only disrupt the family-management procedures themselves, but also amplify the intensity of the struggle during therapy.

For example, Chamberlain et al. (8) found that agency referrals had higher within-session struggle scores than did self-referrals. In addition, cases that dropped out of treatment were characterized by higher initial struggle scores. It is hypothesized that measures of outside stressors and parental depression will covary significantly with both measures of struggle and measures of family-management skills.

It is also assumed that these forces are partially mitigated by the therapist's ability to be supportive, to relate to the client, and to reframe

---

5. *Editor's Note:* In Chapter 11, Jacobson discusses the unresolved question of the optimal level of experience of therapists. When a behavioral approach requiring specific technical skills is used, the therapist's experience with the treatment method may be more important than with models in which flexible use of the therapist's personality is emphasized. "Life experience," rather than experience using the treatment model, may be more relevant in ecosystemic and experiential approaches.

the problem, all of which reduce parental noncooperation. Reframing the child's behavior from a different perspective or reframing what seems to have been a parental failure in the past makes it possible for parents to become involved in the supervised training of parenting skills. It is hypothesized that high rates of therapist support and reframing will be associated with concurrently lower rates of parental struggle. Furthermore, high rates of therapist support and reframing at the midpoint of treatment are associated with greater increases in parental cooperation at termination.

DOES THE PROBLEM BEHAVIOR CHANGE?

Precision in estimating outcome relies entirely on the quality of the assessment procedures employed in measuring the problem behavior. We assume that one of the prime factors for slow progress in treatment research lies in the distortions introduced by the measures of outcome. For this reason, much of this section will be focused on a review of the literature pertaining to the reactivity of parent report (the most frequently used criterion) and observation measures. Three alternative criterion measures for assessing antisocial behavior are presented. The last section briefly reviews the outcome studies that have employed random assignment designs and nonreactive measures.

Parent Report as a Reactive Measure

According to the social interactional model, in distressed couples and distressed families, each member becomes caught in negative exchanges with others. For example, the average correlation between the level of observed coercive behaviors displayed by mothers and by other family members was .40 (22). Given that level of similarity in interaction, one would hardly expect unbiased reports by one member about another.

In addition to parents being enmeshed in the deviant child behavior they purport to describe, their questionnaire and interview data are biased by depressed mood swings of the mother. The studies by Griest, Wells, and Forehand (15) and Patterson and Capaldi (26) showed that measures of maternal depression accounted for at least 15% of the variance in mothers' ratings of deviant child behavior. However, maternal depression does not covary with either observer or teacher descriptions of deviant child behavior (21, 26). It is assumed that both depressed mothers and mothers of problem children tend to be overly inclusive in their schemata for classifying deviant child behavior. In keeping with this, six laboratory studies reviewed in Reid, Baldwin, Patterson, et al. (36) showed that when viewing videotapes of children interacting, mothers of problem children were significantly more overinclusive. Compared to mothers of normal children, they classified more neutral child behaviors as deviant.

Finally, it is also assumed that parent ratings of treatment outcome are highly biased in that they tend to report improvement when in fact no actual changes in child behavior occurred. It is assumed that almost any kind of intervention (or placebo contact) would make the mother feel better, and that the improvement in her mood would be accompanied by ratings of improvements in child behavior as well. One study showed that the majority of the parents in a placebo group rated their children as improved even though the observation data showed no changes (41). A similar effect has been noted by other investigators (3, 5, 16, 34).

It seems reasonable to conclude that although parent reports of treatment outcome should be examined, they cannot serve as the main criterion for evaluating outcome. For reasons already noted, reliance on this as the sole criterion will keep the practitioner permanently locked into ineffective modes of treatment for these children.

An Alternative Criterion

These considerations led us to develop an observation coding system that could be used to collect molecular data describing family interaction. A series of studies showed that it was possible to train (in roughly 40 hours, then retrain every 2 weeks) observers to be highly reliable (35). Three experimental studies were then carried out to determine if it were possible to bias the observation data. In the first study, a group of observers were kept informed about the treatment status of the families observed; the other group was uninformed. Both groups observed the same families. Knowledge of family status (clinical or normal, treated or nontreated) had no effect on the molecular data collected (37). In the second study, one group of observers was told to expect a 30% increase in deviant behavior over the next 12 sessions. A second group was told to expect a commensurate decrease, and a third group was given no biasing instructions. Again, there was no significant effect of the biasing instruction on the molecular data (38). This study of *molecular* ratings was replicated in another laboratory by Kent, O'Leary, Diament, et al. (18). However, when the observers were asked to make *global* judgments about these variables, their ratings perfectly reflected the bias introduced by the experimenter.

The second problem to consider was the reactive effect brought about by the presence of the observer in the home or the classrooms. These studies are reviewed in detail in Patterson (22) and more recently updated in the report by Reid et al. (36). A series of studies carried out in a number of classrooms and in homes showed no support for a habituation hypothesis. There were no significant changes in level of prosocial or deviant behaviors over time. Another series of studies showed no difference in rates of prosocial or deviant behaviors when the presence of observers in the room was compared to the presence of tape recorders that turned on randomly during the day. Perhaps the most interesting of the reactivity studies was carried out by Johnson and Lobitz (17) when parents of problem and nonproblem children were instructed to make their children look good or look bad during observation sessions. These parents were not able to make their children look good, despite being asked to do so.

We conclude that observation in the home is a relatively reliable, unbiased, and nonreactive measure, and consider it as a prime candidate for use in evaluating treatment outcome.

Is Parent Training Effective?

The NIMH-sponsored programmatic studies spanning two decades of outcome studies at the Oregon Social Learning Center (OSLC) have been summarized by Patterson (21, 24). A series of single-case studies in the mid-1960s led to a sequence of group designs in which consecutive cases were treated by the OSLC staff. These early studies, summarized by Patterson (21), showed significant reductions in observed rates of deviant behavior for target children and siblings. Six- and 12-month follow-up studies showed that the effects persisted for the early (21) and for the later (29) studies.

Ensuing studies focused on the question of teachability. Could treatment techniques (unspecified then) be taught to a new group of therapists? Two different studies showed that the techniques could be taught to new therapists, most of whom already had considerable clinical experience (13, 14).

Random Assignment Comparison Studies

The final and most important question concerns the inferences one draws from these studies. Are these promising effects due to some specific treatment factors or could one attribute them to placebo effects? For example, even with no treatment, children might outgrow behavioral problems. It may be that talking to any professional—minister, case worker, therapist, or dentist—would have the same result. Perhaps helping the parent make up an acceptable and coherent story about the problem is all that is necessary.

The first pilot study by Wiltz and Patterson (44) used a waiting-list control design. The second by Walter and Gilmore (41) used a placebo/treatment comparison design. Both studies used pre- and posttreatment observation data and random assignment; in both, the parent-training group improved and the comparison group showed no change. However, there were numerous methodological problems in both studies (small sample size, not a close baseline matching, a time interval of only 4 or 5 weeks), all of thich were corrected in the next study in the series. Patterson, Chamberlain, and Reid (27) randomly assigned 18 families

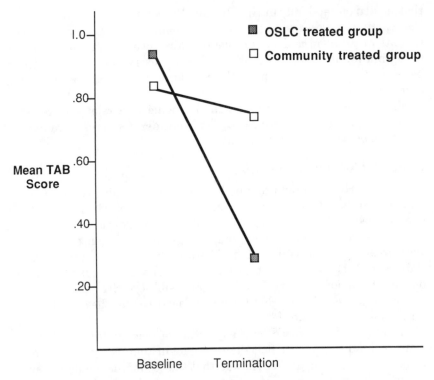

FIG. 2. Total Aversive Behavior (TAB) score comparison between Oregon Social Learning Center (OSLC) and community-treated group.

referred for treatment to OSLC or to community private practitioners. As shown in Figure 2, the pre- and postobservation data showed a significant reduction in observed, deviant-child behavior for the parent-training group and a nonsignificant change for the comparison group. The interaction term, group by phase, was significant; at termination, 75% of the children treated at OSLC were observed to function in the normal range (at baseline, 100% were in the deviant range).

When asked to give a global rating of improvement, 90% of the parents in the OSLC sample rated the outcome as very effective; 20% of the parents in the comparison group rated the outcome as very effective.

A more recent study used a random assignment design for 66 families of chronic offending adolescent delinquents (19). Half the families were treated at OSLC and the other received a variety of treatments provided by the community and the juvenile court for chronic delinquents and their families. The follow-up data showed significant reductions in police offense rates for the OSLC group and no change for the comparison group during the first year of involvement in the program. Even though the effects persisted for the ensuing 2 years, the differences were no longer significant; but there was a significant reduction in the risk of institutionalization for the experimental group that persisted throughout the entire follow-up phase.

These studies lead to the conclusion that parent-training therapy is an effective means for training parents to change their antisocial children. The effects persist, they are replicable, and they cannot be attributable to the usual placebo effects. This therapy approach is a good candidate for the next set of questions concerning the determinants for change.

WHAT DO PARENTS DO THAT PRODUCES THE CHANGE?

One might approach this question at several different levels. Our own social-interactional approach requires a focus at two different levels. On the one hand, there is the question of what parents do that changes antisocial child behavior. That is the level to be considered in this section. On the other hand, there is the question of what therapists do to change the behavior of the parent (and conversely, how do parents change therapists). That will be considered in the next section.

The general formulation to be presented here is taken from the coercion model described by Patterson (22, 25) and by Patterson et al. (32). The general assumption is that disruptions in parenting skills are major determinants for both deviant child behavior and skill deficits such as poor peer relations and academic failure. The disruptions can come about as a function of the parents having ineffective role models or through life stressors such as unemployment, marital conflict, or prolonged illness.

The model specifies that for younger children (ages 3 through 11), disruptions in parental discipline practices will be associated with increases in antisocial behavior occurring both within the home and at school. These disruptions permit coercive interactions between the target child and other family members to increase. The observation studies reviewed by Patterson (22) showed that in unsupervised exchanges, naturally occurring escape conditioning and negative reinforcing arrangements occur. These arrangements can produce rapid increases in observed rates of coercive exchanges. These exchanges provide, in turn, the basic training for antisocial child behavior. Furthermore, it seems that as the child is trained to become more coercive in interpersonal interactions, he or she becomes even more difficult to discipline. For this reason, it is assumed that there is a bidirectional relation between ineffective parent discipline and coercive child behavior.

The last 5 years of the NIMH support has made it possible to translate these clinical formulations into appropriate measurement models. The general approach requires that each concept be defined by more than one reliable indicator. The reason for this is that every measure in social science is assumed to be a biased or distorted definition of whatever variable is being measured. This assumption is in keeping with both traditional measurement theory in psychology (6) and current contributions from structural equation modeling (4). In keeping with this assumption, each of the main concepts, or *constructs*, in the basic

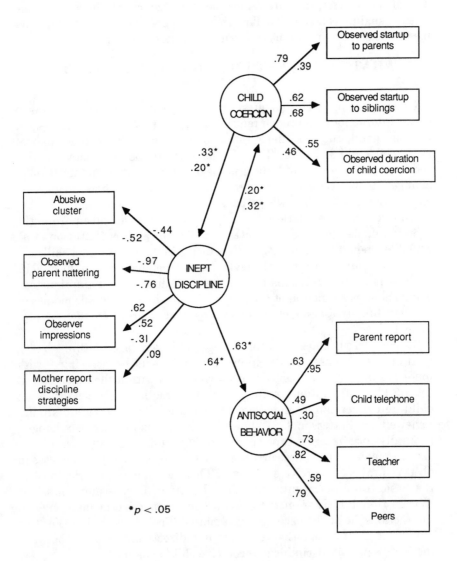

NOTE. Upper number refers to Cohort I and lower to Cohort II.

FIG. 3. Basic training for antisocial behavior: three latent constructs and their multiple indicators.

training model *are defined by multiple indicators* that draw from two or more agents and two or more methods of assessment. Using multiple indicators also makes it possible to specify the relation among the constructs and to address the key question: Do the data fit the clinical model?

Each of the constructs—Antisocial Behavior, Inept Discipline, and Child Coercion—is defined by its own set of indicators. The relation between the indicators and the latent construct are defined by factor loadings. It can be seen in Figure 3 that there is a surprising degree of stability in these definitions between one cohort (upper numbers) and a second (lower numbers) in our longitudinal study of the origins of delinquent behavior (23). Furthermore, the path coefficients also support the theory-driven speculations about both the bidirectional relation between discipline and coercive child and the direct contribution of ineffective discipline to antisocial behavior.[6]

The chi-square analyses (25) showed that for both samples there was a close fit between the measurement model and the clinical model. Furthermore, in each instance the model accounted for about 40% of the variance in the measure of antisocial behavior. Notice that the multiple indicators for this criterion measure drew from both home and school (that is, it was designed to be highly generalizable). At this point, we do not know whether this measure of antisocial behavior is a sensitive measure of treatment outcome. That possibility is currently being examined.

It is also assumed that for older children (ages 11 through 18) the basic training model will be slightly different. As shown in Figure 4, it will be expanded to include the contribution of inept parental monitoring to antisocial behavior. In keeping with the idea of developmental changes, it is also expected that the definition of antisocial behavior will be expanded to include measures of self-reported and police contact data for delinquency. A pilot study by Patterson and Dishion (28) provided a structural equation model that supported both of these assumptions.

The pivotal idea is that pre- and posttreatment measures for discipline and monitoring should demonstrate significant improvements after parent-training therapy. These scores will presumably show no shift for families participating in the comparison groups. It is also assumed that the basic training model will generalize to a clinical sample (the findings presented in Figure 3 were from an at-risk sample). Both of these assumptions will be examined in a later section of the present report.

---

6. *Editor's Note:* The bidirectionality of effects in this example of multivariate data analysis illustrates how hypotheses consistent with family systems theories can be tested empirically.

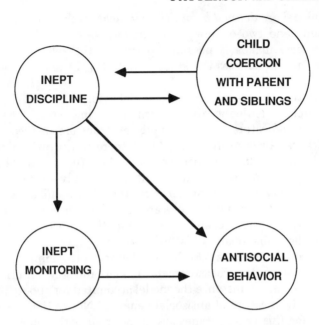

FIG. 4. A developmental model for basic training.

WHAT DO THERAPISTS DO THAT CHANGES PARENTING SKILLS?

It is assumed that the therapy process produces changes in family-management practices. However, the parents' reactions during these exchanges are multiply determined. Parents react cooperatively or non-cooperatively to the efforts of the therapist to change them, but their reactions are also partially determined by forces outside the therapy room (for example, stressors, depression, and marital conflict).[7] In a sense, much of what goes on in the therapy session has little to do with the therapist helping the parents to use better family-management procedures. In the early stages of treatment, the more chaotic the family and the more antisocial the child, the greater the frequency of parent noncooperation (within-session struggle). The therapist's ability to survive and manage these distractions has a great deal to do with therapy outcome.

The concept of noncooperation was introduced into our research after a prolonged immersion in videotaped sessions with families that failed to respond to treatment. Our repeated exposure to these tapes gradually produced the impression, even in the opening sessions, that many of

---

7. *Editor's Note:* This example illustrates how macrosystemic factors can be incorporated into well-designed family therapy research.

these parents were voicing variations on a theme of "I can't" (it's hopeless) or "I won't" (I've already tried it; it's against my religion; and so on). We began counting the variations on these statements, and over a period of months developed a microsocial coding system (see section on Methods) to measure the within-session manifestations of this phenomenon. Each client and therapist verbalization is coded as it occurs into a hand-held computer, and the data are later transferred to the mainframe computer. In addition, the affective valence of each verbalization is rated. Data collected in this sequential format allow for the study of interactional sequences of behavior.

In his review on psychotherapy research, Fiske (12) summarized the problem nicely:

> It is the effects of the therapist's actions, each at its moment in time, which have any possibility of contributing to the patient's immediate benefit. When we look for relationships between two general variables, we are ignoring the fundamental question of how one characteristic of the therapist's act may contribute to one step toward patient improvement. [p. 25; original emphasis omitted]

Empirical studies of client behavior have typically relied on global ratings as a measure for both process and outcome. As noted by Fiske, not only do global ratings tend to be less reliable, they also make it impossible to study client noncooperation as a process of sequential exchanges between client and therapist. Data collected on microsocial interactions such as this allow for the comparison of the base rate of client noncooperation to the conditional likelihood of noncooperation given a specific therapist behavior.

We could also see from the videotapes that some parents would sit and passively listen, then go home and "forget" to carry out the assignment. For this reason, we developed macrosocial measures of noncooperation based on observers' and therapists' global ratings following each taped session. These global ratings reflected reported success in carrying out the preceding week's homework assignments, but also reflected some carryover from the exchange within the session itself. We attempted to untangle the possible "confound" by including a client between-session checklist filled out by the therapist at the end of each session. It included a listing of assignments for the coming week, a listing of assignments from the past week, and a rating of how well those assignments were carried out.

The assumption is that, for the OSLC samples of working-class, chaotic families of antisocial children, the assessment of these micro- and macrosocial variables indicate the same underlying, single-dimension construct. At baseline, the intercorrelations for microsocial measures of "I won't" and "I can't" covaried significantly not only with each other but also with the observers' and therapists' global ratings of between-session noncooperation. It must be said that findings from the pilot studies reviewed earlier are based on very small samples; in fact, we see them as little more than guidelines for analyses we carried out.

The hypothesis that measures of noncooperation would covary was studied by examining the micro- and macrosocial measures for each session in treatment separately for each mother-therapist dyad. On

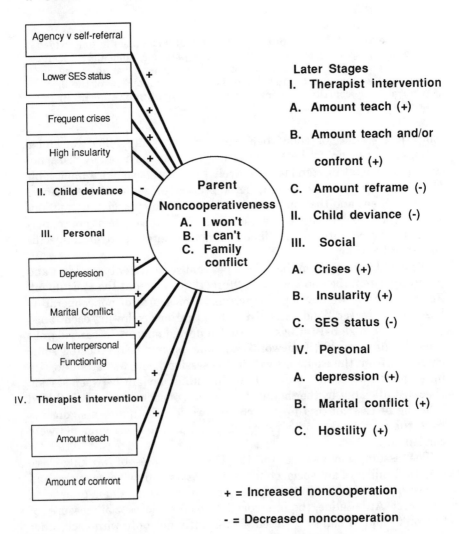

FIG. 5. Multiple determinants for parent noncooperation by stages.

weeks when the mother was noncooperative in the session, was she also noncooperative between sessions? The across-session data were available for only a small number of mother-therapist dyads. The median covariations between micro- and macrosocial measures of mother noncooperation were in the .4 to .5 range (that is, on days that the parent spent considerable time saying "I won't," "I can't," or both, the therapists' and observers' ratings suggested that the parents also had not been keeping up their homework assignment). Our hypothesis would be that a confirmatory factor analysis of the across-subject micro- and macrosocial measures will identify a single dimension.

The second aspect of parental noncooperation became apparent in our supervision meetings when we staffed difficult cases. The study by Chamberlain et al. (8) showed that roughly three-fourths of all cases were noncooperative at some point in treatment. Given that our sample consisted of working-class families with at least one-third of them being father-absent homes, it is not surprising to find that many of them were multiple-problem families. Many were also relatively isolated from the community; they fit the definition of the insular family described by Wahler and his colleagues (39). A large proportion of the cases were confronted daily with ill health, poor housing, and subsistence-level incomes.

People are probably generally noncooperative in the face of efforts to change their behavior, at least in our culture. For example, investigators in behavioral medicine found that, on the average, 44% of medical patients do not fully comply with medical regimens prescribed by their physicians (43). As shown in some of these studies, the noncooperation extends even to those cases in which the prescriptions were designed to treat life-threatening medical problems. Working-class parents' noncooperation during parent training is likely the outcome of this cultural factor, plus the entire array of factors outlined in Figure 5.

For our sample, we perceive the early level of parent noncooperation in treatment to be determined by four clusters of variables, each of which is listed in Figure 5: (a) social variables, (b), child deviance, (c) personal variables, and (d) therapist intervention. It is our suspicion that, given a sample of less-disturbed oppositional children from middle-class families, the network of variables may look somewhat different. We believe that measures of noncooperation must be tailored for different kinds of sample characteristics such as referral problems, levels of socioeconomic status, crises, and insularity.

It is assumed that the determinants for noncooperation vary somewhat as a function of phase of treatment.[8] In the early stages, the social, child,

---

8. *Editor's Note:* This work partially exemplifies the orientation presented in Chapter 13 by Alexander, who demarcates the phases of intervention in greater detail.

and personal variables are thought to play primary roles, whereas the therapist variable plays a secondary one. In later stages, the structure shifts so that the therapist and child-deviance variables are primary, with social and personal variables having a secondary influence. As shown in Figure 5, agency-referral versus self-referral, lower socioeconomic status, high levels of crises, and high insularity all contribute to higher levels of initial noncooperation. The study by Chamberlain et al. (8) provides support for the role played by agency referral. The studies by Wahler et al. (39) provide support for the value of daily reports of contacts with family, friends, and agency staff, as well as for the quality of the communication. These studies showed that highly insular families made fewer gains in parent training and were most likely to return to deviant status at follow-up. In keeping with these findings, we assume that the Wahler insularity variables would account for significant variance in the criteria during early and late stages of treatment.

METHODS

Subjects

At the time of this writing, the 3-year study has been operating for 2 years. Seventy-three percent of the sample has thus far been obtained. The subjects for the study were obtained by screening and recruiting a sample of 70 families of extremely antisocial, preadolescent children referred for treatment. Twenty of these families were assigned to an eclectic family-therapy-oriented community service agency, and the remaining 50 to OSLC.

Subjects and Screening

The sample thus far studied consists of families with at least one child (37 boys and 14 girls) aged 6 to 13 years (mean = 9.5 years) who is judged to be socially aggressive and/or conduct-disordered. The average family income is between $10,000 and $14,000 (ranging from less than $4,999 to $30,000). Mothers and fathers were given the Schedule for Affective Disorders interview (Lifetime version) to determine if they qualified for a current or past psychiatric diagnosis. Of the 49 mothers interviewed, 35 (71%) had a current diagnosis, 44 (89%) had a past diagnosis, and 34 (69%) met the criteria for both past and current diagnoses. Of 25 fathers interviewed, 11 (44%) had a current diagnosis, 19 (76%) met criteria for having a past diagnosis, and 10 (40%) met criteria for both past and current diagnoses. Some form of depression (major, minor, intermittent, or agitated) was the diagnosis for 50% of the cases who qualified for a diagnosis.

Referrals came from pediatricians, school personnel, and parents themselves. Because we anticipated a 26% dropout rate prior to treatment termination, based on our past work and that of other investigators, we initially planned to recruit a sample of 95 families; but, at this point, the actual dropout rate has been much smaller (7%) than expected.

During the parents' initial telephone contact with the clinic, the standard procedure is to collect basic referral and demographic information. Families not appropriate for treatment at OSLC are referred elsewhere. Parents who have youngsters in the stipulated age range, who have a telephone, and who are requesting help because of child antisocial behavior, are given a brief verbal description of the proposed study.

Following that, if they are interested in participation, an appointment is set up for them to come in for a more detailed explanation of study procedures and data collection, as well as completion of consent forms and the first phase of the screening process to determine eligibility, the Child Behavior Checklist (1, 2). All children rated with a t-score of 70 or above on the aggression, hyperactivity, immaturity, and delinquency scales are eligible for Phase 2 of the screening. Phase 2 involves three in-home observations. Using the Family Process Code (10), experienced coders record interactions between a focal subject and all other family members. This coding system is based on earlier work at OSLC with the Family Interaction Coding System (35), which has been used to study clinical outcome (see 20, 42) and to develop theoretical models of social aggression (see 22).

Child scores for the 16 aversive behavior categories on the Family Process Code (FPC) are combined to form a composite labeled *Total Aversive Behavior* (TAB) for which there exist age-equivalent norms. Although it may have been desirable to set a higher cutting score to insure a higher-risk sample, the criterion of only .5 SD above the general population mean was selected to broaden the range of problems studied and to minimize confounding regression effects in the treatment analyses.

Ineligible families are so informed and given an opportunity for OSLC nonstudy treatment if still desired, or for referral elsewhere. Eligible families who remain interested in participation are scheduled for the intake interviews. Prior to the intake, interview families are assigned either to treatment at OSLC or at Looking Glass (a community agency described later in this section). In order to distribute the cases assigned to the two groups evenly, the first 8 cases were alternately assigned to OSLC and to Looking Glass. Next, every fourth case meeting the screening criteria was assigned to Looking Glass for treatment. Given the uneven distribution of cases planned in the final sample (OSLC 50, Looking Glass 20), this system allowed for regulation of the flow of cases and minimized the possibility of historical variables and shifts in community referral patterns differentially affecting the samples.

Intake Interview

The final sample of eligible subjects participate in a 3-hour parent intake interview session and a 2-hour child intake interview. These are scheduled on the same day. Parents are given several questionnaires to fill out in the laboratory on their child's behavior, their sources and level of stress, family activities, insularity, parenting beliefs, and family history. The MMPI is to be filled out at home and returned at the time of the first treatment session. The parents and children are asked in detail about the problems that brought them to treatment. Next, the parents are interviewed using a structured interview assessing their current family-management practices. Their past and current psychological functioning is evlauated using the Schedule for Affective Disorders and Schizophrenia (SADS-L). Children are interviewed using a structured interview that assesses their relationships with their parents, peers, teachers, and significant others. Children who are able to read are given questionnaires to complete; nonreaders have questionnaires read to them.

During the next week, baseline telephone interviews are conducted with 5 children and 5 parents. The child call lasts approximately 8 minutes and obtains information regarding family organization, parental monitoring, and delinquent, aggressive, and prosocial behavior of the target child. The time span for reporting is the prior 24 hours. The child reports on his or her own behavior as well as that of friends and siblings.

The parent call lasts approximately 10 minutes once each week, during which all subscales are obtained, and 5 minutes on each of the subsequent calls. During the 10-minute call, the parent is asked if any one of a list of deviant child behaviors occurred. Next, given the occurrence of any of the problem behaviors, the parent is asked what she or he did about the behavior and what the outcome was. The parent is also asked to describe a discipline event from the preceding 24 hours and to rate the intensity of his or her anger response and perception of the severity of the punishment.

Treatment

The first treatment session is scheduled during the following week. Families are not charged for treatment. Their participation in the screening process, the intake interviews, and the baseline telephone calls are "exchanged" for free treatment. Families are paid for subsequent assessment probes at treatment termination and at 6-month follow-up.

OSLC Treatment (n = 50)

Therapists conducting this treatment have all been thoroughly trained in the approach and have practiced it for at least one year (range = 1 to 10 years). Although the OSLC therapists are trained in social-learning treatment, which emphasizes the role of family-management variables, they have not been aware of how specific hypotheses concerning client or therapist in-session behaviors are being used in the study.

Case assignments are made nonsystematically, based on current therapist caseloads. The treatment approach is derived from a social-learning perspective of families (30, 33). This perspective indicates that behavior patterns develop from learning experiences within the family system. Problem behaviors are the result of previous and ongoing social/environmental contingencies that constantly shape specific reactions. Treatment is focused on training the parents and other family members to alter their nonfunctional styles of interaction. Family-management skills are gradually taught to parents. The execution of this treatment program is complex and requires a careful blend of appropriate behavior-change strategies and therapeutic skills.

The treatment program with families of antisocial children can be outlined as follows. During the initial interview, the clinician asks the family to describe the referral problems and provides clients with information about the social-learning approach. Clients are then helped to pinpoint two problem behaviors and their prosocial opposites. Parents are assigned the task of keeping track of these behaviors at home during the coming week.

The therapist helps parents to learn how to teach their children prosocial skills, beginning with prizes or privileges, later replacing these with social reinforcements for desirable behaviors. Next, parents learn how to use effective discipline techniques for problem-child behaviors. They are taught to apply procedures consistently, such as using time out and withdrawal of privileges, to set house rules and provide appropriate contingencies when these rules are broken, and to monitor the behavior and whereabouts of their youngsters.

As treatment progresses, parents learn to elaborate the incentive and discipline techniques until all the referral problems are included. Problem-solving strategies are practiced in the session each week, with parents taking increasingly active roles in the process. At treatment termination, the families are designing and negotiating their own program with no help from the therapist.

In the past work with families of antisocial youngsters between the ages of 3 and 12 years, the average amount of therapist time required was 17 hours, with a range of 4 to 48 weeks (27). Older children require slightly more time. Because the group to be treated at OSLC are somewhat older, we project that treatment will require between 12 and 20 weeks. Approximately 30% of session time is devoted to treatment of ancillary family problems that influence parent-child relationships, although they may not be directly related to the referral problems.

Treatment termination occurs when the subject family and therapist agree that referral problems have been ameliorated or if the family indicates a desire to stop. Families who complete less than six sessions are considered treatment dropouts, and their data are analyzed separately from completers (those with six or more treatment sessions). Therapists participate in ongoing case supervision for one hour per week.

Comparison Treatment (n = 20)

The Looking Glass counseling program agreed to provide family therapy services for 20 families for 2½ years. This agency has been in operation in Eugene, Oregon, for the past 10 years. Its orientation is an eclectic combination of structural family therapy and Adlerian treatment. Looking Glass regularly offers treatment to families with antisocial children. They are respected in the community and have a well-qualified staff. Therapists are masters-level practitioners with an average of 5 years paid experience. Therapists receive ongoing case supervision one hour a week.

Measures

Therapy Process Coding System

For cases in both groups, the videotapes of sessions 1 and 2, the chronological middle-two sessions, and the last 25% of the sessions are coded using the Therapy Process Coding System (7). The present system is a revision and combination of two codes (the Client Noncooperation Code and the Therapist Behavior Code) that were used in previous studies (8, 31). Nine categories describe the clients' verbalizations: 1) Confront/Challenge, 2) Hopeless/Blame, 3) Defend self/other, 4) Own agenda, 5) Answer for, 6) Not answering, 7) Disqualify previous statement, 8) Interfamily conflict, and 9) Nonresistant. Another eight describe the therapists' verbalizations: 1) Support, 2) Teach, 3) Question, 4) Structure, 5) Disagree, 6) Interpret/Reframe, 7) Talk, and 8) Facili-

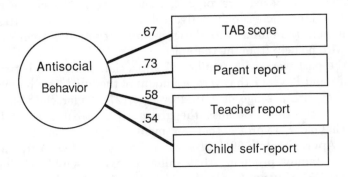

FIG. 6. The Antisocial Behavior construct.

tate. Client and therapist affect and interactional styles are also rated for each response. At the end of each session, coders rate various aspects of the therapy on an impressions form. Coders require an average of 30 hours for training along with biweekly retraining meetings to reach and maintain a minimum of 75% agreement. Of 285 sessions coded to date, 70 have been coded by a second observer to assess interobserver reliability. The average entry-by-entry agreement is 78.5% (range = 75% to 96%), and the average kappa is 72.3% (range = 67% to 88%). A review of the psychometric properties of this coding system and a discussion of its application are presented in Chamberlain and Ray (9).

Construct Development

Constructs used in this study are replications of those built for longitudinal study of antisocial behavior in boys (32). There are four steps in building constructs for the general model. First, it is necessary to list each of the measures thought to define the construct. Second, using data from the sample, each group of items, or scale, is analyzed to determine whether it is internally consistent. In this stage, items that correlate less than .20 with the corrected total score are dropped from the scale. Scales with an alpha value above .60 are retained for the next stage. The third step involves a principal components factor analysis to determine whether the scale loads significantly on the factor. Those scales with factor loadings less than .30 are dropped. Finally, each scale that survives the rigors of a confirmatory factor analysis becomes an indicator for that construct. Indicators for these constructs were analyzed with data from only 35 to 40 cases. Some items eliminated in these early analyses may or may not be included when the total sample data are available. Brief descriptions of the Antisocial Behavior, Inept Discipline, Problem Solving, and Inept Monitoring constructs follow.

Antisocial Behavior

This construct in the longitudinal study is defined by four indicators that reflect the reports of four agents: parents, teachers, peers, and the child. Peer report data were not available for the clinical sample. The Total Aversive Behavior (TAB) score was added as an indicator for this construct. The parent indicator was made up of items from the Parent version of the Child Behavior checklist (2), the Parent Overt-Covert Antisocial questionnaire, and the Parent Daily Report (PDR) that was collected from daily telephone interviews. Items from these measures were selected to form a composite score indicating child overt and covert antisocial behaviors. The teacher indicator was made up of 16 items from the Teacher version of the Child Behavior checklist (11), which measures both covert and overt antisocial behavior. Child self-report is a composite score of 18 items from the Child Interview. The TAB score is described below. Factor loadings from a confirmatory factor analysis are indicated in Figure 6.

Inept Discipline

The home observations form a database for deriving three of the indicators defining this construct: parental nattering, parental explosive punishment, and observers' global impressions concerning the consistency of parental discipline. Items from the Parent Interview formed a fourth indicator. Nattering and explosive discipline are probability scores calculated directly from observation data. Nattering is the probability that the parent will direct low-intensity, negative verbal or nonverbal behaviors toward the target child (scowling, scolding, disapproval). Explosive discipline is the probability that the parent will use more intense, abusive behaviors in dealing with the target child (hitting, humiliating remarks, threats, or yelling). Each of these scores was calculated separately for mothers and fathers; then the mean of the two parents was used for the indicator. The observers' subjective impressions indicator is a composite of 13 items about parental consistency and moderation in discipline. The parent self-report indicator is a composite of 6 items concerning parental discipline practices (for example, following through with punishment, getting angry when punishing the child). Factor loadings from a confirmatory factor analysis are indicated in Figure 7.

Problem Solving

Indicators for the Problem Solving construct reflect the judgment of four agents—parents, child, coders, and observers—across two situations: a laboratory problem-solving task and the home setting. The observer indicator is a composite score of four items of home observers' subjective rating of problem-solving skills in the family. The coder indicator is a composite score of 18 items measuring the coders' subjec-

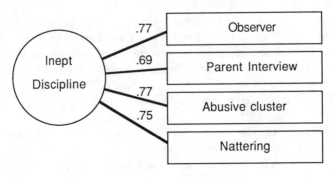

FIG. 7. The Inept Discipline construct.

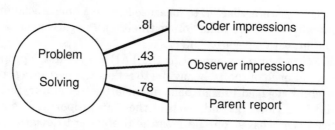

FIG. 8. The Problem Solving construct.

tive judgments of the children's and parents' problem-solving skills from videotaped problem-solving exercises. The family indicator is a composite score of 3 items from the Parent and Child Problem Solving questionnaire, reflecting how each agent thought a particular problem was solved. Factor loadings from a confirmatory factor analysis appear in Figure 8.

Inept Monitoring

The Inept Monitoring construct from the longitudinal study is made up of three indicators: the child's expectation of monitoring rules, parent report of number of hours spent with the child, and interviewers' impressions of how well the child was monitored. One of these indicators, parent report of number of hours spent with the child, did not converge with the other indicators for the clinical sample. We computed two new indicators for this construct: parent report of monitoring from the Parent Structured Interview and child report of parent monitoring practices from the Child Telephone Interview. Factor loadings from a confirmatory factor analysis are shown below in Figure 9.

TAB Score

The Total Aversive Behavior (TAB) score is computed from the home observation data. From the code categories in the Family Process Code

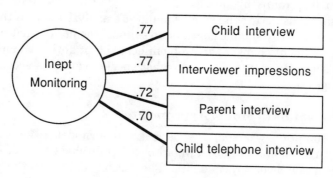

FIG. 9. The Inept Monitoring construct.

(10), 16 behaviors were selected to measure negative microsocial interactions. Generally, these are behaviors with either a negative content or a neutral content with a negative affect.

There are three steps for computing the TAB score. First, a proportion is computed for each of the 16 behaviors to reflect the percentage of time the target child engaged in that behavior relative to the duration of all target-child behaviors. Second, each of these 16 proportions is given a standardized score based on the mean and standard deviation of the corresponding proportion in a sample of 100 fourth-grade boys recruited for a longitudinal study (32). Third, these standard scores are summed and averaged to arrive at the final score.

Because the TAB score is used as a screening and outcome measurement, the same procedures are used to arrive at a TAB score for the longitudinal sample. A cutting score is computed that is .5 SD above the mean of that sample.

RESULTS

Did Behavior Change?

The reported TAB scores can be thought of as reflecting how deviant a child is on these 16 behaviors compared to a normal distribution of children. However, this score is not strictly a z-score with a mean of 0 and a standard deviation of 1. Indeed, the cutting score for boys 10 and over is .217; the standard deviation of this score is not 1, but .434. Although the mean of this distribution is 0, the variance is reduced.

A preliminary set of analyses was conducted on the first portion of the sample to complete treatment in the current study. A series of t-tests showed that cases in the OSLC sample (n = 16) showed significant reductions in the child TAB score from baseline to termination ($p = .03$), whereas comparison group cases (n = 9) showed no change ($p = .69$). The analysis of variance for the 9 OSLC and 4 comparison group cases that have completed 6-month follow-up revealed a near significant interaction term for groups by phases ($F = 3.27$ [2, 10], $p = .08$). This is encouraging considering the small sample size analyzed. Given that the results for the entire sample continue to support the notion that parent-training treatment changes the problem behavior of antisocial children, the next set of questions relates to what specific variables account for that change.

Is the Parent Skill Model Appropriate?

The assumption was that the basic training model, tested against various at-risk samples of boys, would be generalizable enough to apply to a clinical sample of boys and girls. The baseline data from the first 40 families entering treatment were used to examine this issue. The correlational data are summarized in Figure 10. On the left side of the Figure, the factor loadings define the loading of each indicator on the latent constructs. Because of the small sample size at this stage of the study, no effort was made to carry out a structural equation analysis. It can be seen that for this older sample, both Inept Discipline and Inept Monitoring correlate significantly with Antisocial Behavior. Regressing Antisocial Behavior against the three family-management variables provided a value of .581 (p = .03). The Monitoring construct made the largest (and only significant) contribution; Problem Solving variables contributed very little.

The next question concerned the fit of the family-management skills to the TAB score used to evaluate treatment outcome. As shown in Figure

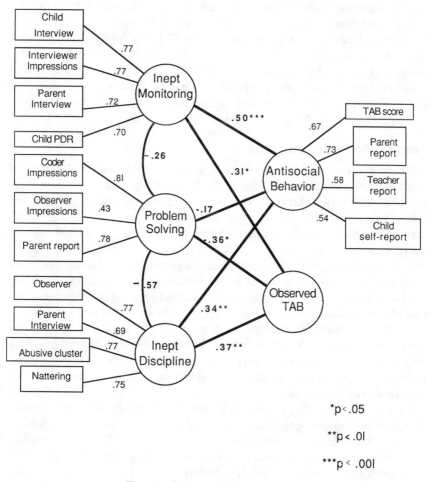

*p<.05

**p<.0l

***p< .00l

FIG. 10. Process during baseline.

10, all three family-management scores covaried significantly with the termination TAB score. Regressing the three parent-skill scores against the TAB score provided a multiple correlation of .572 ($p = .04$). Inept Monitoring made the only significant contribution.

The family-management model provides an appropriate fit to both criterion variables. The amount of variance accounted for was roughly equivalent to what had previously been obtained for at-risk samples. These preliminary findings suggest that it would be appropriate to employ the model as a definition for Level 2.

How Does Parent Struggle Relate to Parent and Child Change?

As discussed earlier, the coding system used to describe client within-session struggle specifies three clusters of client behaviors ("I can't," I won't," and family conflict). One category (Challenge/Confront) defines "I won't." Four categories define "I can't" (Hopeless/Blame, Defend self/other, Own agenda, and Disqualify), and two categories define family conflict (Interfamily Conflict and Answer for). In order to examine whether factors such as daily stress, marital discord, and parental depression relate to the parents' within-session struggle, these factors will be correlated in future analyses.

Covariation among Levels

There are two paths that relate to changes in the rates of observed child behavior. As shown in Figure 11, one path works against the other. It is the task of the therapist to keep both of these in balance. On the one hand, forces outside the therapy session such as parental stressors, marital conflict, and depression appear to increase the within-session conflict among family members. High rates of such conflict are significantly correlated with high antisocial construct scores during both the early and late periods in therapy. For instance, during the last quarter, the correlation between within-session conflict (among family members) and the Antisocial Behavior construct was .37 (n.s.) for fathers and .46 ($p = .01$) for mothers. Evidently, therapy is best served if part of the focus is on reducing the stressors and the accompanying depression. The therapist may also have to design interventions effective in reducing the marital disagreement that may lie behind the observed high rates of conflict during the session.

As noted earlier, the extent to which the therapist actively teaches family-management practices corresponds to an increasing risk of observed rates of parent struggle—"I won't," "I can't," family conflict (31). Similarly, efforts to confront parents for failures to carry out homework assignments produced a similar increase. In the current study, it has been possible to refine the analyses and determine that of these

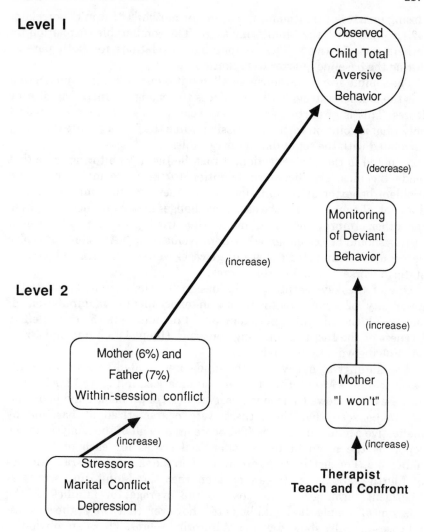

FIG. 11. Covariation among levels.

struggle reactions, it is the parents' "I won't" reaction that seems to play
a key role. To the extent that they disagree, challenge, and confront the
therapist, they are engaged in the work of parent-training therapy and
are actively involved in the change process. The "I won't" reaction is
thought to accompany changes in monitoring practices. During the

closing quarter of treatment, the score for mother's "I won't" correlates .42 ($p = .05$) with the Monitoring score. The comparable correlation for fathers was .55 (n.s.). The comparable correlations for both parents during the baseline quarter were nonsignificant.

The sample size for fathers is small, but it is our growing suspicion that it is the mother's struggle that produces the change in Inept Monitoring scores. This is of particular interest because her score seems to reflect only what is going on within the session, while the father's score is heavily correlated with the set of disrupter variables.

As noted in the earlier section, it was the Inept Monitoring score that made the most significant contribution to the score measuring child problem behavior at termination of treatment. Significant covariation does not, of course, prove the case that changes in one produce changes in the other. Improvements in monitoring from pre- to posttreatment testing should be accompanied by improvements in TAB scores. It is also necessary to demonstrate that failure cases were characterized by either static or worsening monitoring scores.

One of the key features in the design for the current study is the possibility of using treatment as an experimental manipulation. If successful, the clinical experiment would demonstrate the causal effectiveness of the Inept Monitoring construct (Inept Discipline and Problem Solving will also be analyzed).

The findings from seven of the nine cases treated thus far at OSLC (with complete Monitoring data) are summarized in Figure 12. All seven of these cases showed a drop in observed rates of problem-child behavior. It can be seen that these cases were characterized at baseline by ineffective Monitoring scores. The score used in all of the analyses in the report is the mean of the standardized scores for each of the four indicators. The distributions are normed on the sample of at-risk families of fourth-grade boys. It can be seen that the Monitoring scores at treatment termination are close to the average for families in the nonclinical sample. It should be noted, however, that two of the successful cases actually showed worse Monitoring scores. There are obviously some family-management skills other than just change in monitoring that are related to successful outcome. For example, changes in discipline or problem solving may be more important for some families than changes in monitoring. These possibilities will be examined in the coming year.

The crucial test from the experimental manipulation lies in the demonstration that the Monitoring scores did not change for the failure cases. The data showed that in both instances there were only slight shifts in Monitoring scores from baseline for OSLC; one was slightly better and one slightly worse. The two failure cases from the comparison group both showed moderate worsening in Monitoring scores. The pre-

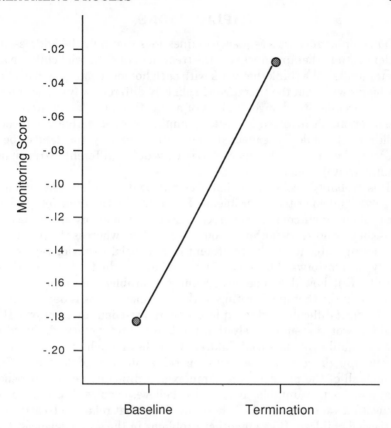

FIG. 12. Covariation of changes in monitoring scores to changes in TAB.

and posttreatment means for monitoring for the four failure cases were .123 and .108 respectively. The trend is for no change or slightly worse.

The preliminary findings are introduced for illustrative purposes. Available findings are supportive of the hypothesized covariation among the three levels. At the close of the study, these complex relationships will be reexamined using structural equation modeling as an analytic format. It is predicted that the path from treatment to family-management variables measured at t_2 and t_3 will be significant; this implies that involvement or noninvolvement in parent-training treatment makes a significant contribution to understanding changes in family-management and problem-child behaviors. The analysis of variance design will also be used to demonstrate that changes in mean level for family-management variables were associated with changes in mean level for child behaviors.

IMPLICATIONS

This report reviews a sequence of questions that must be addressed in order to study therapy process in the treatment of antisocial children and their families. We think that work with each homogeneous group of client problems will train the therapists in slightly different ways. The components necessary to change families of anorectics must be different from the components involved in treating families of hyperactive or antisocial children. It would be expected, then, that one day the landscape of therapy theories will be characterized by quite different performance (multivariate) models.

It is probably also obvious that each narrow-focus treatment will have to solve its own criterion problems. For example, the criterion problem for evaluating outcome for anorectics seems straightforward, at least to those of us who know nothing about the problem, whereas the problem of measuring outcome in the treatment of antisocial behavior seems relatively straightforward to those of us who have studied it for more than a decade. But how does one get around the problem of employing self-report and the therapist's ratings if the treatment focus is depression?

The most difficult level to explore is therapist-client interactions. Here again, it would seem unlikely that the two coding systems designed for chaotic families of antisocial children would be of much use when applied to therapy process with a focus on schizophrenic adolescents. Even though all of the problems are complex and difficult, we do not believe they are insurmountable. Nor do we believe, even within our narrow focus, that we have solved all those problems that relate to treatment of antisocial children. Like any other problems in the social sciences, their eventual solution requires a marriage of clinical experience to measurement theory and application. The present report describes such a marriage, "shaky" but "enduring."

REFERENCES

1. Achenbach, T.M. *Child behavior checklist*. Bethesda MD: National Institute of Mental Health, 1979.
2. _____, & Edelbrock, C.S. The child behavior profile: Boys aged 12 to 16 and girls aged 6 to 11 and 12 to 16. *Journal of Consulting and Clinical Psychology 41:* 223–233, 1979.
3. Atkeson, B.M., & Forehand, R. Parent behavior training for problem children: An examination of studies using multiple outcome measures. *Journal of Abnormal Child Psychology 6:* 449–460, 1978.
4. Bentler, P.M. Multivariate analysis of latent variables: Causal modeling. *Annual Review of Psychology 31:* 419-455, 1980.
5. Bernal, M.E., Klinnert, M.D., & Schultz, L.A. Outcome evaluations of behavior parent training and client-centered parent counseling for children with conduct problems. *Journal of Applied Behavior Analysis 13:* 677–691, 1980.
6. Campbell, D.T., & Fiske, D.W. Convergent and discriminant validation by

the multitrait-multimethod matrix. *Psychological Bulletin 56:* 81–105, 1959.

7. Chamberlain, P., Davis, J.P., Forgatch, M.S., Frey, J., Patterson, G.R., Ray, J., Rothschild, A., & Trombley, J. The therapy process code: A multidimensional system for observing therapist and client interactions. *OSLC technical report* (No. 1Rx), 1985. (Available from OSLC, 207 East 5th, Suite 202, Eugene OR 97401.)

8. _____, Patterson, G.R., Reid, J.B., Kavanagh, K., & Forgatch, M.S. Observation of client resistance. *Behavior Therapy 15:* 144–155, 1984.

9. _____, & Ray, J. The therapy process coding system: Psychometric characteristics and applications, submitted for publication.

10. Dishion, T.J., Gardner, K., Patterson, G.R., Reid, J.B., Spyrou, S., & Thibodeaux, S. The family process code: A multidimensional system for observing family interactions. *OSLC technical report,* 1983. (Available from OSLC, 207 East 5th, Suite 202, Eugene OR 97401.)

11. Edelbrock, C., & Achenbach, T.M. The teacher version of the child behavior profile: 1. Boys aged 6–11, 1983. (Unpublished manuscript available from C. Edelbrock, Ph.D., Western Psychiatric Institute and Clinic, 3811 O'Hara, Pittsburgh PA 15213.)

12. Fiske, D.W. Methodological issues in research on the psychotherapist. In A.S. Gurman & A.M. Razin (eds.), *Effective psychotherapy: A handbook of research.* New York: Pergamon Press, 1977.

13. Fleischman, M.J. A replication of Patterson's "Intervention for boys with conduct problems." *Journal of Consulting and Clinical Psychology 49:* 324–351, 1981.

14. _____, & Szykula, S. A community setting replication of a social learning treatment for aggressive children. *Behavior Therapy 12:* 15, 1981.

15. Griest, D.W., Wells, K., & Forehand, R. An examination of predictors of maternal perceptions of maladjustment in clinic-referred children. *Journal of Abnormal Psychology 88:* 277–281, 1979.

16. Johnson, S.M., & Christensen, A. Multiple criteria follow-up of behavior modification with families. *Journal of Abnormal Child Psychology 3:* 135–154, 1975.

17. _____, & Lobitz, G.K. Parental manipulations of child behavior in home observations. *Journal of Appplied Behavior Analysis 7:* 23–31, 1974.

18. Kent, R.N., O'Leary, K.D., Diament, C., & Dietz, A. Expectation biases in observational evaluation of therapeutic change. *Journal of Consulting and Clinical Psychology 42:* 774–780, 1974.

19. Marlowe, H., Reid, J.B., Patterson, G.R., & Weinrott, M.R. Treating adolescent multiple offenders: A comparison and follow-up of parent training for families of chronic delinquents, submitted for publication. (Available from first author, OSLC, 207 East 5th, Suite 202, Eugene OR 97401.)

20. Patterson, G.R. Retraining of aggressive boys by their parents: Review of recent literature and follow-up evaluations. *Canadian Psychiatric Association Journal 19:* 142–161, 1974.

21. _____. Mothers: The unacknowledged victims. *Monographs of the Society for Research in Child Development 45* (No. 186), 1980.

22. _____. *A social learning approach: 3. Coercive family process.* Eugene OR: Castalia Publishing Co., 1982.

23. _____. Understanding and prediction of delinquent behavior. NIMH Grant No. MH37940, 1982.

24. _____. Beyond technology: The next stage in developing an empirical base

for parent training. In L. L'Abate (ed.), *The handbook of family psychology and therapy.* Homewood IL: Dorsey Press, 1985.

25. _____. Performance models for antisocial boys. *American Psychologist 41:* 432–445, 1986.

26. _____, & Capaldi, D. A comparison of models for boys' depressed mood. In J.E. Rolf, A. Masten, D. Cicchetti, K. Nuechterlein, & S. Weintraub (eds.), *Risk and protective factors in the development of psychopathology.* Boston: Syndicate of the Press, University of Cambridge, in press.

27. _____,Chamberlain, P., & Reid, J.B. A comparative evaluation of parent training procedures. *Behavior Therapy 13:* 638–650, 1982.

28. _____, & Dishion, T.J. Contributions of families and peers to delinquency. *Criminology 23:* 63–79, 1985.

29. _____, & Fleischman, M.J. Maintenance of treatment effects: Some considerations concerning family systems and follow-up data. *Behavior Therapy 10:* 168–195, 1979.

30. _____, & Forgatch, M.S. *Family learning series* (five cassettes). Champaign IL: Research Press, 1975.

31. _____, & Forgatch, M.S. Therapist behavior as a determinant for client noncompliance: A paradox for the behavior modifier. *Journal of Consulting and Clinical Psychology 53:* 846–851, 1985.

32. _____, Reid, J.B., & Dishion, T.J. *A social learning approach: 4. Antisocial boys.* Eugene OR: Castalia Publishing Co., in press.

33. _____, Reid, J.B., Jones, R.R., & Conger, R. *A social learning approach to family intervention: 1. Parent training.* Eugene OR: Castalia Publishing Co., 1975.

34. Peed, S., Roberts, M., & Forehand, R. Evaluation of the effectiveness of a standardized parent training program in altering the interaction between mothers and their noncompliant children. *Behavior Modification 1:* 323–350, 1977.

35. Reid, J.B. (ed.). *A social learning approach to family intervention: 2. Observation in home settings.* Eugene OR: Castalia Publishing Co., 1978.

36. _____, Baldwin, D.V., Patterson, G.R., & Dishion, T.J. Some problems relating to the assessment of childhood disorders: A role for observational data. In M. Rutter, A.H. Tuma, & I. Lann (eds.), *Assessment and diagnosis in child and adolescent psychopathology.* New York: Guilford Press, in press.

37. Skindrud, K.D. An evaluation of observer bias in experimental field studies of social intercourse. Unpublished doctoral dissertation, University of Oregon, Eugene OR, 1972.

38. _____. Field evaluation of observer bias under overt and covert monitoring. In L. Hamerlynck, L. Handy, & E. Mash (eds.), *Behavior change: Methodology, concepts, and practice.* Champaign IL: Research Press, 1973.

39. Wahler, R.G., Leske, G., & Rogers, E.S. The insular family: A deviance support system for oppositional children. In L.A. Hamerlynck (ed.), *Behavioral system for the developmentally disabled: 1. School and family environments.* New York: Brunner/Mazel, 1978.

40. Walker, H.M., Shinn, M.R., O'Neill, R.E., & Ramsey, E. A longitudinal assessment of the development of antisocial behavior in boys: Rationale, methodology, and first year results. *Remedial and Special Education 8* (4): 7–16, 1987.

41. Walter, H.I., & Gilmore, S.K. Placebo versus social learning effects in parent

training procedures designed to alter the behavior of aggressive boys. *Behavior Research and Therapy 4:* 361–377, 1973.

42. Weinrott, M., Bauske, B., & Patterson, G.R. Systematic replication of a social learning approach to parent training. In S.L. Bates, P.O. Sjoden, & W.S. Dockens, III (eds.), *Trends in behavior therapy.* New York: Academic Press, 1979.

43. Wills, T. The study of helping relationships. In T. Wills (ed.), *Basic processes in helping relationships.* New York: Academic Press, 1982.

44. Wiltz, N.A., & Patterson, G.R. An evaluation of parent training procedures designed to alter inappropriate aggressive behavior in boys. *Behavior Therapy 5:* 215–221, 1974.

PART V

DATA ANALYSIS

15

TOWARD A COHERENT METHODOLOGY FOR THE STUDY OF FAMILY THERAPY

FREDERICK STEIER

Old Dominion University
Norfolk, Virginia

I
N THIS CHAPTER I shall address several concerns regarding the methodology and paradigmatic basis of family therapy research. I believe that we are getting considerably better at using research methods for examining specific questions with statistically appropriate research designs. However, we must realize that we can become still better at investigating family structure and how change in family structure co-occurs with certain interventions. In addition, we must become more concerned with the question of evaluation of an entire research program, including aspects of the research context. That is, the entire research situation, together with its natural feedback loops, must be considered as part of what is being evaluated.

STRUCTURE AND CHANGE

An underlying question in family therapy research is: What is the family structure that is changing with an intervention? Embedded within this question is the issue of what characteristics of the family are relevant to the research investigation. These characteristics can be seen as properties of the family that covary with the intervention process, or as concomitant variables whose relationship to change must be controlled for. I think it is generally agreed that family covariates should be included in an assessment of family therapy efficacy. What seems not generally agreed upon is the manner in which family covariates should be employed, as well as what dimensions of family structure should be used as covariates. Here is where our theories of family process and family therapy need to reveal themselves in the research design.

An underlying notion here is that the family (or any social system) is always in flux or process. This view generates a problem that is often manifested in the following question: If a system is constantly changing, what is the system that is changing? Or, more importantly, how does one study this changing "system"? A distinction made by Maturana (5), the biologist and cybernetician, is particularly relevant. He distinguishes between the *organization* of a system, which is the set of *invariant* relations by which it constitutes itself as a system, and the *structure* of the system, which is the *varying* set of relationships realized in that system. The reader should be aware that throughout this chapter the term "structure" will be used in Maturana's relational sense.

In a three-person family, for example, mother, father, and child, the organization may be thought of as the relations that define it as a family, for example, as husband-wife, father-child, and mother-child. For this family to remain as this particular family, its organization must not change. However, the particular relationships within this family system are continuously evolving—for example, the child may become less enmeshed with mother, or become more independent with respect to both parents. It is this evolving, structuring process that we seek to examine in family therapy research.

COVARIATES IN FAMILY THERAPY RESEARCH

It must be understood that each family at the time of intake to therapy or therapy research carries with it its own structure, which may to a certain extent be uniquely associated with that family. Most good comparative or control-group research studies have realized this to some degree by including analyses of covariance to control for differences between groups on certain structural variables (such as family socioeconomic status, ethnicity, race, and so on) that may be related to the outcome. That, however, is not enough. The difficulty is that most demographic characteristics traditionally employed as covariates are those that are consistent with a notion of a family defined from *outside* that family. Although these traditional covariates are useful for some investigations, their exclusive use in the context of family therapy research is not consistent with the theoretical bases that provide the power of family therapy. I refer here to the notion of a family as a system defined by its transactions—in Dewey and Bentley's (2) sense—and by its own construction of reality—in von Foerster's (3) or Reiss's (7) sense. These transactional covariates may well be the context in which therapeutic change occurs.[1]

In order to appreciate fully the possible efficacy of family therapy as an intervention aimed at the level of a transactional social system, we must think of, as relevant family characteristics, those family processes that are essential to the therapy itself. Because many family interventions are at the level of the *communication process* (for that is what underlines family structure), various dimensions of communication ought to be

---

1. *Editor's Note*: The project example described by Patterson and Chamberlain in Chapter 14 illustrates how microsocial measures of family transactions can be integrated with macrosocial covariates such as SES status.

considered as essential covariates. For example, dimensions of family rigidity and adaptability of communication, which are certainly relevant to an intervention, may be fruitfully examined as covariates. (Do the treatment groups differ in dimensions of rigidity? Do these dimensions relate to outcome?) "Communication" variables should be examined through direct observation in accord with how family therapists work. This is not to dismiss the possible value of self-report measures of family communication. It is merely to emphasize a needed coherence between how researchers observe family structure and how therapists make those observations in the practice of an intervention.

Especially for the more traditional covariates, two components may be of use: (a) the value for that covariate and (b) the importance of that covariate as a context for change in a given family—a measure not often used to date. For example, suppose that we are interested in using ethnicity as a covariate and have coded ethnicity as a series of "dummy" variables. One of these may be a yes or no question as to whether the family is German. However, this approach loses the richness of variety present within an ethnic group in that it assumes that all families answering yes are equally "Germanic." I am not using the term "equally" in the sense of "percentage of German blood," but in the sense that family researchers must be concerned, for example, with the extent to which transactions and constructions that characterize that family may be considered as typically "Germanic," and the extent to which this "Germanness" is a useful descriptor of that family. A reliable coding scheme would have to be developed in order to construct a "weighting" method that would assess the degree of this variable's importance. Todd and Bleyer (1) have already developed such a weighting technique for global family interaction variables. This procedure assesses, with statistical reliability, the extent to which any dimension represents an area of "importance for change" in a given family structure.

It must be further noted that some covariates, as properties of family structure, are not constants but will vary over time. This lack of invariance must be understood in order to evaluate "treatment" effects more fully. Other covariates are constant (for example, race, ethnicity) for a given family; still others vary in some constant fashion (for example, age); still other covariates may change in interaction with the intervention itself. Thus, in order to evaluate properly the contribution of a covariate, we need to obtain both its value pretreatment and its change. Some changes in a family's outcome variables may take place only with change in certain covariates; to look at only the value of a covariate pretreatment may obscure its contribution over time. From a traditional statistical perspective, this last is a problem in that it creates a blurring of distinctions between sources of effects—we must recall that traditional experimental analysis of covariance requires covariates to be unrelated to treatment; however, such effects can be seen not to occur in independent increments.

Family therapy, as a systemic intervention, is not reducible to component effects that can be isolated (for example, increased flexibility, decreased enmeshment). Moreover, treatment variables include the whole situation of the therapy program. Thus, if a family in a control or comparison group shows increased flexibility and also improves on an outcome measure, we may reasonably expect a family in the index group showing similar increased flexibility to indicate even greater improvement. We may think of these co-occurring changes in family structure as necessary but not sufficient conditions for outcome change for a given family.

Additionally, even for covariates that are constant (and more so for those that vary), the importance of that covariate as a context for change for that family may itself change—that is, the parents may still be separated but this "problem" no longer looms large in the picture. This type of change must be also taken into account.

ASSESSING SEQUENCES OF CHANGE

All of the above points suggest a research program that involves a close examination of the data prior to the application of specific techniques, rather than just using those techniques "blindfolded." Change in families is a complex, multivariate phenomenon. I do not, however, believe that understanding the outcome of family therapy will be attained by tossing a large number of structural and contextual variables into a hat and studying what is pulled out. We need an approach that uses a smaller number of dimensions that fit with a specified theory and allow interpretable results. (This is not to rule out serendipitous findings, but more to clarify the sense-making process and consequent interpretations.) It should be clear that the use of covariates merely to control for unwanted "noise" in the data does not fit with a theory of change in family therapy. I am not saying that analysis of covariance should not be used; rather, I argue for the importance of redefining covariates to be coherent with the process being assessed—family change.[2]

More importantly, these points suggest the importance of investigating the sequences of change for families, for both outcome variables and covariates. A reasonable expectation is that family therapy efficacy research should examine not only whether change takes place, but also *under what (changing) contexts certain processes of change are*

---

2. *Editor's Note*: The participants in the research conference and the contributors to this volume strongly agreed upon this important point (see chapters 2, 8, and 12).

revealed. The importance of including contextual change as a factor in the therapy process itself is evident.

What methods are appropriate for assessing change in family therapy research? I submit that for family therapy research the strength of data lies in *sequences* of change for individual families. By sequences of change, I refer to the patterns generated by the key variables over time. For example, for a family with an alcoholic father, we would want to know how measures of the father's alcohol consumption change over time, together with associated relevant changes in family structure. It is true that we are interested in group differences (for example, family therapy versus comparison group), but the "things" on which the groups should be compared are *processes* of change, not merely aggregate scores. This suggests that methods akin to *time series analysis* be used instead of only aggregate forms of data analyses.[3]

In terms of sampling design, I think that the emphasis must be on *longitudinal* forms of design, including several follow-up periods. This now seems to be well accepted in the family therapy research community. In addition, increased emphasis on sequences of change argues that the distinction between therapy process research and outcome research is an artificial one, and that the process of change during treatment must be included in the assessment of "outcome." This is especially so when investigating under what conditions and in what contexts improvement (if any) took place in a group of families who received family therapy.

Forms of data analysis that examine sequences of change must be employed in addition to the more traditional group-change measures. For example, it is important to assess whether long-term improvement is most clearly evident after an initial worsening of a problem; positive processes of change need not be linear or even monotonic. The sequences of change can be understood only by employing techniques that use the family as the unit of analysis, and that allow for an examination of changes in family structure in concert with (or at some lag with) outcomes.

I believe that family therapy researchers have been to some extent imprisoned by what Monge and his colleagues (6) have called "methodological determinism." By this I mean that the reciprocal effect of traditional design methodologies (and statistical methods) and of questions asked by family therapy research have put undue constraints upon both. This has been especially so in investigations of processes of change in the family system. All too often, researchers have restricted themselves only to questions that can be answered by those special techniques already known to them or, even worse, by only techniques available

---

3. *Editor's Note*: See Chapter 16 for further discussion of this approach.

through some canned statistical package (the "if package X doesn't do it, I won't ask it" approach), instead of developing a coherent theory and initial set of hypotheses. A productive research program will involve an examination of the relationship between theories and their consequent hypotheses and, only then, be concerned with which statistical techniques are available through canned packages.

This of course raises the obvious question of what techniques are useful in the study of processes of change in "presenting problems" and family structure that co-occurs with family therapy. Many such techniques are available, with several of them falling under the general category of repeated-measures design models with multiple analysis of variance/covariance. This would include methods such as profile analysis and trend analysis. Time-series models, if enough time periods are studied (which is not often the case in most family therapy research programs), and lagged sequential analysis also are applicable. In addition, discrete parameter models, such as those based on Markov analysis or information theoretic techniques have demonstrated usefulness in addressing the process issue (9), and they can be further developed to address specific questions in family therapy research.

Finally, I believe it is important to emphasize the relevance of good, naturalistic observation in conjunction with any of the above methods, especially if the researcher realizes that the known techniques will not do justice to the richness of certain kinds of data. In fact, it is often through naturalistic observation that new forms of questions are generated that may lead to the development of new statistical techniques.

FEEDBACK LOOPS BUILT INTO RESEARCH DESIGNS

What is the nature of change in an intervention embedded within a research program? What role should various feedback mechanisms play within a coherent research paradigm? Programs in family therapy rsearch have for the most part focused upon only one order or aspect of the data emerging from an intervention, and I suppose that this has been a consequence of an overly strong, positivist tradition of dealing only with measurable results. For example, a study comparing some form of family therapy with nonfamily intervention on a similar sample may be concerned with differences in outcome or with the differences in sequences of change in individual and family systems during and following the intervention. It must be realized that although comparisons of this sort are necessary for an understanding of the effects of treatment, these data are only a part of what family therapy intervention programs are really about, especially if one is concerned with replicability and adaptability of the overall methods and results of the program.

The call here is for the adoption of a paradigm more consistent with a *cybernetic* perspective, which I think underlies the cyclical nature of any research program concerned with social interventions. This perspective would include both an awareness and an investigation of the various feedback loops that are an integral part of any research process involving family therapy. These loops include: (a) the continual evolution and refining of techniques in the family intervention itself, as information gets shared between therapists, supervisors, and researchers as to what is happening with the various families in treatment; (b) periodic monitoring of results, including outcome, from earlier cohort families, with results being made available to therapists, supervisors, and researchers; and (c) the loop connecting the results of the family therapy effectiveness and family structure change data to the theories that motivated the study in the first place. This loop includes an examination of the consequences of the results of treatment.

What I am suggesting for inclusion as "data" from family therapy "experiments" are analyses and explanations of how these various processes proceed as a part of the overall research program; without an understanding of these larger processes, the specific results of the "efficacy of family therapy" within any study will lose much of their meaning. Let me elaborate on these various feedback processes:

1. I think we would agree that family therapy, from any school, is not an invariant or monolithic process. Interventions evolve over the life of a research program (as they do outside any formal research program). Information about the apparent success of various techniques will be shared by all program staff, with the interactions generating a possibility of increased variety in the therapy process. In short, the program staff (therapists, supervisors, and researchers)/family system could be examined as a self-organizing system characterized by its own internal transactions. Study of such a reflexive process is similar to Schön's (8) concept of "Reflection-In-Action," which, as Schön notes, derives from Wittgenstein's (10) idea of "seeing-as." The importance of reflexivity in sense-making of family therapy research is key.

2. Whereas many research programs wait until most or all of the results are in before analysis proceeds (perhaps under some false idea of objectivity, or perhaps because it is easier to "keypunch" the data all at once), the value of analyzing available data at various times during the course of a program and feeding back those results to all concerned cannot be overstated. Realizing that our data do not exist apart from the instruments with which they are measured, we must ask ourselves if the instruments are eliciting the kinds of information we want. Are certain interviewers picking up additional information that may be more useful if obtained more uniformly? How can information from follow-up interviews be used to improve the treatment process? I am not only arguing that information of this kind should be fed back, but also that *the manner in which this process proceeds is itself data* and must be examined to understand fully any "results."

3. An analysis must be made of the consequences of the results. This can refer to several levels. The first, and the one to which I think most good research programs adhere, involves the way in which theories and methods of the research program are to be reinterpreted in light of the final results (suggestions for future research, and so on). The second, which is certainly much less followed, involves an analysis of the consequences of any interventions judged to be "successful." For example, if the stated goals of family therapy are met and persist over time, what then happens to the family that presumably no longer has a "presenting problem" about which to organize itself? And how does that family then interact with larger systems of which they are a part? In fact, one could argue that the process of redefining "success" in light of such consequences is also "data" of the family therapy research endeavor. I believe this is where the notion of the *responsibility* of an intervention research program enters.

In summary, I am arguing that the data of a study include the process by which the data are generated, as well as the consequences of the program results. To perform such analyses requires methods of participant observation. I must stress, however, that only through these "meta-data" can any of the more traditional results be appreciated. We must include, as von Foerster (4) has stated, the study of the observing system—the research/therapy system observing itself in the act of performing an intervention.

REFERENCES

1. Bleyer, R. An assessment of pre-post treatment, family interactional change, and its relationship to post-treatment I.P. outcome. Unpublished doctoral dissertation, Georgia State University, 1984.
2. Dewey, J., & Bentley, A. *Knowing and the known.* Boston: Beacon Press, 1949.
3. Foerster, H. von. On constructing a reality. In F.E. Preiser (ed.), *Environmental design research. Vol. 2.* Stroudberg: Dowden, Hutchinson, and Ross, 1973.
4. _____. *Observing systems.* Seaside CA: Intersystems Publications, 1981.
5. Maturana, H.R. Neurophysiology of cognition. In P.L. Garvin (ed.), *Cognition: A multiple view.* New York: Spartan Books, 1970.
6. Monge, P.R., Farace, R.V., Eisenberg, E.M., Miller, K.I., & White, L.L. The process of studying process in organizational communication. *Journal of Communication 34*: 22–43, 1984.
7. Reiss, D. *The family's construction of reality.* Cambridge: Harvard University Press, 1981.
8. Schön, D. *The reflective practitioner.* New York: Basic Books, 1983.
9. Steier, F., Stanton, M.D., & Todd, T.C. Patterns of turn-taking and alliance formation in family communication. *Journal of Communication 32*: 148–160, 1982.
10. Wittgenstein, L. *Philosophical investigations.* New York: Macmillan, 1953.

16

STATISTICAL METHODS FOR STUDYING FAMILY THERAPY PROCESS

KURT HAHLWEG

Max Planck Institute of Psychiatry
Munich, West Germany

C LINICAL RESEARCH is torn between two equally attractive strategies of collecting evidence: the group experiment that, if properly done, offers statistical evaluation and generalizability, and the case study that offers a more thorough understanding of individual processes and dynamics. Researchers seem to be divided in their adherence to these two strategies, with a slight tendency lately to prefer the single-case study. It is as if group statistics have not quite fulfilled their promises in clinical research, especially in therapy research. The reasons for this are well known: it is often difficult to collect homogeneous, large clinical samples that are statistically efficient; it is often impossible to have genuine control groups that make up for all the nonspecific experimental effects; and randomization is seldom rigorously possible, especially in clinical samples (21).

The single-case study may be a means of minimizing the difficulties in studying patients and families under control and experimental conditions. One way to conduct single-case studies is to experiment with treatment using a withdrawal or reversal design (that is, deliberately including or excluding treatment) in order to study the effect of treatment on the dependent variable. If it is not possible to withdraw or reverse the treatment effect, a multiple baseline design can be used whereby the treatment is applied to several aspects of behavior or to the same behavior in several situations (11). This approach is conceptually sound, but thus far it has not been successfully applied in family therapy research. Efforts to do so are clearly warranted. Two other methods, time series analysis and sequential analysis, have recently been used in studies of family and marital process. The results appear promising, although the most appropriate methodologies are still undergoing active investigation.

TIME SERIES ANALYSIS

The techniques of time series analysis (TSA) were developed quite apart from family therapy research (1). In order to apply TSA to therapy data, it is necessary to assess patient or family variables continuously over an extended period of time, preferably over a baseline (for example 20 days before treatment) and during treatment. In marital therapy, both spouses can be asked to keep a diary for daily ratings of their relationship, for example, happiness, time spent together, feelings of acceptance, tenderness or closeness (see 19). In family therapy with schizophrenics, family members can be asked to rate specific behaviors of the patient such as amount of time spent sleeping or in social activities, or their changing feelings toward the index patient.

Evaluation of Change

One way to evaluate a time series is by inspection. By merely "eyeballing" the data, one can see whether there is a general trend, positive or negative, in the data. One can see whether there is a change in the time series due to treatment after an initial baseline (in terms of a step function). One can see whether the daily fluctuations are so large that any detection of change seems questionable. One can also see whether the ups and downs in the several variables covary (whether the time series are correlated). All of these evaluations are done on individual cases as opposed to aggregated groups (19). By counting positive and negative trends or shifts in level, the effects of therapy may be evaluated without the risk of the fallacies of group statistics.[1] It is well known that in group statistics, opposite trends in individual cases may cancel out each other and contribute to variability but not to mean levels—thus, rendering the data analysis statistically inefficient. It is also well known that simple pre/post measurements may not be sensitive to the actual changes that took place (19). According to a hypothesis of the evolution of the therapy process (7), there may be an initial deterioration effect (sensitization) followed by an overly optimistic view of the success of therapy. It is only after a period of settling down that the net effect of the treatment becomes visible.

There are, however, limitations to the inspection method of evaluating time series. First, variations in the time series may be considerable and trends and shifts may not be easily detected (signal-to-noise ratio is low). Furthermore, as has been repeatedly shown (3, 6), sequential dependence of consecutive measurements from one data generator make judgments of change difficult and misleading in time series analysis. Due to the inertia of the system, consecutive data points are not independent of each other; the system—that is, the spouse or the couple—has a "memory"

---

1. *Editor's Note*: See Jacobson's discussion in Chapter 11 in which he criticizes traditional inferential statistics and the measures of statistical significance that are ordinarily reported. Clinical significance has usually been neglected in psychotherapy research reports.

that influences behavior ratings sequentially. This sequential dependence works against random fluctuations of the residuals about their local mean. Thus, both inspection and simple statistical evaluation of, say, a difference of levels at two phases of therapy may be misleading (19).

A more elaborate statistical methodology has been developed to analyze time series with tools that take into account the sequential dependence (1, 3). Afterwards, statistical analysis of level, level shifts, trends, variations, and correlations can be conducted. The sequential dependence may come from several sources; for example, a consistent upward or downward trend in the data disturbs local independence of the time series data. If the data increase or decrease steadily, they may not vary freely, as would be the case if the data points were drawn at random. Another source of sequential dependence is periodicity. For example, in family data, weekly fluctuations are likely; "time spent together" is probably higher on weekends. A further reason for sequential dependence is a day-to-day relationship in the data. Consecutive data points may be either close together, due to inertia of the system (positive autocorrelation), or they may tend toward alternating extremes (negative autocorrelation). Trends, periodicities, and day-to-day dependence may take several forms, which are discussed comprehensively by Box and Jenkins (1). Moreover, the time series may not be stationary and may show gross fluctuations over large segments of time. These fluctuations may not be predictable from trend, periodicity, or day-to-day dependence (19).

In summary, the basic procedure in time series analysis is to build a mathematical model for sequential dependence in the data, eliminate the model from the empirical data by checking the sequential independence of the residuals, and then (if independence is achieved) treat them as independent sample points by classical statistics.

Evaluation of Relationships

Changes in the series, like those mentioned above, may be interpreted as effects of the treatment. Another point of interest is the interrelation of the various time series. Do changes in one aspect of the relationship parallel similar changes in other areas? Or do certain events in the relationship precede others? Questions related to this kind of dependence and interdependence may be analyzed by means of cross-correlations (22, 23). Whereas in normal correlational analysis the direction of causality may not be inferred, time series allow for a special kind of correlation. Two time series may be correlated synchronously, for example, today's "negative symptoms of the patient" with today's "feeling angry at the patient." If this correlation is substantial, no causal inference is warranted because of the synchronicity (interdependence).

However, one may also correlate today's "negative symptoms of the patient" with tomorrow's "feeling angry at the patient," or yesterday's "feeling angry at the patient" with today's "negative symptoms of the patient." These time-lagged correlations have direction because one can exclude that today's events influenced yesterday's events (19). One can compute cross-correlations between time series with one family member as well as between family members in order to assess the family dynamics.

In summary, time series analysis seems to be an alternative in family therapy research whenever group experiments are not feasible. It is useful to evaluate change brought about by family therapy and to evaluate family structure. Time series analysis seems especially useful in studying the process of change. In order to understand fully our complex treatments, both strategies (single-case and experimental-group design) should be considered and sometimes combined.

SEQUENTIAL ANALYSIS OF SYSTEM INTERACTION

Up to the present, most studies using the methods of sequential analysis in marital and family therapies have examined some form of communication-skills (CS) training. At least for marital therapy, there is convincing evidence that the CS training has received consistent empirical support as facilitating outcome (8). Therefore, the assessment of CS probably should have high priority in family therapy research. Some of the problems in the assessment and subsequent statistical analysis of CS will be addressed here. Because much methodological progress has been recently made in the study of the communication patterns of couples, special reference will be made to modifications that are necessary when more than two persons are involved in the interaction.

Assessment of Communication Skills

The most fruitful approach in the assessment of CS is behavioral observation by trained observers using some form of coding system. With regard to the subsequent statistical analysis, such assessment flexibly allows frequency measures as well as sequential analysis; the latter cannot be done when using rating scales or questionnaires.

Two major issues have to be dealt with in the assessment of CS: the selection of an assessment procedure and a coding system. With regard to the assessment procedure, a high-conflict task should be chosen in order to stimulate family interaction, whether this takes place in the laboratory or in the home. Discussion of a conflict relevant to the family has yielded the best discrimination between criterion groups. In order to facilitate the family's habituation to the procedure, a low-conflict task, for example, reaching consensus on the meaning of a Rorschach card, should precede the more intense discussion.

At least five behavioral observation systems for coding CS have been reported in the literature: (a) Coding System for Interpersonal Conflict (CSIC; 18); (b) Marital and Family Interaction Coding System (MFICS; 17); (c) Marital Interaction Coding System (MICS; 13); (d) Couples Interaction Coding System (CICS; 4); and (e) Kategoriensystem für interpersonelle Kommunikation (KIK; 27). Unfortunately, all of these systems have some conceptual and/or psychometric problems (see 9, 10, 14, 15, 26). Following the suggestions of these authors, a coding system should meet all of the following criteria:

1. *Coding unit:* One of the major decisions in devising a system is the definition of the coding unit, that is, how to unitize the stream of interaction. Two methods are frequently employed: interval (for example, coding every 6 seconds) and event (units of speech or meaning). Because event coding is more congruent with the flow of interaction, the coding unit may be defined as the "thought unit."

2. *Double coding:* This occurs when one person changes the content of his or her speech one or more times, and the other participants merely listen. When analyzing response chains by sequential analysis, double coding should be avoided because it complicates the analysis and leads to noncomparable results of frequency and sequential analysis for the same data set.

3. *Operationalizing interaction constructs/content validity:* The family field is characterized by an extreme lack of clarity with regard to its most core theoretical constructs. This is also true for the term "communication." Researchers developing a system to assess this construct should describe the theoretical assumptions underlying their approach and provide rationales for various code definitions in order to establish content validity.

4. *Independent nonverbal coding:* Both from a theoretical and clinical point of view, nonverbal behavior is regarded as very important. Moreover, it has been shown to be a powerful discriminator between criterion groups, especially between distressed and nondistressed couples. Therefore, the nonverbal behavior of the participants should be assessed.

5. *Discriminative validity:* The coding system, especially the theoretically important codes, should discriminate between criterion groups of families or couples.

6. *Validity as a measure of change:* The coding system should sensitively monitor the changes produced by the family therapy in the CS patterns of the family members.

7. *Summary codes:* For purposes of sequential analysis, it is necessary to collapse or combine subcategories into larger summary codes. The

summary codes should be made on the basis of content (adding semantically similar codes) and function (for example, the codes should positively correlate with each other or relate significantly to each other when analyzed sequentially).

An Example of a Coding System to Assess Communication Skills

With the above criteria in mind, we (9) developed the Kategoriensystem für partnerschaftliche Interaktion (KPI) or Interaction Coding System (ICS).

Rationale: The aim of the KPI is to assess empirically the CS that are manifest in various treatment programs. Although the different CS components differ somewhat with regard to content and technique, there are some common assumptions. Generally, communication will be enhanced when the family members are using the following skills: (a) *speaker skills*—use "I" messages, describe specific behaviors in specific situations, and stick to the here and now; (b) *listener skills*—listen actively, summarize and check the accuracy of a partner's remarks, ask open questions, and give positive feedback. Family members who use these skills should also avoid blaming, criticizing, and sidetracking. The core skills are reciprocal self-disclosure of feelings, attitudes, and thoughts, as well as the acceptance of (not necessarily agreement with) a partner's utterance.

Coding unit: The basic unit is a verbal response that is homogeneous in content without regard to its duration or syntactical structure. For each code, a nonverbal rating (negative, neutral, or positive) is assigned (see 4). If there is a sequence of codes for one speaker (double coding), a nonverbal listening code (LI) is assigned to the listeners, thus guaranteeing alternate coding. This procedure is necessary for interactions among three family members (mother, father, patient). The verbal responses of each family member are coded as described. Whenever double coding of mother/father occurs, or both parents are talking to each other, LI plus the nonverbal rating for the patient is coded. In case of double coding for the patient, LI is coded for the parent whom the patient is addressing.

Description of categories: The KPI consists of 12 categories that have been derived primarily from the previously mentioned assumptions about effective communication, and they were supplemented by some of the more salient categories and definitions from other coding systems, notably the MICS (13), CISS (4), and KIK (27). The positive codes are Self Disclosure, Positive Solution, Acceptance, and Agreement. The neutral codes are Problem Description, Metacommunication, and Rest. The negative codes are Criticism, Negative Solution, Justification, and Disagreement. (For a more extensive description of these categories, see 9.)

Psychometric properties of KPI: Several *reliability* studies in Germany, England, and the United States yielded satisfactory results.

Kappa statistics were usually well over .80, indicating that the interrater agreement is acceptable for frequency and sequential analysis. The discriminant *validity* of the KPI could be established using criterion groups of (a) distressed and nondistressed couples (9) and (b) depressed patients with relatives high and low on expressed emotion (12). Results of another study investigating the effects of behavioral marital therapy on the couples' CS showed that the KPI is also a sensitive instrument for monitoring change after treatment (10).

STATISTICAL ANALYSIS

In the following section some options and problems associated with the statistical analysis of observational data are discussed; the emphasis will be on treatment efficacy research.

Frequency Analysis

Treatment efficacy is basically evaluated by comparing groups of treatment and control families before and after treatment. Typically, multivariate analysis of covariance is used despite the problem that the low quality of observational data (for example, homogeneity of variance, skewed distribution of variables) often prohibits the use of parametric statistics. But the major problem in dealing statistically with family data is the nonindependence of the data, which precludes straightforward analysis of the individual family member as the unit of analysis. Several options have been considered, including (a) summing data for all family members per given variable (unit = family), and (b) treating each member separately in an analysis of variance design, but evaluating factors such as sex and generational status as separate effects. The latter approach is problematic when family size varies.

Sequential Analysis

Using frequency (baserate) analysis, certain limited conclusions can be reached, for example, that treated couples show significantly more positive and less negative behaviors than the control couples (10). This is a satisfying result in itself, but it does not answer the more interesting question—do partners also learn to respond adequately to the stimuli presented by their spouses; that is, do they change their *interaction pattern*. To answer this question, sequential analysis of the interaction sequences is necessary.

Analyzing Lag-1 Contingencies

As a first approach to sequential analysis, one can inspect the likelihood that particular sequences will immediately occur. These are known as lag-1 contingencies. The basic question is: Given a specific antecedent (for example, self-disclosure), what is the likelihood (conditional probability) that a specific response (for example, acceptance) will immediately follow (lag-1)? Is the conditional probability of acceptance higher or lower at lag-1 than the unconditional probability (baserate) of acceptance? To test the statistical significance of this difference, one form of critical ratio (see 16, 25) can be used: $z = (\text{ObsF} - \text{NP})/\text{NP} (1 - \text{P})$. In this z-value, the difference between observed frequency (ObsF) and expected frequency (NP) is divided by the standard deviation—NP (1 − P)—of expected frequency.

Analyzing Longer Sequences

Because the responses as coded by the KPI last only six seconds on the average, computation of simple stimulus-reaction patterns (lag-1 contingencies) seemed inadequate to depict a meaningful interaction pattern of the spouses. Therefore, longer sequences need to be considered. A major difficulty with data analysis of longer sequences is the increasing paucity of data points. There are two ways to overcome this problem. One way is to use lagged sequential analysis (5, 25) in which responses are considered in relation to antecedents more than one step back in time, irrespective of what happens in between. Unfortunately, it is doubtful whether the resultant sequences accurately portray what is occurring in the interaction. The second approach is to look at real, but generalized, behavior patterns (k-Gramm-Analysis; see 20, 24).

The following *observed behavior sequence* demonstrates how the data are analyzed with the K-Gramm method. (The first letter indicates the person—H = husband, W = wife. The second and third letters represent content codes):

1	2	3	4	5	6
HDE	WAA	HNI	WCR	HRF	WRF

The sequence is analyzed by looking at the frequency of the following patterns:

2-Gramm: HDE—> WAA; WAA—> HNI; HNI—> WCR . . .
3-Gramm: (HDE, WAA)—> HNI; (WAA, HNI)—> WCR . . .
4-Gramm: (HDE, WAA, HNI)—> WCR; (WAA, HNI, WCR)—> HRF . . .

For each K-Gramm pattern, the conditional probability is computed. Because the number of observations for each couple is rather small, analysis is based on aggregate data (summed across couples in each group). Unfortunately, statistical evaluations of the differences between groups are not possible when aggregate data are used (see 20).

Classification of Interaction Patterns

When analyzing longer sequences, the longest patterns usually have a sequence length of 10. Because the average duration of a KPI-code is roughly 6 seconds, such a pattern has an average duration of one minute—rather a short time for human communication. Furthermore, the described methods are based on group data that do not permit the identification of individual couples. However, the analysis of individual couple or family data is possible when their total interaction pattern for the entire discussion is graphically depicted, using cumulative response curves as suggested by Gottman (4).

In order to plot the couple's interaction pattern, the behaviors of the partners are coded as positive, negative, or neutral. Positive behavior will result in an increase, and negative behavior will result in a decrease of the graph. When there is neutral behavior, the graph will stay at the same level. By this method, it is possible to group couples or families visually, according to the individual response curves (see 12).

Sequential Analysis with Family Data

Sequential analysis is only possible when dyadic data are available. Whenever families with more than two members are under study, it is necessary to reduce the data to a two-member interaction. Basically, the responses of both parents are combined and the parent-patient dyad is analyzed sequentially. Although we have no experience with families with more than three members, it is doubtful that sequential analysis can be usefully applied in such a context.[2]

Analyzing Data on Family Alliances

A convincing approach to the analysis of observational data on families with three or more members was recently developed by Gilbert, Christensen, and Margolin (2). The goal of their study was to investigate empirically the differences between distressed and nondistressed families in the strength, patterning, and cross-situational consistency of alliances. Data from two structured interaction tasks were analyzed by the Family Alliance Coding System, which consists of 16 positive and negative alliance codes (for example, Affection, Defend/Protect, Attack). Each event or speech act was coded; the coders rate *whom* the speaker was addressing, the *content* of the communication, and its *affective* quality.

In order to analyze the data, each content/affect code was weighted

---

2. *Editor's Note*: It is desirable that the communications of the therapist be included in the sequences of interaction in family therapy research on the conceptual grounds that the therapist is participant in the observing therapeutic system. However, in attempts to apply the methods of sequential analysis beyond dyads, the addition of the therapist further complicates the difficulties that Hahlweg has described. One solution, applicable to marital therapy, would be to combine the responses of the spouses and to analyze couple-therapist dyad data sequentially.

numerically according to its degree of positive or negative alliance. For each event, an *alliance score* for the dyad was computed using the weighted values (for example, mother attacks daughter would be coded as -9; father defends mother as $+5$). All alliance scores were summed to yield a set of "Total Alliance Scores" for each dyad in the family.

After adjustment of the Total Alliance Scores for differences in family size and amount of speech, frequency analysis can be used to test differences between groups of families or changes after therapy. One hypothesis tested by Gilbert et al. (2) was that nondistressed families are characterized by stronger alliances than are distressed families. This hypothesis was confirmed.

Another hypothesis was that in distressed families the relative strength of the marital alliance would be lower and there would be a skewed pattern of parent-child support (discrepancy between mother-child and father-child alliances). In order to test the hypothesis concerning the relative position of the marital alliance, the dyads were ranked according to their Total Alliance Scores. The obtained score reflects the percentage of communication pathways in the family that are more positive than those in the dyad alone. By employing this measure, it is possible to evaluate the intrasystem position of the marital (or any other) alliance independently of the overall level of positivity or negativity of the family. Group comparisons on an "Alliance Rank Percentage Score" can be obtained using analysis of variance.

Gilbert et al. (2) also describe other forms of analyses using the "alliance" approach, for example, computing a single measure to describe the whole family structure ("Maladaptive Family Structure Index"). In general, this methodology seems useful whenever larger family systems are studied. Furthermore, it is an innovative way to test some of the abstract structural concepts in family therapy, and the method of analysis can be easily applied to data obtained with other coding systems.

CONCLUSION

A great deal of methodological progress has been made recently by using behavioral observation in the study of communication patterns. It now seems possible to assess communication skills in a reliable and valid way, and to analyze the data with meaningful statistical methods— especially with sequential analysis. The methods to assess CS also can be applied in a family therapy context after slight alteration of the coding procedure. Although it seems difficult to apply sequential analysis to family data, the problems are not insoluble. An innovative procedure to analyze family structure, developed by Gilbert et al. (2), can easily be applied to communication data.

Whereas the analysis of CS seems fruitful in family therapy research, the described methods are costly and time-consuming, which limits their use in many projects. Depending on the research hypotheses, the use of self-report and/or questionnaire data often will be sufficient. However, observational measures are critical in the evaluation of specific questions, for example, whether family therapy produces change in the system's interaction pattern.

REFERENCES

1. Box, G.E.P., & Jenkins, G.M. (eds.). *Time series analysis: Forecasting and control.* San Francisco: Holden-Day, 1970.
2. Gilbert, R., Christensen, A., & Margolin, G. Patterns of alliances in nondistressed and multiproblem families. *Family Process 23:* 75–87, 1984.
3. Glass, G.V., Wilson, V.L., & Gottman, J.M. (eds.). *Design and analysis of time series experiments.* Boulder: Colorado Associated University Press, 1975.
4. Gottman, J.M. *Marital interaction: Experimental investigations.* New York: Academic Press, 1979.
5. _____, & Bakeman, R. The sequential analysis of observational data. In M.E. Lamb, S.J. Suomi, & G.R. Stephenson (eds.), *Social interaction analysis.* Madison: University of Wisconsin Press, 1979.
6. _____, & Glass, G.V. Analysis of interrupted time series experiments. In T. Kratochwill (ed.), *Strategies to evaluate change in single subject research.* New York: Academic Press, 1977.
7. _____, & Markman, H.J. Experimental designs in psychotherapy research. In S.L. Garfield & A.E. Bergin (eds.), *Handbook of psychotherapy and behavior change: An empirical analysis.* New York: John Wiley & Sons, 1978.
8. Gurman, A.S., & Kniskern, D.P. Family therapy outcome research: Knowns and unknowns. In A.S. Gurman & D.P. Kniskern (eds.), *Handbook of family therapy.* New York: Brunner/Mazel, 1981.
9. Hahlweg, K., Reisner, L., Kohli, G., Vollmer, M., Schindler, L., & Revenstorf, D. Development and validity of a new system to analyze interpersonal communication: Kategoriensystem für partnerschaftliche Interaktion. In K. Hahlweg & N.S. Jacobson (eds.), *Marital interaction: Analysis and modification.* New York: Guilford Press, 1984.
10. _____, Revenstorf, D., & Schindler, L. The effects of behavioral marital therapy on couples' communication and problem solving skills. *Journal of Consulting and Clinical Psychology 52:* 553–566, 1984.
11. Hersen, M., & Barlow, D.H. *Single case experimental designs: Strategies for studying behavior change in the individual.* New York: Pergamon Press, 1976.
12. Hooley, J.M., & Hahlweg, K. The marriages and interaction patterns of depressed patients and their spouses: Comparison of high and low EE dyads. In M.J. Goldstein, I. Hand, & K. Hahlweg (eds.), *Treatment of schizophrenia: Family assessment and intervention.* Berlin: Springer-Verlag, 1986.
13. Hops, H., Wills, T.A., Patterson, G.R., & Weiss, R.L. Marital interaction coding system. Unpublished manuscript, Oregon Research Institute, University of Oregon, 1972. (Available from ASIS/NAPS, c/o Microfiche Publications, 305 East 46th St., New York NY 10017.)
14. Jacobson, N.S., Elwood, R.W., & Dallas, M. Assessment of marital dysfunc-

tion. In D. Barlow (ed.), *Behavioral assessment of adult disorders.* New York: Guilford Press, 1981.

15. Markman, H.J., Notarius, C.I., Stephen, T., & Smith, R.J. Current status of behavioral observation systems for couples. In E.E. Filsinger & R.A. Lewis (eds.), *Observing marriage: New behavioral approaches.* Beverly Hills CA: Sage, 1981.

16. McNemar, Q. *Psychological statistics.* New York: McGraw-Hill, 1959.

17. Olson, D.H., & Ryder, R.G. Marital and family interaction coding system (MFICS), unpublished manuscript, 1975. (Available from first author, 290 McNeal Hall, University of Minnesota, 1985 Buford Ave., St. Paul MN 55108.)

18. Raush, H.L., Barry, W.A., Hertel, R.K., & Swain, M.A. *Communication, conflict, and marriage.* San Francisco: Jossey-Bass, 1974.

19. Revenstorf, D., Hahlweg, K., Schindler, L., & Kunert, H. The use of time series analysis in marriage counseling. In K. Hahlweg & N.S. Jacobson (eds.), *Marital interaction: Analysis and modification.* New York: Guilford Press, 1984.

20. _____, Hahlweg, K., Schindler, L., & Vogel, B. Interaction analysis of marital conflict. In K. Hahlweg & N.S. Jacobson (eds.), *Marital interaction: Analysis and modification.* New York: Guilford Press, 1984.

21. _____, Kessler, A., Schindler, L., Hahlweg, K., & Bluemer, E. Time series analysis: Clinical applications evaluating intervention effects. In O.D. Anderson (ed.), *Analyzing time series: Proceedings of the Second ITSM Conference.* Amsterdam: Elsevier North Holland, 1980.

22. _____, Kunert, H., Hahlweg, K., & Schindler, L. The use of cross-correlation and other time series parameters in clinical analysis. In O.D. Anderson (ed.), *Time series analysis: Theory and practice 1. Proceedings of the Third ITSM Conference.* Amsterdam: Elsevier North Holland, 1981.

23. _____, Schindler, L., & Hahlweg, K. Lead and lag in aspects of marital interaction. *Behavior Analysis and Modification 2:* 174–184, 1978.

24. _____, Vogel, B., Wegener, C., Hahlweg, K., & Schindler, L. Escalation phenomena in interaction sequences: An empirical comparison of distressed and nondistressed couples. *Behavior Analysis Modification 4:* 97–115, 1980.

25. Sackett, G.P. (ed.). *Observing behavior. Vol 2: Data collection and analysis methods.* Baltimore: University Park Press, 1978.

26. Schaap, C. *Communication and adjustment in marriage.* Lisse: Swets & Zeitlinger, 1982.

27. Wegener, C., Revenstorf, D., Hahlweg, K., & Schindler, L. Empirical analysis of communication in distressed and nondistressed couples. *Behavior Analysis Modification 3:* 178–188, 1979.

PART VI

RECOMMENDATIONS

17

AN OVERVIEW OF THE STATE OF THE ART:
What Should Be Expected in Current Family Therapy Research

LYMAN C. WYNNE
Editor

THE NIMH/*Family Process* conference from which this volume derived was approached by the family therapy participants with apprehensive optimism. The therapists appeared to share anxiety that their scientific interests in strengthening family therapy research would be compromised by their responsiveness to unstated but anticipated pressures from two audiences: (a) family therapy colleagues who hold conflicting views about clinical practice and theoretical premises, and (b) diverse policymakers, funding organizations, grant reviewers, and journal reviewers. I think it is fair to say that the family therapists feared that they would become cooks who were expected to produce fast food of gourmet quality in an antiquated, poorly equipped kitchen. Clearly, this volume is not a cookbook but, instead, a collection of thoughts about the kinds of things that the family therapy kitchen can realistically provide, given the current state of the art. The overview in this concluding chapter is intended to be a fair consensus of the recommendations of the contributors to the volume. Necessarily, it is a selective and personal interpretation of the consensus of the conference. Additionally, the chapter incorporates more recent revisions in my thinking, which have been influenced by the research literature, developments in mental health care and research programming, and conversations and correspondence with the contributors and other colleagues. Some of my more idiosyncratic views are conveyed in the Editor's Comments at the end of the volume.

THEORY IN FAMILY THERAPY RESEARCH

Given the pragmatic concerns that led to the NIMH/*Family Process* conference, it is understandable that contributors expressed fears that family therapy research, under pressures for funding and credibility, already was or would become "politically motivated." Therapy outcome research—if reduced to the question "Does it work?" and if it neglects the question "How does it work?"—was viewed as providing justification for therapy, not information about therapy (25). Therefore, it was surprising yet greatly reassuring, to me at least, that both the family therapists and NIMH staff participants thoroughly agreed that theory is not a research nicety, not merely a delicacy for gourmet appetites. A primary recommendation from the conference was that family therapy research should be theory-based and theory-driven; the selection of research goals, problems, and methods should be clearly linked to a matrix of hypotheses, concepts, and theories. Research designs, it was agreed, are not worth implementing unless they are embedded in a context of theory. Further, the relationship between research design and theory should be reciprocal: research findings should serve as feedback to clarify and strengthen the theories and hypotheses that have generated the designs.

Although high-level epistemologies have been popular in family therapy, most of the participating group of researchers agreed with Reiss (Chapter 2) that theories and hypotheses should include a middle level of abstraction that facilitates linkage of theory to clinical observations and practice. It is not always clear how some formulations of family systems theory and ecosystemic theory can in fact be connected to clinical observations. (See Editor's Comments, 2, at the end of the volume.) However, the expectation that therapy research designs be clinically relevant certainly seems to be justified.

There also was specific interest in strengthening theories about the processes of family change, both with and without therapeutic intervention. The overarching conceptual goal is to develop a theoretical matrix that will facilitate building cumulative knowledge, small step following small step. It must be recognized that any single study is necessarily limited in scope and can deal with only a small, selected portion of the variables and issues of interest in this field.

A Research Definition of Family Therapy

Family therapists have long agreed that this field should be regarded as an approach or a paradigm, and not as just another treatment modality. It would be operationally easier (for research purposes) to define family therapy as a modality in which two or more family members interact with each other and a therapist. However, to press for such a restrictive definition would no doubt be like trying to divert a broad river of definitional discussion into a narrow sluiceway. Perhaps we should turn from this issue and heed an admonition attributed to Nietzsche, that anything with a history cannot have a definition.

Nevertheless, a conference consensus, reached somewhat begrudgingly, favored a definition such as the following: *Family therapy is a psychotherapeutic approach that focuses on altering interactions between a couple, within a nuclear family or extended family, or between a family and other interpersonal systems, with the goal of alleviating problems initially presented by individual family members, family subsystems, the family as a whole, or other referral sources.*[1] This definition does not specify whether a solo therapist or a therapeutic team participates, nor does it specify whether all family members, only some of them, or only one, participate in meetings with the therapist(s). Family therapy with a single family member present in the session can be differentiated from individual psychotherapy by evidence that the family therapist actually makes interventions oriented primarily to altering interaction patterns of the family regardless of who is present in the meeting.

From a research standpoint, there is no need to legislate a more restrictive definition of family therapy. No matter what definition is used by therapist and researcher, a minimal research description of the therapy should specify who the participants are—family members, treatment team members, and researchers. Additionally, clinical and research understanding of the therapy certainly should be enhanced by descriptive information about the therapists' goals, the family members' expectations, and the researchers' concepts and methods. Because of considerable variation across different family therapy models, settings, problems, therapists, and families, the details of therapeutic methods must be specified within each study anyway and, hence, do not need to be part of a definition of family therapy.

Exploratory Versus Confirmatory Studies

The term "research" is often understood by psychotherapists as referring to confirmatory studies, such as comparative studies of the outcome of two methods of therapy. In sharp contrast to this usual view, the conference participants strongly recommended that, at the present stage of development of the family therapy field, a strong emphasis should be given to exploratory, discovery-oriented, hypothesis-generating research, rather than primarily or exclusively to confirmatory research. This implies major attention at present to methodologic research and to studies of therapy process in which links to multiple aspects of outcome are considered. In the study of most therapy issues, large-scale, confirmatory clinical trials of family therapy were regarded as premature and likely to be wasteful of funds and effort at the present stage of research development.

---

1. See Stanton (Chapter 1), Epstein (Chapter 9), Gurman (Chapter 10), and Pinsof (Chapter 12) for similar versions of this definition.

CRITERIA OF THERAPEUTIC CHANGE

There can be no doubt that a pivotal issue in family therapy research is criteria for change. Unless change criteria are specified, it is impossible to know whether improvement, no change, or deterioration has taken place at the termination of therapy. Also, without checkpoint data on change during the course of therapy, the study of therapeutic process becomes an academic exercise without clear import for therapists.

On the one hand, the principle that treatment research should be embedded in a context of theory implies to some systems theorists that *family system change* should constitute the primary change criterion. If the same measures of family system change were applied consistently across studies, with different kinds of treatment problems, techniques of intervention, treatment settings, treatment characteristics, and so on, then generalized conclusions could begin to emerge. On the other hand, despite this argument, there was a strikingly high degree of consensus at the research conference that change in the *presenting problem* must be an essential change criterion in family therapy research, as it is in most other forms of treatment research. The chief controversy that sifts out of discussion in the current literature, as well as from this conference and its aftermath, is concerned with how much weight should be given to *other* criteria of change, including family systems change.

A number of family therapists, ranging from behavioral therapists, such as Jacobson (Chapter 11) to strategic/structural therapists, such as Haley (13), tend to regard change in the presenting problem as the only important criterion. Other therapists, more concerned about criteria of change in family system patterns, do not give primary attention to symptoms and illness. These therapists include, for example, those whose concerns are mainly theoretical (18, 19); those who emphasize experiential growth (30); and those who stress connectedness within the family unit (1) or family enrichment (20).

Part of the controversy can be resolved by recognizing that the concept of presenting problems can be broadly construed and not restricted to symptoms or diagnosable distress. The "problem" for which a couple or family seeks professional assistance may be a relational difficulty without significant individual symptoms, or it may represent a need for help, for example, in coping with a life event or a stalled developmental transition, or a wish for more satisfying relationships.

If this broad view of the concept of presenting problem is adopted, then I believe that substantial consensus does exist about its centrality for family therapy and family therapy research. Indeed, I contend that therapists and researchers have an ethical responsibility to give priority to assessment of change in the presenting problem that is desired and perceived by family members themselves, that is, to a change in "what they are coming for."

At first glance, assessing whether or not the presenting problem is alleviated or eliminated seems simple and straightforward. Actually, a great deal of methodologic work on how to make the presenting problem a researchable concept is still necessary and should be given a high priority. In this summary, only a small sample of the methodologic issues can be mentioned (see Chapter 7 for further discussion).

First of all, the act of selecting a "presenting problem" is a form of punctuation, to use the term introduced by Bateson and Jackson (2). A sequence of reformulations of the presenting problem ordinarily has begun before treatment, typically in family discussions and in discussions with other professionals and referral sources. The specification of the "presenting problem" is not a single punctuation but, rather, a process that continues during the intake telephone call to the family therapist or family clinic. Usually, it continues to be modified or clarified during the initial consultations or assessments with the family, during which alternatives for how to proceed are discussed. Still more drastic changes often take place during the reframing of the problem by both therapist and family during the therapeutic process itself, and may be reframed again in retrospective views of the treatment at follow-up.

Thus, the presenting problem can be regarded as a still picture, or snapshot, or series of snapshots, selected from the flow of an evolving motion picture or videotape. Such issues as who is taking the picture, the setting for the picture-taking, who is included in the frame and who is left out, and how representative can any snapshot of family process be, are some of the questions that should be specified if the presenting problem is used as a change criterion for research. In most research designs and reports, there is far too little description of the timing and context of the presenting problem.

My tentative solution to the dilemmas created by the many changes of problem definition over time is to recommend that two primary baselines be given priority in family therapy research: (a) the multiple versions of the family members' "initial" presenting problems, and (b) the problem identified by consensus of family and therapist.

The first baseline includes the multiple perspectives of the various family members at the time of first contact with the family therapist (or the therapist's intake person). The views of each family member should be recorded separately, with the content, timing, and circumstances carefully specified. Family therapy researchers have not developed a consensus about how to deal with discrepancies between the perspectives of family members and therapists. With such a consensus still lacking, it is crucial that explicit descriptions be reported of the rationale for selecting one perspective while ignoring others, of the method for grouping or aggregating perspectives, and of the procedure, if any, for eliciting quantified ratings from family members regarding both family problems and family strengths.

Because family therapists have insisted upon the distinctiveness of their interest in interpersonal contexts and relational issues rather than in individual illness, there has been a tendency to ignore the obvious fact that many, if not most, problems presented for family therapy are initially viewed by the family members (and often by referral sources) as problems of a person or patient, not as relational problems. However, it is quite consistent with theories of open-linked systems, ranging from the biologic to the societal, for family therapists to proceed to work, and to work successfully, with problems defined at *any* system level—including that of a biologically described illness.

The issue of multiple perspectives poses a more difficult dilemma for researchers than for clinicians. On the one hand, how to carry out empirical research with diverse, individualized information and not reductionistically drain it of clinical, relational "juice" is a major methodologic/conceptual difficulty for family therapy research. As soon as the therapist and family together constitute the therapeutic system and have achieved a consensus about their goals, this constitutes a primary baseline perspective for assessment of family therapy change. However, the therapist, even when he or she has become an "insider" (23) member of the therapeutic "observing system" (6), may have a different long-range perspective than do the family members because of the therapist's concepts about developmental processes and the family life cycle.

The researcher, often inaccurately viewed as an "independent" evaluator, helps shape the research system that constitutes still another observing system, which is meta to the therapeutic system. The researcher's view of the presenting problem usually is an interpretation of the statements or actions of the family members, the therapist, and the referring persons. Therefore, the sources and rules for the researcher's formulation should be carefully specified and reported for each study.

It must be conceded that the public (as consumers) and nonfamily therapist professionals are more interested in the initial presenting problems, that is, in change in those problems for which the family came, rather than in change in the redefined family problem, which is of special interest only to the family therapist and family researcher.

No matter how the presenting problem is incorporated into the therapeutic plan and the research design, information about how and when baseline data were obtained should be reported for other therapists and researchers. These procedures may range from standardized family assessment tasks evaluated with microanalytic, quantitative coding (10) to broadly exploratory approaches. For example, Auerswald (Chapter 4), who uses an ecosystemic paradigm, has suggested that "as data accumulate, clusters of similar types of problem definitions are formed, and a spontaneous classification system emerges that differentiates forms of distress germane to all families, to families from differing ethnocultural and socioeconomic environs, and, idiosyncratically, to families who reside in the community served by the delivery system."

All too often, reports of treatment research have been uninformative about the criteria and procedures whereby the therapists and researchers inducted some families into the study and excluded others. For example, in accord with customary practice in some settings, a presenting problem of "schizophrenia" is regarded as an indication for family therapy, even before the views of the family members about their needs and wishes have been ascertained. But who in the family regards "schizophrenia" as a problem for family therapy? Indeed, does *anyone* in the family actually want family therapy? Or do they want therapy for the patient but something else, such as information, for the other family members? Until a number of studies provide methodologic and descriptive groundwork about varieties of presenting problems *as perceived by family members,* generalizations seem premature about how to incorporate the initial presenting problem as a change criterion into family therapy research.

Pending an examination of this issue in greater depth, a global distinction proposed by Grunebaum (11) seems useful for classifying families' initial presenting problems: (a) families with a problem person and (b) families with a relational problem. Additionally, the "problem persons" can usefully be subdivided into those who have presented with (a) a diagnosed physical or mental illness, or disorder, such as cancer, Alzheimer's disease, or schizophrenia, or (b) problematic behavior, described and located in an individual family member, such as adolescent school-underachievement or truancy. Research procedures for describing and grouping these problematic behaviors are, of course, much less established than are the typologies of psychiatric and medical diagnosis.

Bear in mind that after the focus has shifted from a "problem person" to a "relational problem," with consensus achieved by the therapist(s) and family members, this relational consensus can be used as a second major baseline. For some therapists, this may take place only after many family therapy sessions. Other family therapists implicitly or explicitly redefine and reframe the presenting problem as "relational" by the end of the initial meeting or even by the end of the intake phone call. In this pretreatment reframing, the process of defining the problem as relational has been condensed. Nevertheless, for research purposes, information should be recorded about what each family member initially said, and the therapist should obtain firsthand evidence from the family members before concluding that a consensus with them about a relational problem has in fact been reached.

My own preference is to regard family therapy "proper" as starting only when a consensus about a relational problem has been reached, together with a decision or contract (formal or informal) to treat this relational dysfunction. I prefer to regard the important preliminary work as pretreatment family consultation and/or assessment (31). However, the specific terminology is not important if the clinical and research procedures and definitions are clearly specified for each study so that replicability and comparison become possible.

Other Baseline Variables

Multitudinous, potentially confounding variables, apart from those directly associated with the presenting problem as described above, have been recommended for incorporation into family therapy research designs. Presumably the simplest are the *demographic variables* that are obtained at intake or during pretreatment consultation or assessment ("baseline"). Also there are the variables used to characterize the *treatment setting,* the *referral process,* and *family composition.*

In addition to these "factual" variables, many researchers strongly recommend that pretreatment assessment include systematic study of *relational variables* such as emotional bonding or attachment, cohesion, problem-solving and communicational skills, and so on. Self-report instruments (12, 21, 22, 24, 26, 28), family rating scales (3), and coding of standardized samples of family interaction (10) can be used for this purpose.

Baseline *therapist characteristics* have been less consistently considered, but they should be given equal weight if the concept of therapeutic system is to be taken seriously. The demographic characteristics of the therapist, particularly gender and age, have been shown to make a difference in the therapeutic process (Alexander, Chapter 13). The *therapist's experience* with the particular treatment model applied to the specific problems under study presumably is important, but it is still controversial how and if the amount of experience of the therapist actually influences outcome (Epstein, Chapter 9; Jacobson, Chapter 11). This remains an empirical question that deserves further study, without any specific recommendations possible at present.

Even with this schematic and partial listing of baseline variables and procedures that have been regarded as significant by many researchers, it is clear that families, therapists, and researchers would be overwhelmed if an effort were made to incorporate all of these items into a therapy research design. My suggestion is that baseline variables, in addition to those that can be nonintrusively and routinely obtained, be limited to those for which a hypothesis has been advanced that would indicate that the variable has a *theory-based relationship to therapeutic process or outcome* (see Chapter 7). If researchers took this suggestion seriously, it could be a stimulus to theory building in relation to empirical measures; it also would curtail the "raw" empiricism that makes some research proposals elaborate and expensive, but difficult to interpret. To be sure, after focused research findings are reported, critics will always point out that there are other, unmeasured variables that confound the interpretation of the results. Such critiques should stimulate fresh research with improved, additional features, but apprehension by investigators that they may be criticized for omitting variables does not justify their endless proliferation, as if it were research malpractice to leave any test out.

SPECIFICATION OF MODELS OF INTERVENTION

Several contributors to this volume, especially Epstein and Gurman (chapters 9 and 10), boldly recommended that research priority be given to certain models of family therapy in preference to other models. The criteria for these judgments hinge upon such issues as clarity of description of a model's procedures, the number of current practitioners and ease of teaching other practitioners, and the availability of specific measures of process and outcome relevant to the model. Behavioral, structural, strategic, problem-solving, and psychoeducational approaches have been recommended as "ready" for empirical research. However, if exploratory and single-case research designs are applied, I believe that other current models are also amenable to research.

Within-Model Versus Between-Model Research

It should be recognized that the kind of research that is feasible with different models varies considerably. Within-model research—for example, dismantling the components of interventions (15) and single-case designs (17)—is especially appropriate at present. Elaborate clinical trials with global outcome comparisons between models are not only expensive and difficult to organize, but they are apt to be less informative than is hoped unless component variables relevant to competing hypotheses first have been identified and included in the study.

The specific features of some family therapy models make between-model comparisons especially difficult. For example, family therapy models that emphasize changes in behavior and communication enacted within sessions require different process measures than do approaches that expect change to take place primarily during homework outside the sessions. Comparisons between such models will be difficult because the process is so different. Also, as noted earlier, in proposing a definition of family therapy, the number and roles of persons who participate in sessions varies across treatment models—and, for some models, from one part of the treatment process to another.

At the research conference, a preference was expressed for giving priority to the study of well-differentiated, specific therapy models, versus combining them in order to study common features. It is argued that the common or nonspecific features that possibly are important across models will be examined more fruitfully after specific treatment approaches have first been delineated.

Although the issue of feasibility is usually an important consideration in selecting one kind of research design rather than another, it should be recognized that creative research cannot be neatly pigeonholed in advance. The first priority always should be to promote well-designed, high-quality studies that will illuminate the processes of change and the degree of efficacy of family therapies for specified problems.

Combined and Integrated Treatment Approaches

The preference for within-model research reflects concern that the components of intervention be well specified. Such specification is possible in certain combinations of family therapy models with one another and of family treatment with other approaches. Stanton (27) has described a combination of structural and strategic family therapy models integrated over time. Using a concept of phases of treatment comparable to that described by Alexander in Chapter 13, Stanton keeps the structural and strategic components well delineated but brings them sequentially into play. In the initial phases, structural methods are used, followed by a switch to strategic methods if treatment is not succeeding during the phase of Behavior Change (applying Alexander's terminology). During Alexander's phase of Generalization and Termination, Stanton suggests reverting once again to a structural approach. Research on such a combination of family therapy models would need to include phase-specific criteria of change. In principle, this would appear to be a sensible research application of a creative clinical approach.

In recent years, several studies have combined family therapy and pharmacotherapy, especially for the presenting problem of schizophrenia in a family member. The first of these studies was conducted by Goldstein and his colleagues (8). Two dosage levels of an antipsychotic medication were studied with and without a crisis-oriented, psychoeducational model of family therapy. The results clearly showed a favorable interaction effect of combining high-dosage medication and family therapy. Falloon and Others (5) compared a combination of drug therapy, case management, and behavioral family therapy with a combination of drug therapy, case management, and individual supportive psychotherapy. The family therapy component, as compared to individual psychotherapy, was clearly superior in this integrated treatment approach. Hogarty, Anderson, Reiss, et al. (14) used maintenance chemotherapy with alternative combinations of psychoeducational family therapy or individual social-skills training, or both. Again, the family therapy made a distinctively valuable contribution.

At present, medication is generally viewed as the baseline component in treatment for schizophrenia. For this and other complex difficulties, a combination of treatment approaches appears essential. Well-specified family therapy models can be integrated into the design of these research programs. However, the clinical integration of the team members responsible for the different components of care is not easy to achieve or maintain. Additionally, as Goldstein (Chapter 8) and Pinsof (Chapter 13) have pointed out, even in the recent studies of family treatment of schizophrenia, which have been at the cutting edge of methodology, the interpretation of the findings would have been clarified and enhanced by further specification of family-process variables.

Treatment "Manuals"

The question of specification of interventions relates to the highly controversial topic of the need for treatment manuals in family therapy research. Some researchers strongly contend that manuals are only appropriate for procedurally well-specified models such as behavioral family therapy. They contend that most nonbehavioral family therapy approaches allow and encourage such great flexibility, innovativeness, and creativity that therapists would be stifled by the use of treatment manuals (Stanton, Chapter 1). In English, the word "manual" connotes a step-by-step set of instructions to be used in operating a computer or constructing a piece of machinery. Treatment research can use but does not require instructions in such detail. It would be more accurate to describe the therapy framework as "treatment guidelines," rather than to use the term "manual." At the research conference, Waskow of the NIMH staff described written guidelines and strategies, combined with videotape examples and supervision, that were flexibly and successfully used as "manuals" in recent collaborative, individual psychotherapy research on depression.

In any event, if research with any treatment approach is going to be carried out at all, it would be appropriate to describe, as specifically as possible, the range of components and options that are compatible and incompatible with this approach. For example, with an ecosystemic approach, focusing reductionistically and persistently on a detail of a symptom would be incompatible with this approach. As guidelines for a number of family therapy models are spelled out, those features that are relatively specific for a given approach, as well as the features that are common across approaches, will gradually become clarified.

Treatment Integrity

A closely related issue is whether the treatment has actually been carried out in accord with the guidelines specified for the model. Such accord has been called treatment integrity. Was the therapy carried out as intended or described? Attention to this issue should become part of the state of the art in all family therapy research, but as yet has received insufficient attention. Methodologically, further work will be needed within each approach to consider how treatment integrity can be evaluated in studies that compare videotaped research treatment sessions during therapy research with manual guidelines and tapes of "model" sessions used to train and supervise therapists.

PROCESS/OUTCOME RESEARCH

An extremely strong consensus emerged from this group of researchers that primary attention needs to be given to therapeutic process and not to study of outcome disconnected from process measures. However, process should not be studied in isolation either; processes such as qualities of the therapist-family alliance need to be examined in relation to serial measures of "outcome." Thus, there may be "outcomes" at the conclusion of each phase of the therapeutic process, as well as immediately posttreatment and at various points during follow-up. In short, the process/outcome distinction is now regarded as highly arbitrary.

Pretreatment Processes

Processes that appear to be highly important conceptually and pragmatically, but which are more difficult to tap systematically, are the pretreatment processes mentioned above. In the stocktaking of what I, McDaniel, and Weber (31) have called family consultation, the actions taken in response to similar presenting problems of families at time of first contact with a family clinician can be compared. The decision of whether or not to proceed with family therapy is an "outcome" of the pretreatment process that deserves much greater scrutiny. If feasible, in some settings it also would be desirable to move the starting point for study of pretreatment processes back to the stage of referrals, for example, to a referring crisis clinic or a family medicine program. Even though the family's presenting problem may be similar, some of these cases may be sent to family therapy clinics, others to a biologic psychiatrist, and still others to a school psychologist (Stanton, Chapter 1).

Phases of Treatment Process

As indicated above, the amount of time allotted in different treatment models for consultation or assessment after initial contact or intake varies tremendously and greatly affects the kind of research data that can be obtained at baseline and later reviewed for the study of change. There also are variations across models in the specificity of treatment contracts. Some models have written contracts and others a fluid, informal relationship that is never labeled as "therapy." These many variations would seem to create a morass for the researcher, but I believe that most if not all of what actually takes place can be described and differentiated.

The processes after the therapist or therapeutic team start to meet with family members face to face are more fully amenable to research, but they should be regarded as a continuation of a process that is already underway. Alexander (Chapter 13) makes a valuable contribution by delineating the phases of family therapy process beginning after a decision has been made to proceed with therapy.

The Therapeutic Alliance

What can no longer be accepted in family therapy research, in my opinion, is a concept of the therapist as an outsider, separable from the family. Instead, the therapeutic alliance of therapist and family interacting with one another is crucial for the study of process. The therapist is not an external observer, but, rather, is participant in the observing system (6). The extensive work on the therapeutic alliance in individual psychotherapy research is beginning to receive comparable attention in family therapy research, led by process researchers (9; Pinsof, Chapter 12).

Varieties of Family System Measures

With the proviso that measures not be incorporated promiscuously into research designs simply because they exist or can be obtained, the question remains about how to select hypothesis-generated, study-appropriate measures of the family system. In the not-distant past, many family therapy researchers have taken rather doctrinaire positions about the kind of family measures they regard as worth obtaining. Some researchers have used only self-report measures. Others, impressed by the merits of studying interaction sequences directly, in videotaped interviews and in periodic research assessments of interaction, have been disdainful of self-report measures. Ratings of families in therapy, including global ratings of family functioning as well as more specific dimensions, such as range of affect expressed and clarity of communication, have had their strong advocates. In recent times, it seems to me that there has been a distinct softening of exclusive preferences for any one of these three main approaches. Indeed, there is now an almost universal acceptance of the need for multiple measures—self-reports, macro-family ratings, and micro-interaction studies. Each kind of measure has both advantages and difficulties. For all kinds of measures, there needs to be more consistent emphasis on obtaining measures not only from all family members, but also from the therapist—and, I would add, the researcher. The problems of aggregating data using any of these methods and comparing families with different constellations again involve methodologic studies that deserve high priority. Although multiple measures are widely advocated, the difficulty of deciding what to do about discrepancies between measures and how to interpret them and handle them statistically, should give researchers pause before proliferating their use of multiple measures. Once again, the principle that I would advocate is that measures be included only when a well-formulated, theory-based hypothesis supports their inclusion.

The Core Battery Issue

Several of the contributors to this volume, as well as others represented in the literature, have strongly recommended that a core battery of family measures be included in all family therapy research, similar to the recommendations by Waskow (29) for individual psychotherapy research. The failure of individual psychotherapy researchers to follow those recommendations and their objections that some of the core measures were not appropriate and meaningful should give pause to those who recommend a similar core-battery approach at the present time for family therapy research.

Although a core battery would provide an appealing consistency across studies, I believe that the state of the art calls for more limited efforts to have some measures overlap across only those studies and settings that share certain specified features. For example, it might be possible to specify measures that would be "core" for studies of treatment of families with a schizophrenic member, another set that would be appropriate for studies of treatment of marital conflict, another for studies in which there is an adolescent problem offspring, and so on. I believe that the state of the art is some distance from achieving a satisfactory core battery for *all* family therapy research. However, respected colleagues sharply disagree with this conclusion.

DATA ANALYSIS

At the same time that variables and measures are being selected, the data analysis procedures that will be used later also should be mapped out. Doing so early in the research process makes it more likely that the data analysis becomes an integral part of the overall research design rather than a post-hoc add-on. Although this principle is applicable to all forms of research, it is easily overlooked in exploratory studies of new fields, such as family therapy research.

In evaluating treatment outcome, there still is a tendency to overvalue statistical significance of group differences, using inferential statistics, and too little emphasis upon assessment of clinical significance (Jacobson, Chapter 11). Jacobson, Follette, and Revenstorf (16) have recommended a two-fold criterion of therapeutic improvement: (a) the client or family has shifted from the distribution of dysfunctional clients or families to a distribution of healthy functioning subjects, and (b) the amount of change during therapy exceeds chance expectations, as assessed with a new standardized index of significant change (4). These statistical methods will need more extensive trial before it is clear how widely applicable they will be in family therapy research. At present, the important issue is that methodologic studies are actively underway for assessing *clinically* significant therapeutic change.

Multivariate techniques with structural equations and path analysis are now being successfully used by some family therapy researchers such as Patterson and Chamberlain (Chapter 14). These methods are beginning to cope with some of the complexities that have worried family systems theorists. Further work is needed, of course, on ways to apply these methods in research on the diversity of family therapy processes linked to the course and outcome of treatment across the great variety of problems, populations, and treatment settings that remain to be studied.

Single-case research designs are favored at this time in family therapy research by a number of investigators (17). Coded observational measures of family interaction patterns are especially valuable in the assessment of whether specified interventions have led to hypothesized family changes. The statistical techniques of lag sequential analysis and time-series analyses have been most successfully adapted for the study of sequences of marital interaction (Hahlweg, Chapter 16). Innovative methods for studying alliances in larger family systems are also being developed (7). It should be noted that these new methods provide opportunities both for testing old hypotheses and for generating new ones.

CONCLUDING COMMENTS

In the 1950s, family therapy began with discovery-oriented research observations of meetings with family members, with therapeutic goals, if any, only vaguely specified. These early research hypotheses generated clinical enthusiasm and, in the 1960s, were incorporated into a diversity of family therapy models. Family therapy teaching and theorizing has continued to flourish, but it became disconnected from its research base during the late 1960s and most of the 1970s. Meanwhile, research in individual psychotherapy and pharmacotherapy was developing new approaches and achieving credibility with health care professionals and policy-making and funding organizations.

In the late 1970s, family therapy researchers began to critique the field and concluded that although the overall thrust of preliminary reports and unreplicated studies was clearly positive, there was a paucity of good-quality, sustained research. Also, the special conceptual and methodologic difficulties of conducting research on family therapy began to be identified. During the last decade, a new wave of family therapy research has begun to emerge, especially using therapy models with structural, behavioral, problem-oriented, and psychoeducational approaches applied to relatively well-defined problems such as anorexia nervosa, substance abuse, schizophrenia, preadolescent and adolescent conduct disorders, and marital conflict.

Although the predominant thrust of this volume has concerned recommendations for empirical research on circumscribed family treatment programs, my hope is that the reader can apply these suggestions to broader contexts, both in theories and in clinical work on difficult problems for which our approaches have been ineffective or, more dismayingly, only distantly relevant. For example, how can the field of family therapy facilitate more research in which family therapy and other approaches are integrated to bring about change in a wider array of medical and social problems? How can family therapy sensibly relate to major societal problems such as the feminization of poverty and changing patterns of health care? How can we think more creatively and constructively about the problems of families that are, for example, poor and disadvantaged? How can we as family therapists learn from and contribute to the burgeoning variety of family self-help groups and marital enrichment programs? But do we have the courage and skill to evaluate and specify our limitations and failures as well as our aspirations and successes? These and similar questions deserve our sustained scrutiny, our inquiry as both clinicians and researchers.

It seems timely for the family therapy field to reconsider and reassess its missions, its conceptual base, and its mode of relating to families. In this process of self-scrutiny, family therapy research should contribute. Collaboration between family clinicians and researchers is essential in setting priorities for family therapy research that optimally will be: valued by families, significant to practitioners, credible to health care policy-making and funding organizations, methodologically feasible, and conceptually interesting and/or provocative.

REFERENCES

1. Allman, L.R. The aesthetic preference: Overcoming the pragmatic error. *Family Process 21:* 43–56, 1982.
2. Bateson, G., & Jackson, D.D. Some varieties of pathogenic organization. In D. McK. Rioch & E.A. Weinstein (eds.), *Disorders of communication. Proceedings of the Association for Research in Nervous and Mental Disease, Research Publications, Vol. 42.* Baltimore: William & Wilkins Co., 1964.
3. Carlson, C.I., & Grotevant, H.D. A comparative review of family rating scales:

Guidelines for clinicians and researchers. *Journal of Family Psychology 1:* 23–47, 1987.

4. Christensen, L.C., & Mendoza, J. A method of assessing change in single subject designs: An alteration of the RC index. *Behavior Therapy 17:* 305–308, 1986.

5. Falloon, I.R.H., & Others. *Family management of schizophrenia: A study of clinical, social, family, and economic benefits.* Baltimore: Johns Hopkins University Press, 1985.

6. Foerster, H. von. *Observing systems.* Seaside CA: Intersystems Publications, 1981.

7. Gilbert, R., Christensen, A., & Margolin, G. Patterns of alliance in nondistressed and multiproblem families. *Family Process 23:* 75–87, 1984.

8. Goldstein, M.J., Rodnick, E.H., Evans, J.R., May, P.R.A., & Steinberg, M.R. Drug and family therapy in the aftercare of acute schizophrenics. *Archives of General Psychiatry 35:* 1169–1177, 1978.

9. Greenberg, L.S., & Pinsof, W.N. (eds.). *The psychotherapeutic process: A research handbook.* New York: Guilford Press, 1986.

10. Grotevant, H.D., & Carlson, C.I. Family interaction coding systems: A descriptive review. *Family Process 26:* 49–74, 1987.

11. Grunebaum, H., personal communication, 1986.

12. Hahlweg, K., Schindler, L., Revenstorf, D., & Brengelmann, J. The Munich marital therapy study. In K. Hahlweg & N.S. Jacobson (eds.), *Marital interaction: Analysis and modification.* New York: Guilford Press, 1984.

13. Haley, J. *Problem-solving therapy: New strategies for effective family therapy.* San Francisco: Jossey-Bass, 1976.

14. Hogarty, G.E., Anderson, C.M., Reiss, D.J., Kornblith, S.J., Greenwald, D.P., Javna, C.D., Madonia, M.J., & Environmental/Personal Indicators in the Course of Schizophrenia Research Group. Family psychoeducation, social skills training, and maintenance chemotherapy in the aftercare treatment of schizophrenia. *Archives of General Psychiatry 43:* 633–642, 1986.

15. Jacobson, N.S. A component analysis of behavioral marital therapy: The relative effectiveness of behavior exchange and communication/problem-solving training. *Journal of Consulting and Clinical Psychology 52:* 295–305, 1984.

16. ———, Follette, W.C., & Revenstorf, D. Toward a standard definition of clinically significant change. *Behavior Therapy 17:* 308–311, 1986.

17. Kazdin, A.E. Single-case experimental designs. In P.C. Kendall & J.N. Butcher (eds.), *Handbook of research methods in clinical psychology.* New York: John Wiley & Sons, 1982.

18. Keeney, B.P., & Sprenkle, D.H. Ecosystemic epistemology: Critical implications for the aesthetics and pragmatics of family therapy. *Family Process 21:* 1–19, 1982.

19. Kniskern, D.P. Climbing out of the pit: Further guidelines for family therapy research. *Journal of Marital and Family Therapy 11:* 159–162, 1985.

20. L'Abate, L. Skill training programs for couples and families. In A.S. Gurman & D.P. Kniskern (eds.), *Handbook of family therapy.* New York: Brunner/Mazel, 1981.

21. Locke, H.J., & Wallace, K.M. Short-term marital adjustment and prediction tests: Their reliability and validity. *Journal of Marriage and Family Living 21:* 251–255, 1959.

22. Moos, R.H., & Moos, B.S. *Manual for the Family Environment Scale.* Palo Alto: Consulting Psychologist Press, 1981.

23. Olson, D.H. Insiders' and outsiders' views of relationships: Research studies. In G. Levinger & H. Rausch (eds.), *Close relationships*. Amherst: University of Massachusetts Press, 1977.

24. _____, Russell, C.S., & Sprenkle, D.H. Circumplex Model of marital and family systems: VI. Theoretical update. *Family Process 22:* 69–83, 1983.

25. Ryder, R.G. Coherent diversity: Views and recommendations following the NIMH/*Family Process* workshop on efficacy research in family therapy, 1984. (Unpublished manuscript, available from author, Department of Child Development and Family Relations, University of Connecticut U-58, Storrs CT 06268.)

26. Skinner, H.A., Steinhauer, P.D., & Santa-Barbara, J. The family assessment measure. *Canadian Journal of Community Mental Health 2:* 91–105, 1983.

27. Stanton, M.D. An integrated structural/strategic approach to family therapy. *Journal of Marital and Family Therapy 7:* 427–439, 1981.

28. Van der Veen, F. The parent's concept of the family unit and child adjustment. *Journal of Counseling Psychology 12:* 196–200, 1965.

29. Waskow, I.E. Selection of a core battery. In I.E. Waskow & M.B. Parloff (eds.), *Psychotherapy change measures* (DHEW Publication No. ADM 74-120). Washington DC: US Government Printing Office, 1975.

30. Whitaker, C.A., & Keith, D.V. Symbolic-experiential family therapy. In A.S. Gurman & D.P. Kniskern (eds.), *Handbook of family therapy*. New York: Brunner/Mazel, 1981.

31. Wynne, L.C., McDaniel, S.H., & Weber, T.T. Professional politics, and the concepts of family therapy, family consultation, and systems consultation. *Family Process 26:* 153–166, 1987.

EDITOR'S COMMENTS

LYMAN C. WYNNE
University of Rochester
Rochester, New York

I NCLUDED HERE is a potpourri of: my views on various topics that are too lengthy for footnotes and probably do not represent a consensus of conference participants; my postconference correspondence with authors (primarily Auerswald); and a few miscellaneous thoughts expressed by participants during the research conference. In other words, these Comments are a postscript.

1. The "Identified Patient" in Family Therapy

"Identified patient"—often abbreviated as I.P.—is a traditional term in family therapy practice and family therapy research. Because its meaning and implications are ambiguous and outdated, it is not used in this volume. Early family therapists introduced the term to indicate that one of the family members had been identified *by the family,* or by the referring person or facility, as "the sick one" or patient. The term implied that the family therapist was withholding agreement with this view held by the family or the referral source. Family therapists assumed that some other presenting problem, usually involving the family as a system, was going to be more central for family therapy and that the "identified patient" would later be viewed as only a start-up reference point.

My impression is that, historically, the concept of identified patient was derivative from the earlier, widely accepted concept of family scapegoat. A number of influential family therapists, such as Ackerman in 1958 (1), and family researchers, such as Bell and Vogel in 1960 (5), had persuasively described cases in which individual family members appeared to be family scapegoats. These family members, most commonly children, were blamed by others in the family for causing trouble, tensions, or conflicts in the family or between the family and persons in the community. In these families, the child who was brought to the professional was identified by the family as the symptom-bearing patient who needed treatment.

In an era when clinical generalizations held sway and systematic research sampling was not considered, the concept of "identified patient" quickly caught on as a standard, descriptive component that was applied to all families entering therapy. For example, by 1964 the term was so well established that Satir (28) began her textbook on *Conjoint Family*

Therapy" as follows:

> Many therapists have found it useful to call the member who carries the
> symptoms the "Identified Patient," or "I.P.," rather than to join the family
> in calling him "the sick one," or "the different one," or "the one who is to
> blame." This is because the therapist sees the Identified Patient's symptoms
> as serving a family function as well as an individual function .... The
> Identified Patient is the family member who is most obviously affected by
> the pained marital relationship and most subjected to dysfunctional par-
> enting .... His symptoms are a message that he is distorting his own growth
> as a result of trying to alleviate and absorb his parents' pain. [pp. 1-2]

Over the ensuing years, the "family function" of individual symptoms
became axiomatic. Possible independent sources of individual biological
factors (as well as extrafamilial factors) often were dismissed except
when they were conceptualized as incorporated into primary, circular
(nonlinear) family system patterns. The concept of an individual patient
was often regarded as a hangover from an outmoded "medical model,"
and in many programs the term "identified patient" became a record-
keeping device for insurance and research purposes.

Gradually, however, in the late 1970s, family therapists began to be
more involved with families of medically ill patients with, for example,
cancer and Alzheimer's disease, in which there could be little doubt about
who was identified as the patient. Furthermore, the biopsychosocial
version of the medical model (9, 10) became more widely accepted as
compatible with attention to multiple systems levels. And, finally,
research on major psychiatric disorders, such as schizophrenia, provided
indisputable evidence for biological factors and meant that a specific
family member with such a diagnosis was indeed a "real" patient whose
difficulties were appropriately regarded as a stressor and source of
substantial burden for the other family members.

Meanwhile, family consumer advocates were becoming a potent political force. They complained angrily that early concepts about families as
"pathogenic systems" were still being employed, and that the blaming of
families for causing the patient's illness added to the burden. Furthermore, family consumer advocates have protested that family therapists
regard the other family members as *un*identified patients, with the
unwarranted presumption that they are sick and hence need family
therapy.

These charges have been startling to those family therapists who still
thought of themselves as undoing blame directed toward the family
scapegoat or identified patient. When family therapists have responded
that they are not blaming *any* individual in the family when they view the
family *system* as dysfunctional, family advocates object that the use of

the system concept is pejorative about them as families. They also contend that the maxim, "The family is the (real) patient," implies a primary, unidirectional (and nonsystemic!) impact of family upon the symptomatic family member, without adequate attention to the reverse direction of effects of a patient's symptoms upon the family system.

This brief historical account should make it obvious that the term "identified patient" at best can be regarded as having outdated, overgeneralized implications, and at worst can be taken as evidence that family therapists are disrespectfully insensitive and demeaning toward family members whom they claim they want to help. A further discussion of the treatment implications of the identified patient concept has recently been published by Johnson (12).

Therefore, the ambiguities of the term "identified patient" and its abbreviation "I.P." are avoided in this volume in favor of one of three alternatives: (a) *"patient"* (when a family member has in fact been formally diagnosed by a professional), (b) *"index person"* or *"index patient"* (when used as a record-keeping term), or (c) *"problem person"* (when a family member is perceived by other family members as having a presenting problem but who may or may not have been formally diagnosed by a professional as a "patient").

2. Systems Theory: A Shaky Framework for Family Therapy and Family Therapy Research

During the early development of the family therapy field, systems theory provided a thought-provoking, widely accepted and unifying rationale for bold hypotheses and seemingly radical treatment methods. Indeed, for a number of years systems theory seemed so dominant in family therapy that only refinements and elaborations, rather than challenges, prevailed. In Chapter 4, Auerswald differentiates three versions of what he collectively labels family systems therapy: a family system paradigm, a general systems paradigm, and a cybernetic systems paradigm. What these approaches have in common are quite general formulations that have provided a broad orientation for therapy and research. Some therapy models, such as those labeled communicational, structural, strategic, triadic, Bowenian, and Milan approaches, have most explicitly emphasized some version of systems principles, but essentially all other family therapy models have incorporated various ideas from systems theories. Family research, too, has drawn heavily upon systems principles in studies of family interaction and communication.

The concepts shared across these diverse approaches are quite simple and straightforward, especially the concept of family and family subsystem boundaries and the basic principle that change in one subsystem or component is reciprocally associated with change in other components. A central difference from individual therapy has been the conceptualization that family system functions are more than and different from the sum of the functioning of the individual participants.

Auerswald has proposed that an ecosystemic paradigm would go beyond any "standard" version of family systems therapy. In Chapter 4, he provides a beginning for the application of these principles to clinical practice and research. Further examples and details will be needed before it will be clear how this theory translates into research methods that are distinctively different from what is included in the application of present-day multivariate concepts and methods. In Chapter 14, Patterson and Chamberlain provide a sophisticated example of how systemic principles, such as multidirectionality and the sequential unfolding of treatment processes, can now be incorporated into family therapy research.

Systems theory, in its various forms, has been both criticized and praised because it is content-free; any kind of specific content, including emotional functioning, can be encompassed within its framework. But increasingly high levels of abstraction in the elaboration and refinement of systems theory has left many family clinicians and researchers dissatisfied. It has been difficult, as Reiss points out in Chapter 2, to formulate middle-level hypotheses that relate both to clinical observations and highly abstract theoretical proposals.

I wish here to express some views that undoubtedly do *not* represent a consensus of the contributors to this volume, but which reflect growing discontent and dissension with certain aspects of systems theory as it has been applied in the family field. These points include disagreement with a number of prevailing concepts that family therapists have derived from systems theory, sometimes with misapplication of terms, sometimes with overgeneralizations about the relevance of systems concepts to families, and sometimes with constrictive overemphasis on the family level in systems theory. In my view, "systems theory" may still be viable, but a great deal of conceptual clarification is urgently needed. Systems concepts have all too often been used so carelessly that communication among theorists, clinicians, and researchers has been seriously impaired. Conceptual confusion has more visible, negative consequences in research publications than in clinical work in private offices. Hence, researchers should be in the front lines of those who are scrutinizing and reformulating systems concepts.

Terminologic Misfortunes

Circular Causality: The concept of circular causality has had the status of an axiom in family therapy. Many writers have asserted that the enlightened recognition of circular causality is what best differentiates family therapists from the benighted adherents of lineal causality. (It has been regarded as even more enlightened to drop the allegedly antiquated notion of causality altogether and to speak only of circular processes, cybernetic circuits, or structural determinism.)

Writing primarily as a clinician, I concluded a commentary upon concepts of "circularity" as follows:

> Today, a "circular" epistemology has become such an article of faith that it has not been reconsidered in relation to two lineal processes that are therapeutically crucial: (1) The *time line*, which prevents truly circular processes from *ever* occurring. When one becomes concerned about treatment and developmental outcomes (an idea embedded in time), then the concept of *spiral rather than circular transactions* makes a crucial difference. Also, (2) family therapists are directionally (lineally) oriented, whether to goals of symptom relief [13, 21], growth [30], or balancing the ledger of merit and obligation [7] . . . . [I]n actual practice my goals and those of other therapists unbalance the therapeutic process so that it is dominantly a lineal thrust from therapist toward family. Indeed, if it is not, the process becomes too nearly circular, "homeostatic," and ineffective. The effective therapist, by and large, is personally forceful and pragmatically lineal; unsuccessful therapists are wishy-washy and let therapy swirl in circles. In my view, teaching and practice of family therapy and its early reconciliation with theory will be facilitated by dropping its ritualistic pretense that therapy proceeds, or should proceed, in accord with a circular epistemology. [32, p. 259]

Recently, Dell (8) has elaborated a similar viewpoint, pointing out that Bateson's authoritative pronouncement that lineal causality is an "epistemological error" has "bred confusion (and occasionally terror) in the minds of clinicians about how they should talk about families and family therapy" (p. 513). Dell suggests that in the *description* of human experience, we use lineal concepts. Viewed from the more abstract metadomain of Batesonian epistemology, unilateral causality, or what Maturana (22) calls instructive interaction, is incomplete as an *explanation*. Keeney (16) accepts lineal interventions and lineal thinking as long as we do not forget "that these 'partial arcs' are always approximations of the more encompassing circles that incorporate them" (p. 58).

These distinctions may suggest that for purposes of research, which presumably is concerned with explanation, a circular epistemology may be appropriate. I think not. On the terminologic level, the metaphor of circularity ignores the lineality of time and therefore is inaccurate. Additionally, circularity (and recursiveness), exemplified in sequences such as A leads to B leads to C leads back to A, is *uni*directional. The path is indirect but in one direction; *bi*directionality and *multi*directionality are *not* included in the image conveyed by circularity. Thus, the term is too narrow, even on a descriptive level, to represent the complexity of the processes with which both clinicians and researchers in the family field are concerned.

Recursiveness: Keeney and Bateson, in his later years, have preferred the term "recursive" to "circular." However, recursiveness is explicitly unidirectional and misrepresents phenomena in the same way that circularity does. Family theorists may be chagrined to realize that a distinction between unidirectional recursiveness and *bi*directional *non*-recursiveness has been the subject of thousands of publications in mathematics. In an overview for social scientists, Berry (6) writes:

> Recursive causal models have been used often by sociologists and political scientists over the last two decades . . . To be recursive, a model must satisfy several conditions that together ensure that all causal effects specified in the model are "unidirectional" in nature, i.e., that no two variables in the model are reciprocally related, with each affecting the other . . . . [T]he assumptions made in recursive models are often at odds with our understanding of the nature of the social science process being studied. In many cases it is unrealistic to assume that no two variables in a model are reciprocally related; furthermore, given our generally high degree of ignorance about the factors represented in a model's disturbance terms, it is often impossible to provide a convincing justification for an assumption that each error term in a model is uncorrelated with all other error terms in the model. In such cases, we must abandon recursive models, and employ *nonrecursive* multiequation (or simultaneous equation) models. These models allow for both patterns of reciprocal causation among variables and assumptions that one or more pairs of error terms in the model have nonzero correlations. [pp. 8-9]

In this volume, Patterson's report in Chapter 14 expertly exemplifies how nonrecursive, bidirectional processes can be examined in the design and data analysis of family therapy research.

Bateson (4) decried the concept of power as lineal and epistemologically erroneous. On this issue he split from Haley (13) who has emphasized the clinical significance of hierarchy within families and therapeutic systems. Those family therapists who, despite Bateson, have been highly directive and lineal, such as Minuchin (24), are among those for whom the best evidence for therapeutic effectiveness can be found. Nevertheless, the Batesonian systemic view has been commonly accepted by many clinicians to mean that concepts of victim-victimizer, for example, are incorrectly lineal and that the proper systemic therapist will therefore regard the "victim" as having contributed as much as the "victimizer" to such phenomena as spouse battering. These clinical interpretations have outraged and alienated feminists, advocates for families of the mentally ill, and others who are concerned with comprehensive health care and with political and social injustice.

Family clinicians are still fumbling with how to reconcile their avowed systemic principles with clinically effective interventions. As a result, family therapy—and family therapy research—has not forthrightly addressed important issues of concern to families such as family violence and major mental or physical illness. Also, some of the interventions that research has shown to be effective, especially behavioral and psychoeducational approaches, are viewed with suspicion by theorists as insufficiently systemic. What needs to be reexamined is the interpretation and application of theory in order to catch up with clinical practice. Systems theory lags behind and does not yet adequately encompass these clinical problems and some of the current approaches for dealing with them.

Not all of my colleagues in this volume will agree, but I contend that in terms of theory, problem selection, and data analysis, *the state of the art in the family therapy research field has moved beyond the constricting and misleading implications of the "circular" and "recursive" versions of systems theory.* These versions of systems theory fail to incorporate what Dell (8) has called the lineal, descriptive aspects of human experience, and they do not readily encompass the clinical, social, and value-laden complexity of such problems as biologic illness and death, gender inequality, individual psychodynamics, loosely connected family and community networks, cultural variations in power allocations within occupational and family hierarchies, and entrenched social class and racial disadvantage. These problems have clear relevance to families and to professionals working with them. For the field of family therapy to maintain or regain its earlier vitality, these topics *must* be addressed clinically by family clinicians. At the same time, the theory (relabeled as ecosystemic or whatever) and the research methods for the study of these issues must be relevant to the broadened scope of clinical practice. Systems theory provided a powerful start-up orientation for family therapy, but major reconstruction of this theoretical framework is now required.

Isomorphism of Physical and Social Systems: A major feature of the general systems paradigm as adapted by family therapists is that families share isomorphic characteristics with other systems arranged in a hierarchy of inclusiveness ranging from quarks to the universe. The concept of isomorphism has been attractive partly because biologic and physical systems can be readily shown to function in patterns that are analogous to certain family patterns and patterns of intervention. Also, it has been interesting to note analogies between patterns found in a hospital program, in the relationship of therapist with family, and in the relationship of therapists with one another. These kinds of observations have been most persuasive in instances in which interpersonal relationships have been tightly or rigidly contained without much linkage to other persons or systems, either within the individual or outside in the community. The links between system levels has been illustrated most clearly in Engel's (10) biopsychosocial model in the relationship between biologic and personality functions, and, to some extent, in treatment relationships.

The evidence for isomorphism, however, becomes implausible when the analogies are extended to so-called macro-systems. On the broader level of family and community networks and the broader society, it is easy to show that events and factors such as poverty have powerful influences upon the smaller systems of the family, individual person, and biology. But this does not establish that the larger social matrix is truly organized as a series of functional system levels in which relationships between components can be identified as they can be in a steam engine or in the neuroendocrine system. To be sure, family therapists often have actively worked with larger networks, but systems *theory* has not satisfactorily encompassed these macrosystems. Also, as most families become dispersed geographically, as well as through divorce and remarriage, the meaningfulness of systemic principles becomes blurred at what can only loosely be called the family systems level. In other words, the hypothesis of isomorphism of general systems theory has probably been overgeneralized.

Etiology: Partly as an effort to avoid attributing blame to anyone, systems theorists have emphasized the idea that punctuation of sequences is arbitrary and that etiology is a tenuous or fallacious concept. This view is closely related to the concept of circular causality, but carries the further implication that studies of etiology are meaningless or misguided. It is quite true that many formulations in medicine and psychiatry have been excessively simplistic, particularly when they emphasize single rather than multiple causes. However, from the standpoint of clinical and research studies, it is obvious that new inputs from outside the family system do take place and alter the course of events. In that sense, they can be viewed as etiologic or causative. These inputs include biologic illness, independent extrafamilial events, and enduring cultural circumstances that have discontinuous effects that are enduringly disequilibrating.

An overreaching emphasis upon earlier family systems concepts such as homeostasis led some family therapists and researchers to neglect the contribution of these nonfamilial "etiologic" factors. More recent attention in theory building to catastrophes and discontinuities has as yet not been much applied clinically. The formulation that individual symptoms are a function of family disorder continues to be interpreted as meaning that family dysfunction is the primary factor leading to a great variety of illnesses and problems. This has led to unrealistic, excessively exclusive reliance upon trying to change dysfunctional family patterns. In recent years, fortunately, greater care is being used in describing how these variables—familial and nonfamilial—relate to one another, and in developing more comprehensive treatment plans. However, the era of misunderstanding is not yet over.

3. Case Descriptions in the Development of Family Theory

Reiss (Chapter 2) is indisputably correct that the theory of family therapy, unlike psychoanalytic theory, did not build upon a few widely read case descriptions. On the other hand, family therapists have long prided themselves upon their willingness, in contrast to the extreme reluctance of psychoanalysts, to make their work visible to colleagues and trainees who view family therapy through one-way windows or on videotapes and read verbatim transcripts of therapy sessions. Indeed, it could be said that early family theory was erected on a scaffold of many case vignettes, written and electronic. For example, extensive excerpts from family therapy were published by many therapists such as Ackerman (2, 3), Laing and Esterson (19), Minuchin and his colleagues (25), Weakland and Jackson (29), and Wynne (31).

These vignettes, however, have not satisfied latter-day methodologists who attend to case selection and research design. In addition, the vignettes did not provide extensive enough material, or were not studied sufficiently to sustain discussion and theory building. To be sure, a few early films and videotapes were widely viewed, but were used primarily to demonstrate the distinctive techniques of virtuoso therapists and the immediate responses of families, not to document the repetitious patterns of special interest for theory.

Partial, noteworthy exceptions to the lack of more lengthy case studies was the influential book by Haley and Hoffman (14) in which five family therapy transcripts were presented and discussed, but, once again, primarily from the vantage point of therapeutic technique. Three more recent book-length case descriptions that warrant careful attention are those by Paul and Paul (27), Napier and Whitaker (26), and Keeney and Silverstein (17).

4. Losing the Family's Definition of the Presenting Problem

Several authors in this volume, such as Wynne (Chapter 7) and Jacobson (Chapter 11), have strongly urged on conceptual and ethical grounds that change in the initial problem as presented by the family should be a primary consideration and criterion in family therapy research. In Chapter 7, I have described some of the methodologic difficulties in implementing this concept. In Chapter 4, Auerswald used case examples to illustrate vividly the ways in which the family's definition of the presenting problem can disappear from the view of therapist and researchers. Probably, families themselves often become muddled about what were their initial, relatively straightforward concerns. In a note to Auerswald, I said, in effect, "Yes, Dick, there *is* a danger, both for clinicians and researchers, of losing sight of the family's definition of the problem. But let's at least urge that this not happen and see what can be done not to let it happen."

Auerswald, in a personal communication (1987), responded with pragmatic pessimism, softened by the more hopeful possibilities that he believes can be achieved by a shift to what he has called an ecosystemic epistemology:

> I would contend that once the information generated in any helping effort, in or out of a research framework, becomes part of a formal response to required procedures, that attention to problems as presented by the family is not recorded. Record-keeping and other forms of data collection reflect the reductionistic, institutionalized "professionalization" of the information collected in the language used. For example, third-party payers pay according to diagnosis in institutionalized language (DSM-III); researchers use language to remain "legitimate" in their professional surroundings. It is not enough to urge attention to this matter. In fact, I doubt that many would disagree with that message, but nothing will change with urging. The problem is not found in the intent of therapists or researchers. It is found in the institutionalized structures of the health-care delivery system and in research methodologies that are rooted in the "objectivist," reductionistic "Western" edition of reality with its linear view of time and causality.

5. Single-Case Approaches to Family Therapy Research Design

Goal Attainment Scaling (GAS) has been enthusiastically recommended for therapy research ever since Kiresuk and Sherman (18) introduced the approach in 1968. It must be acknowledged that its implementation in psychotherapy studies with individuals or families has been disappointingly infrequent. It appears that preliminary groundwork on methodologic details was insufficient and that procedures for obtaining reliable measures were not first established. Recent, renewed attention to solving these methodologic problems is highly promising (see, for example, 20, 23). High priority should be given to making GAS a full-fledged component of state-of-the-art family therapy research.

In a personal communication (1987) to me, Auerswald took issue with my comparision of Goal Attainment Scaling and his "ecosystemic" method of record-keeping (which he has described in Chapter 4):

> While I can see the similarities between the system I present and GAS, especially in terms of sequencing, the use of my system is not geared to reductionistic definition of goals. It is, instead, designed to facilitate centrifugal generation of the story, a description of an "event-shape" in timespace, with the common goal always being to intervene in such a way as to evolve an ending to the story in which the distress has been attenuated or disappeared. Each story is different. The "presenting complaint" may state a goal, but more often it does not. Other targets of intervention arise, and the presenting complaint may simply become irrelevant. There is no way to deal

with reliability in my system. The only judge of reliability is the family, and each situation is unique.

Therapy research is undoubtedly made difficult by the changing view of the "presenting problem" and the "story" held by the family and therapist (see Chapter 7). With Goal Attainment Scaling and other single-case research designs (15), a new baseline *could* be designated whenever a new or redefined primary problem has emerged, with "outcome" defined as that point when "the distress has been attenuated or disappeared," as Auerswald recommends. Using Goal Attainment Scaling, the family's stepwise movement through therapy could be assessed either in their own terms or in terms of goals identified by a therapist, treatment team, or researcher. Therefore, I disagree mildly with Auerswald and believe that his approach and GAS are compatible.

A pragmatic difficulty, obviously, for *any* record-keeping is that therapy often moves with such rapidity and fluidity that no one can "catch" these multiple "baselines" and "outcomes." However, the strategy of studying therapeutic episodes or small chunks of therapy, as recommended by Pinsof (Chapter 12), perhaps can partially cope with this difficulty. Also, many major problems, unfortunately, change only slowly, and for such problems I believe that we can and should try out single-case research methods that study evolving, "centrifugal" processes (in Auerswald's sense). To be sure, any such method *can* be used reductionistically, but they *need not* be, as Auerswald's proposal for a single-case design illustrates.

The question of interrater reliability in single-case research has as yet been little studied even in the simpler field of rating change of target complaints in the context of individual psychotherapy (23). How or if "reliability" measures are obtained would depend on how and by whom the GAS guide has been constructed for a given case study. In studies of individual therapy, this has been done diversely by: therapist alone, client alone, staffing conference, research team, or patient-therapist negotiation. In single-case studies the key issue of reliability concerns "test-retest" comparisons. That is, are the persons who assessed the problem reasonably consistent with themselves in the way that they use the same scale over time, and when they rate degrees of distress or coping in relation to specific treatment goals? The first task in GAS or related approaches to single-case studies, as yet rarely attempted in family therapy research, is, in Auerswald's terms, for "client and helper" to match "actual outcome" and previously specified "desired outcome." Another version of this approach has been suggested by Feldman (11), using family self-report checklists initially and repeated subsequently, in which individual, subgroup, and total family ratings of presenting problems and strengths are assessed.

6. Relevance of Therapy Research for Clinicians

Traditionally, therapy researchers have mournfully taken a rather martyred view of themselves as perpetually neglected by clinicians. At the NIMH/*Family Process* conference, Goldstein took exception to this view and noted that clinicians *do* pay attention to resarch, but only under certain conditions. First, research on easily identified problems is more readily understood and applied by clinicians. Goldstein noted that clinicians have paid a lot of attention to research on treatment of phobias and that the research on psychoeducational and behavioral approaches to family therapy has generated considerable response among those treating chronic schizophrenics. He commented that it is difficult for clinicians to know whether "vaguely defined problems of living" and research on their treatment relate to the specific issues seen in their daily clinical practice.

A second reason why clinicians probably have ignored research is that the reported results usually have not shown high magnitude of effects. This relates to the issue of clinical significance discussed by Jacobson (Chapter 11). Goldstein stated that he did not think we should underestimate the clinician's desire or willingness to use research if really clear differences are demonstrated with treatment.

A third reason why clinicians may not have attended to therapy research is that the traditional research emphasis upon improvement rates ("outcome") has neglected attention to the clinical events or processes that lead to one outcome versus another. Clinicians would be more interested in research on therapy if the circumstances of treatment and the processes of treatment are clearly specified. As Pinsof (Chapter 12) has especially emphasized, process research in the context of outcome studies generates clinical interest and meaningfulness. On the other hand, if *only* process is studied, without a context of outcome, it is easy to be skeptical as to whether these processes "mean" anything.

Finally, Goldstein noted another factor that has discouraged clinicians from attending to family interaction research, namely, the tendency of some research reports to list too many variables without highlighting a few key variables in a theoretically relevant hierarchy.

REFERENCES

1. Ackerman, N.W. *The psychodynamics of family life: Diagnosis and treatment of family relationships.* New York: Basic Books, 1958.
2. _____. *Treating the troubled family.* New York: Basic Books, 1966.
3. _____. To catch a thief. In N.W. Ackerman, J. Lieb, & J.K. Pearce (eds.), *Family therapy in transition.* Boston: Little, Brown & Co., 1970.
4. Bateson, G., Weakland, J.H., & Haley, J. Comments on Haley's "history." In C.E. Sluzki & D.C. Ransom (eds.), *Double bind: The foundation of the communicational approach to the family.* New York: Grune & Stratton, 1976.

5. Bell, N.W., & Vogel, E.F. *A modern introduction to the family.* New York: Free Press, 1960.

6. Berry, W.D. *Nonrecursive causal models.* Beverly Hills CA: Sage Publications, 1984.

7. Boszormenyi-Nagy, I., & Ulrich, D.N. Contextual family therapy. In A.S. Gurman & D.P. Kniskern (eds.), *Handbook of family therapy.* New York: Brunner/Mazel, 1981.

8. Dell, P.F. In defense of "lineal causality." *Family Process 25:* 513–521, 1986.

9. Engel, G.L. The need for a new medical model: A challenge for biomedicine. *Science 196:* 129–136, 1977.

10. _____. The clinical application of the biopsychosocial model. *American Journal of Psychiatry 137:* 535–544, 1980.

11. Feldman, L.B. Assessment instruments for family therapy: Clinical and research applications, 1984. (Unpublished manuscript available from author, Chicago Family Institute.)

12. Johnson, H.C. Biologically based deficit in the identified patient: Indications for psychoeducational strategies. *Journal of Marital and Family Therapy 13:* 337–348, 1987.

13. Haley, J. Development of a theory: A history of a research project. In C.E. Sluzki & D.C. Ransom (eds.), *The double bind: The foundation of the communicational approach to the family.* New York: Grune & Stratton, 1976.

14. _____, & Hoffman, L. *Techniques of family therapy.* New York: Basic Books, 1967.

15. Kazdin, A.E. Single-case experimental designs. In P.C. Kendall & J.N. Butcher (eds.), *Handbook of research methods in clinical psychology.* New York: John Wiley & Sons, 1982.

16. Keeney, B.P. *Aesthetics of change.* New York: Guilford Press, 1983.

17. _____, & Silverstein, O. *The therapeutic voice of Olga Silverstein.* New York: Guilford Press, 1986.

18. Kiresuk, T.J., & Sherman R.E. Goal Attainment Scaling: A general method for evaluating comprehensive mental health programs. *Community Mental Health Journal 4:* 443–453, 1968.

19. Laing, R.D., & Esterson, A. *Sanity, madness, and the family. Vol. 1: Families of schizophrenics.* London: Tavistock Publications, 1964.

20. Lewis, A.B., Spencer, J.H., Jr., Haas, G.L., & DiVittis, A. Goal Attainment Scaling: Relevance and replicability in follow-up of inpatients. *Journal of Nervous and Mental Disease 175:* 408–418, 1987.

21. Madanes, C. *Strategic family therapy.* San Francisco: Jossey-Bass, 1981.

22. Maturana, H.R. Biology of language: The epistemology of reality. In G.A. Miller & E. Lenneberg (eds.), *Psychology and biology of language and thought.* New York: Academic Press, 1978.

23. Mintz, J., & Kiesler, D.J. Individualized measures of psychotherapy outcome. In P.C. Kendall & J.M. Butcher (eds.), *Handbook of research methods in clinical psychology.* New York: John Wiley & Sons, 1982.

24. Minuchin, S. *Families & family therapy.* Cambridge: Harvard University Press, 1974.

25. _____, Montalvo, B., Guerney, B.G., Jr., Rosman, B.L., & Schumer, F. *Families of the slums: An exploration of their structure and treatment.* New York: Basic Books, 1967.

26. Napier, A.Y., & Whitaker, C.A. *The family crucible.* New York: Harper & Row, 1978.

27. Paul, N.L., & Paul, B.B. *A marital puzzle: Transgenerational analysis in marriage counseling.* New York: W.W. Norton, 1975.

28. Satir, V. *Conjoint family therapy: A guide to theory and technique.* Palo Alto CA: Science and Behavior Books, 1964.

29. Weakland, J.H., & Jackson, D.D. Patient and therapist observations on the circumstances of a schizophrenic episode. In D.D. Jackson (ed.), *Communication, family, and marriage. Vol. 1: Human communication.* Palo Alto CA: Science and Behavior Books, 1968.

30. Whitaker, C.A., & Keith, D.V. Symbolic-experiential family therapy. In A.S. Gurman & D.P. Kniskern (eds.), *Handbook of family therapy.* New York: Brunner/Mazel, 1981.

31. Wynne, L.C. The study of intrafamilial alignments and splits in exploratory family therapy. In N. Ackerman, F.L. Beatman, & S.N. Sherman (eds.), *Exploring the base for family therapy.* New York: Family Service Association of America, 1961.

32. _____. Structure and lineality in family therapy. In H.C. Fishman, & B.L. Rosman (eds.), *Evolving models for family change: A volume in honor of Salvador Minuchin.* New York: Guilford Press, 1986.

NAME INDEX

Italicized page numbers refer to references at the end of each chapter.

SUBJECT INDEX

Affective Style (AS), 101, 111, 112, 114
Alcoholism, 25, 96
Alliance for the Mentally Ill (AMI), 89
Anatomy of Intervention Model (AIM), 177
Anorexia nervosa, 38, 39, 103, 133–135, 264
Anthropic cosmological principle, 61
Antisocial (delinquent) children/ adolescents, 96, 190, 192, 199, 203, 206, 209, 214–216, 220
Aversive behavior (see Total Aversive Behavior)

Baseline measures, 81, 83, 86, 90, 256
    multiple, 75, 76, 79, 85, 100, 134, 201, 235, 262, 277
    primary, 100, 105, 253, 255
Beavers Systems Model, 102
Biopsychosocial model, 92, 268, 273
Blame/blaming, 24, 40, 268

Case descriptions of families, 37, 57, 58, 68–70, 275
Causality, 9, 50–54
    bidirectional, 201, 268, 271
    circular, 10, 190, 270, 271
    directional, 273, 271
    linear/lineal, 11, 270, 271
    multidirectional, 270, 271
    nonlinear/nonlineal, 10, 268
    spiral, 271
    statistical, 192
Circumplex Model, 102
Client
    characteristics, 145
    measures, 145
    system, 160, 161
Clinical trials, 144, 164, 172, 228, 230, 251, 257
Coding System for Interpersonal Conflict (CSIC), 239
Coevolution, 61
Coercion model, 199
Communication-Skills (CS) Training, 238
Community, 37, 38, 40–42, 56, 66, 68, 72, 76, 79, 96, 103, 105, 255, 267, 273, 274
Costs (see Treatment, costs)
Couple Communication Program, 127
Couples Interaction Coding System (CICS), 239

Cultural issues, 16, 37, 41, 49, 69, 205
Cybernetics, 24, 25, 37, 61, 232, 269, 271

Depression, 96, 122, 135, 146, 147, 195, 206
Deterioration (negative effects), 25, 50, 115, 134, 236
    in control group, 140
    while on waiting list, 140
Diagnosis, diagnostic criteria (also see Disorders and Family typology)
    family, 109, 110
    individual, 23, 56–59, 81, 82, 99, 105, 109–111, 166, 252, 255
DSM-III, 76, 81, 103–105, 110, 113, 135, 276
Dismantling strategies, 128, 144, 147
Disorders
    of individual (index/"problem person") family members, 3, 81, 92, 99, 100, 109–111, 113, 135, 255, 264
    relational (of family systems), 3, 81, 99, 103, 110, 135, 255, 256
Disassembly, 38–40
Dyslexia, 57, 58

Epistemology, 1, 37, 52, 55, 60–65, 129, 175, 250, 272
    Batesonian, 271
    circular, 271
    of ecosystemic/ecological systems, 60, 64, 71, 276
    esthetic, 89
    new science, 63
Event-shapes in timespace, 62, 67–69, 276
Experiencing Scale, 167
Expressed Emotion (EE), 101, 111, 112
Extra-session change, 16, 100, 160, 162, 203

Family
    adaptability, 77, 229
    addiction cycle, 101
    change processes, 34, 37, 38, 230
    chaotic, 109
    cohesion, 77, 103
    communication, 77, 206, 228, 229, 238–240, 243–244, 261
    composition, 20, 114, 251, 256
    connectedness, 90, 252

287